Inspiring
Women

Every Day

One-year devotional
by women for women

WAVERLEY ABBEY

RESOURCES

The readings in this compilation were originally published 2006, 2007 by CWR as bimonthly Bible
reading notes, *Inspiring Women Every Day* as Jan/Feb, Mar/Apr, May/June, July/Aug, Sep/Oct, Nov 2006
and Dec 2007. Previously published as *Inspiring Women Every Day Book 1*.
First published in this format in 2010 by Waverley Abbey Resources, Waverley Abbey House, Waverley
Lane, Farnham, Surrey GU9 8EP, UK. Registered Charity No. 294387. Waverley Abbey Resources is the
trading name of CWR. Registered Limited Company No. 1990308.

For a list of National Distributors visit: waverleyabbeyresources.org/distributors
Unless otherwise indicated, all Scripture references are from the Holy Bible: New International Version
(NIV), copyright © 1973, 1978, 1984 by the International Bible Society.
Other versions used: *The Message*: Scripture taken from *The Message*. Copyright © 1993, 1994,
1995, 1996, 2000, 2001, 2002. Used by permission of NavPress Publishing Group.

Concept development, editing, design and production by Waverey Abbey Resources
Cover image: Getty Images/Rubberball Productions/Mike Kemp
Printed in the UK by Yeomans.
ISBN: 978-1-85345-568-1

Contents

Introduction   4

Celtic Prayer Weave   5

A time for everything   7
Abidemi Sanusi

Onwards and upwards – reflections on 1 Timothy   35
Christine Platt

Living a life of wisdom   61
Ruth Valerio

Angels on standby   89
Christine Orme

From fear to faith   115
Rebecca Lowe

Spirit-inspired confidence   143
Wendy Bray

The Lord's Prayer   171
Alie Teale

Encounters   199
Chris Ledger

Ephesians – seeing the full picture   227
Anne Le Tissier

Pioneering   253
Marion Stroud

The power of praise   281
Helena Wilkinson

Titus – a call to radical discipleship   309
Heather Coupland

It is our huge joy and privilege to introduce you to twelve wonderfully gifted and inspired women who have authored the notes in this one-year compilation. The variety of themes, styles and approaches covering a range of Bible books and practical biblical topics, will help open your mind and heart to God's Word each day. We encourage you to dwell on the Scripture verses and the biblically based thought, and then turn that thought into prayer. The structure of the weekday and weekend readings vary slightly – but each will, in their different ways, enrich your personal time with God.

Time spent with the Bible is never wasted; so amidst the busyness of your day, we pray these short meditations will help you journey with many other women on a life lived in the knowledge of God's love for you, and in passing that love on to those around you.

You may notice some seasonal references here and there – but we pray that whenever and wherever you read these devotions, the Lord will bless, inspire and challenge you.

The *Inspiring Women Every Day* Team
Waverley Abbey Resources

The prayer-poem opposite was written by Julie Steadman while on a day of reflection here at Waverley Abbey House. It is based on the idea of the Celtic weaving prayers, weaving God into your very being, your life. Julie has very kindly allowed us to include it at the start of this year of devotions.

Celtic Prayer Weave

Into my life I weave the
love of God

Into my striving and my being
I weave the peace of God

Into the frayed edges of my life I weave
the crimson thread
of His forgiveness and strength

Into my stony heart
I weave His kindness
melting me into love

Into my darkness I weave
His light and life

Into my time I weave
His eternity

Julie Steadman

A time for everything

everything

Abidemi Sanusi

Abidemi Sanusi (www.abidemi.tv) is the author of several books. Her book, *Eyo*, was shortlisted for the Commonwealth Writers' Prize 2010. Abidemi runs her own copywriting company, www.thereadywriter.co.uk, which delivers corporate content to commercial companies. She is also the editor of www.readywritermag.com, an online magazine for Christians who write. She enjoys cooking, photography and running, although not necessarily in that order, and certainly not all at the same time!

WEEKEND

A time for everything

For reflection: Psalm 31; Ecclesiastes 8:7

The start of something, whether a new year or not, appears to me to be filled with undiscovered possibilities and new beginnings. The Bible says that, 'With the Lord a day is like a thousand years, and a thousand years are like a day' (2 Pet. 3:8). This means that the Lord is not on our timetable or calendar and therefore can create new beginnings at any time.

Over the next few weeks, we will be looking at the seasons of our life, specially the tough ones, and how God uses them to draw us closer to Him and in the process enable us to find out more about ourselves. Our study will be drawn from the book of Ecclesiastes which was written by Solomon, a man who knew only too well the value of seasons. We will be looking at the all too common issues of pain, bereavement, disappointment, as well as joy and forgiveness, and how we can use each experience as an entry into the new season to which God is calling us.

By the end of the month, I pray you will have come into a greater understanding of the current season of your life and how God wants to mould your character during it.

Holy Spirit, I ask You to give me a greater understanding of life's seasons as I journey with the Lord, and prepare my heart to hear from You afresh.

Joy indescribable

We will start by looking at joy. What it is, what the Bible says about it and how to sustain it, whatever the season we're in, even in the midst of suffering.

It is a proven fact that money can make our lives more comfortable but it doesn't necessarily make us happier. It is also usually the simple things that make our hearts sing; the sun rising over a new day, a loved one's reassuring touch ... these are the things that money cannot buy.

Often we do things because we have to. Necessity dictates how we lead our lives; the mortgage has to be paid and we have to put food on the table – so we work. I've often wondered about those women, especially in foreign countries, who literally have their choices taken away from them. In my days as a human rights worker, I met many such people. They've experienced enough tragedy in their lives to wither most people, yet they carry on, praising God and with the peace that defies all understanding emanating from their very hearts. How do they do it? The answer lies in their faith and the One they serve. They've followed their heart which is not swayed by changing circumstances or the horrors of war. I learned a lot from these women about true joy and following the Lord – no matter the cost.

Secular society has different ways of measuring joy. Money, influence and fame top the list each time. It is most peculiar then to discover that the people who have all three are often the unhappiest people on earth. A life without Christ is not worth living. When we give Him our hearts, we are trusting in something infinitely bigger than ourselves, money or influence. Now that is what I call following your heart.

Ecclesiastes 11:7–10

'Follow the ways of your heart and whatever your eyes see ...' (v.9)

For prayer and reflection

I give my heart, my being and my all to You, Jesus. For You alone are worthy of it all. Amen.

Joy demystified

Ecclesiastes 2:1–9

'... Come now, I will test you with pleasure to find out what is good.' (v.1)

There is much mysticism associated with joy nowadays. To a certain extent, this mysticism has entered the Church and created quite a bit of confusion. Some people think it's a kind of happiness – mythical, pure, yet probably unachievable.

People take pleasure in many things. For some, their pleasure is in their children. For some, it's in alcohol, and for others, exercise. What is true is that most of these pleasure-inducing situations are only temporary measures. They do not last.

We see the Teacher attempting to find some pleasure in whatever form was available to him. He tried to find it in many ways, including alcohol, but discovered they were all meaningless. In the end, he was forced to admit that his pursuit of pleasure was altogether fruitless because he didn't gain anything. Neither did its pursuit add anything to his life.

Real joy, however, is not dependent on situations or emotions. It is not shaken by changing circumstances nor is it dependent on others.

Real joy – that comes from the Holy Spirit living inside us – enables us to live freely and face whatever comes our way with the certainty that the Saviour is in control. It does not take pleasure in painful situations but it does take comfort from the One we look to to sustain us.

We cannot buy or sell the joy that Christ gives because it is free, like our salvation gift. This joy is not limited to the purest saint but is available to all who believe in Jesus Christ as their Lord and Saviour.

What blessed relief!

For prayer and reflection

I thank You, Father, for this peace and joy that surpasses all understanding. Amen.

Joy does not equal drudgery

There is a misconception in secular society that is a little like this: if something doesn't benefit you, then it's of no use to you.

Christ-followers are offered an alternative aim to live by: even if it doesn't benefit you, there is good reason to do it. Sometimes, we call it the 'cost'. And when we come to making choices do we count the cost?

We've all had to make choices in our lives. Should we do something which brings us instant gratification or do we look at the eternal significance and happily pay the price? Do we bless someone who is in more need than we are?

The Bible tells us that the Lord desires obedience rather than sacrifice. Sometimes it is easier to sacrifice than it is to obey. But obedience has its own reward; namely, doing the right thing. Sometimes, of course, obedience requires making sacrifices but in doing that, we have the reward of knowing we've obeyed the Lord. This brings with it joy and fulfilment.

We also have the added pleasure of knowing that obeying God brings visible rewards – wisdom, knowledge and happiness (Eccl. 2:26). And there is more.

Today's reading challenges us and confirms what the world still needs to grasp. A life without God is an empty one. A life in God enables us to find enjoyment and satisfaction in our work. It enables us to be content with our lot even as we strive to reach the next level of whatever He has in store for us.

A lifetime full of self profits no one. A lifetime of service to God and others profits humanity. And in this there is joy: in serving others, we serve God.

Have you ever done something that wasn't of visible benefit to you? How did it make you feel?

Ecclesiastes 2:17–26

'To the man who pleases him, God gives wisdom, knowledge and happiness ...' (v.26)

For prayer and reflection

Father, help me to live a life that pleases You, through loving You and serving others. Grant me Your wisdom, knowledge and joy. Amen.

My joy **is in the Lord**

**Ecclesiastes
5:1–7**

'Much dreaming
and many words
are meaningless.
Therefore stand in
awe of God.' (v.7)

There comes a point in all Christians' lives when they have to make a choice regarding whom they will serve. I suspect we've all been there. Some people call it the crossroads of life. I like to call it a major life choice.

Today's Church in some ways is better equipped than ever before. We are abundantly blessed with many resources. We have more Bible translations than Wycliffe ever dreamed possible. A quick click on the internet will bring up a multitude of Christian websites all designed to aid us in our Christian walk. They are in essence all pointing us towards a central truth: namely, that in order for us to grow as Christians, we have to make a conscious decision to follow Christ every day.

In doing that, we must consciously bring all our 'life choices' under Christ's lordship. Choices that will be influenced by whether we really believe God's Word – what He says about life, joy and how we live our life. And by standing firm on what the Bible says, we can learn to master our emotions, instead of allowing our emotions to master us. I don't know why we women tend to have more self-esteem issues than men. Perhaps it's because of the abundance of hormones we have been blessed with! One thing is certain, though, if we do not make a conscious effort to grow in our knowledge of God and in our relationship with Him, our faith will be ruled by our circumstances and we will be left wondering where our supposed joy is.

A little time set aside for prayer will never go to waste. Make that effort to spend time alone with God. For it is usually in the secret place that our joy is refreshed, our faith is strengthened, our hope is renewed and we are given enough grace to face the day.

For prayer and reflection

I thank You, Lord, that Your joy is my strength. Amen.

Rejoice and be happy!

W hat a great God we serve! There are many people who have both fame and riches yet who are unhappy and insecure. They spend their lives in gilded cages and behind security guards. They do not sleep because they are too busy worrying about 'what ifs'. God promises peace of mind to those who serve Him. This is the peace of mind that accepts each season we're in with perfect equanimity knowing that the best is yet to come. This is the peace that does not rely on human logic but instead relies on what the Bible says. There is true joy in having the peace of mind to appreciate the present with assured hope for the future. It doesn't allow room for negative retrospect because God has filled the heart with gladness and fullness of joy.

The Lord promises us His peace which is like a running river. Even in the midst of great trouble He offers this gift of peace. So, if you're depressed, hold on. If you're going through a financial challenge, keep on praying, keep on believing and be faithful with your tithes, for God sees it all. If you're in need of physical healing and it's a long time in coming, it's not because God has forgotten about you. The Bible says that He has our names written on the palms of His hands so it stands to reason that He *cannot* forget about you. No matter your season, whatever you're going through, know that the Lord is faithful and He will never, ever give you more than you can bear.

And that is one of Christianity's unexplainables: the guarantee of a peaceful heart despite the challenging situations we face. A gift from a loving Father to His children. All we have to do is reach out and accept the gift offered.

Ecclesiastes 5:13–20

'He seldom reflects on the days of his life, because God keeps him occupied with gladness of heart.' (v.20)

For prayer and reflection

Forgive me, Lord, for those times when I haven't taken Your peace offering. Fill me with Your peace. In Jesus' name I pray. Amen.

WEEKEND

It's the weekend – I'm thankful!

For reflection: Psalm 138

There is something about weekends that makes most people positively joyous. Perhaps it's the relief of surviving the onslaught of the past week. Perhaps it's the sheer joy, for those who don't have to work at weekends, of knowing that we have two full days to devote to our life and people outside work.

Weekends are celebrated differently in different countries. In the UK, some people celebrate it by getting inebriated beyond reason. In some Muslim countries, the weekend starts on Thursday while the week starts on Sundays. For many of us weekends can provide a welcome opportunity to spend time with family, and fellow Christians in church or other environments.

Whatever our experiences of the past week, or however we choose to spend this weekend, let us determine within our hearts to bless the Lord for His help throughout the week. Next week as we look at tough seasons, we see that nonetheless, because of our Lord, we have reason to rejoice and to hope for what He has in store for us. So rejoice and be glad!

Spend some time listing all the good things in your life – all the blessings God has given you. I guarantee you will find some if not many!

What joy in the Lord?!

I begin today with a personal confession. Last year was a bit of a strange one for me. I didn't welcome in the New Year on my knees as has been my custom. I don't make New Year resolutions but I do set personal targets for myself in certain areas. Last year, I didn't do that. I simply woke up and wondered what had happened to my joy in the Lord.

As I write these words, I'm faced with a new challenge; I've determined within myself to be thankful even if I don't feel like it or even if I don't feel that God cares for me. There are days when I am overwhelmed by loneliness, restlessness and disappointment. My self-esteem plummets and I am left wondering what use the Lord could possibly have for me in His kingdom. Surely, I shouldn't be going through this. I'm a Christian. I should be happy! Happy! Happy!

I'm not alone in this. I've spoken to fellow believers – male and female – and they understand. They've been there. They even had a name for it: 'The wilderness'. I'm relieved. I'm not a sad excuse for a Christian. God sees me and yes, He does care for me. He will restore my joy. He will see me through this wilderness season.

So I will keep on thanking and praising Him, even when I don't feel like it. Even if I have to do it through gritted teeth. Even when – *especially when* – I hear that little voice telling me God doesn't love me. Because my joy in the Lord is not dependent on external circumstances, or feelings. It is a joy that comes from knowing Him.

Ecclesiastes 9:1–10

'This is the evil in everything that happens under the sun …' (v.3)

For prayer and reflection

Have you ever lost your joy in the Lord? Spend a minute again reflecting on the good things you are thankful for and thank God just for being Him.

A time for everything

**Ecclesiastes
3:1–14**

'I know that
everything God
does will endure
forever ...' (v.14)

Today's Bible reading is a well-known one. I suspect it's because it is a gentle reminder of how transient life is. Having begun to understand what true joy is, this week we will be looking at the issue of pain; what the Bible has to say about it, why God allows it and how we can use it to strengthen our faith and Godlike character.

I live in the UK where January is generally agreed to be the coldest month of the year. In fact, it makes me long for spring, not least because then the days are longer, the flowers and plants begin to bud and, most of all, the weather is not so dreary! Life's seasons are a lot like that, particularly the painful experiences. We long for them to be over, and in some cases ask if there is any point to it all.

There are some who believe that pain is not a Christian's 'portion'. However, a quick look through the Bible will reveal that almost everyone mentioned in it went through painful seasons in their lives. The reason for this is simple: although we are citizens of heaven, we still have to live on earth and deal with the consequences of living in a fallen world. The fact that we are also humans thus inherently fallible also leaves us open to pain.

The good news is that God's grace is able to sustain us in the painful situations we're going through. The even better news is that God in His infallible grace knows just how much we can take of a situation and He assures that He will never give us more than we can bear. That is the hope of Christianity. What blessed assurance!

For prayer and reflection

'My grace is sufficient for you, for my power is made perfect in weakness' (2 Cor. 12:9). Thank You, Lord, for Your amazing grace. Amen.

No pain, **no gain**

Being a Christian offers genuine peace and joy, but one thing it doesn't do is protect us from facing the harsh realities of life. As a young Christian, I really believed that I would be shielded from life's tragedies and be cocooned in the embrace of the Holy Spirit while I waited out my life on earth. The Lord didn't wait long to disabuse me of that notion!

When we are going through trying times, it is easy to believe that the Lord doesn't see our pain and our challenges; after all, He's up there in heaven. We are the ones battling it out on earth. It doesn't help when people come out with well-meaning platitudes: *'I just know that God's name will be glorified when all this is over'*, *'If you just have a little bit more faith, then maybe your miracle will not be blocked'*. They fail to lift us up. So we try a little harder; more prayer confessions, more fasting, more casting and binding of demons. And all the while, it might just be that the Lord wants us to be still and abide in His presence, yes, even in the midst of the storm we're facing.

Nobody likes to go through painful times. A quick look through the Bible will show that characters are moulded, legends created and life-changing encounters with God experienced more during those painful times than at any other season in our life. Often, when it seems we have no comforter, it is simply that the Comforter is waiting to make Himself known and He dares us to believe in Him when everything rational tells us to do otherwise.

Ecclesiastes 4:1–3

'Again I looked … I saw the tears of the oppressed – and they have no comforter …' (v.1)

For prayer and reflection

Dear Lord, I may not understand everything that is happening to me right now but I know and I am reassured that my life is in Your hands and that gives me peace. Amen.

In **all things**

Ecclesiastes 7:12–14

'… God has made the one as well as the other.' (v.14)

Nobody likes to endure pain of any kind. That's perfectly natural and human. Indeed, the Bible recalls that when Jesus was going into Jerusalem for what He knew would be His journey to the cross, He set his face like a flint. He was unyielding in His approach to the pain He knew He would face at the cross. He understood what He was going to accomplish at the cross and set His mind accordingly. Although we might not have the same understanding about the situation we are going through Jesus' approach teaches us a lot about attitude adjustment and the way God expects us to handle adversities.

As today's verse reminds us; in good times and in bad, in good decisions and the consequences of bad decisions, nothing is beyond the grace-filled arms of God. We might not know the full details of every single thing that will happen in our lifetime (and I wonder if we would really want to!) but the Bible is resoundingly clear on one thing; God has nothing but good planned for us. That knowledge alone should comfort us in our time of need when everything else fails.

Does that mean that we should not grieve or show emotion when we're hurting? No! It means that we have the liberty to acknowledge and express our emotions yet, at the same time, we can rejoice in the midst of our pain and suffering because we understand that our faith is not dictated by our circumstances.

Ultimately God's way will triumph.

For prayer and reflection

Dear Jesus, I know that in You everything exists. I give You my present situation knowing that You are in control of my life. Thank You.

It's **not my strength!**

There are different kinds of pain. There is the pain of betrayal, the pain of a broken heart and the pain of physical illness amongst many. Anyone suffering from any of these 'pains' knows the depths to which they've suffered. At times, emotional pain can even feel like physical pain.

For those suffering from a broken heart, the inclination is to build a hedge of 'protection' around it so we won't ever be betrayed by it again. That seems entirely normal. But we must remember the psalmist's cry, 'a broken and contrite heart, O God, you will not despise' (Psa. 51:17).

For those of us suffering from betrayal, we strengthen ourselves with the thought that we need never trust again – forgetting the countless times we've abused the Lord's trust in us.

And for those suffering from the pain of physical illness, we wonder why the healing miracle seems so long in coming. We berate ourselves for lacking faith, forgetting that sometimes the Lord in His own wisdom chooses not to reveal why healing does not take place for some people.

If we are not careful, these situations which could be used to glorify God and purify us can turn us into hardened vessels unfit for God's use, sometimes without us knowing. How do we prevent that? By maintaining close contact with God.

Jesus Himself knew pain and betrayal. God does not despise a broken heart because broken hearts are devoid of self and require heavy (if not total) reliance on Him to heal. He understands our struggles and will be there for us to make us strong when we are weak. When we lack physical strength we can ask the Lord for *His* strength to keep us emotionally and spiritually strong.

Ecclesiastes 7:3–9

'Do not be quickly provoked in your spirit …' (v.9)

For prayer and reflection

Forgive my pride, Lord, in thinking I could do it all by myself. You alone are my source. I repent of my pride now in Jesus' name. Amen.

WEEKEND

What use pain?

For reflection: Psalm 30; Ecclesiastes 2:23

This past week, we have been looking at pain and how God can use it for His own glory. Perhaps we have also discovered how He uses it to reveal to us something of our own character and our relationship with God. How would we know what is wrong with us if we didn't experience pain? People who lose all sense of pain or are oblivious to it, are at high risk of irrevocable damage, because one of their senses and therefore a defence is not working.

There are times when God does not answer our questions. Could it be He is asking: *Regardless of how this situation turns out, will I still be Lord of your life? Will you still trust Me and believe that I know best and have nothing but good planned for you?*

Consider this and be honest – can you trust Him, whatever?

It is a tough one but it is made easier by knowing that ultimately we are not alone in our challenges, in our pains and in our journey. We have God Himself in the Person of the Holy Spirit helping us to make sense of the chaos. What use pain? In the hands of the Master, it is worth its weight in gold.

Thank You, Jesus, for allowing the challenges that have come my way to reveal something of Your character to me. Amen.

Not knowing it all

I n trying to make sense of particular seasons of our life we seek understanding.

As born-again Christians, we have the assurance that we have a relationship with God. This gives us the freedom to seek answers from Him regarding any situation in our lives. I believe that this is one of the most liberating things about Christianity. At the same time, this freedom can unknowingly act as our albatross.

My church tradition is Pentecostal which encourages and challenges me to look to God and God alone for answers in all situations of my life, while at the same time examining myself to find out if there are areas where I have gone wrong and which are contributing to my particular challenge. If I have financial problems, I examine my finances to see where I've gone wrong or where I'm not honouring God with them. When I'm facing emotional challenges, I examine my life to see in which areas I've taken idols instead of focusing on God. And on it goes. But sometimes, when this approach does not work, I'm flummoxed, perplexed and work even harder to get to the root of my challenge.

While self-examination, wisely interspersed with the Word of God is the right approach (see also 1 Cor. 11:26–32), when it doesn't work, we unknowingly revert to works to 'earn' God's favour. So we actually miss out on what the Lord is trying to teach us – that He wants us to be still and enjoy being in His presence regardless of what we're going through. The Father of all creation yearns for relationship with us and enjoys being with us.

Ecclesiastes 7:19–29

'So I turned my mind to understand, to investigate and to search out wisdom …' (v.25)

For prayer and reflection

Lord, teach me to be still and to enjoy being in Your presence not only today but all the time. In Jesus' name. Amen.

Not just a **state of mind**

**Ecclesiastes
10:5–9; 11:1–2**

'Cast your
bread upon the
waters …' (11:1)

We are now going to look at the issue of disappointment – a powerful emotion and one that needs to be dealt with before God. When we are let down, we feel hurt. And if not dealt with, this hurtful feeling can actually progress into something infinitely more harmful – bitterness. I've observed that bitter people did not start out being bitter. Somewhere along the way they have been let down and disappointed by people or institutions they trusted.

Disappointment is usually with individuals, the Church or even God. Some people have believed God for physical healing but haven't received anything. Some have diligently served the Lord only to face walls wherever they go. Some have simply endured far too much pain in their lives. All these people are wondering where God's 'good plans and future' are and they're left wondering why their breakthroughs appear to be permanently stuck between heaven and earth.

Today's reading bemoans the terrible consequences that can arise from having unwise rulers. The wise man comments that, 'I have seen slaves on horseback while princes go on foot like slaves' (v.7). However, we are not serving an unwise ruler; neither are we slaves. We are serving a heavenly Father who sees all our disappointments and has promised to steer us through the maze of hurt that comes with it, if only we would allow Him. In our disappointment, if we do not take appropriate measures, we can shut out – partly to shield our hearts from further disappointment – the voice of the Lord asking us, 'Do you still trust Me and believe that I have nothing but the best in store for you?'

For prayer and reflection

Lord God, grant me the courage to face up to my feelings and disappointments. I know that You will never let me down. Thank You. Amen.

Disappointment with God

S ome simply cannot understand a faith that makes people stronger when they're 'down' but that is precisely what our Christian faith teaches, for when we are weak, Christ is strong (2 Cor. 12:9-10).

But what do we do when we're disappointed, especially when we're disappointed with God?

On the whole, we are mostly disappointed when people let us down or situations do not pan out the way we expect them to. And so it is with God. Many a time when we are disappointed with Him, it is simply that He hasn't 'behaved' in a way we expect Him to; He hasn't 'answered our prayer', for example, or He's let things happen to us that we feel He 'shouldn't have'; or our dreams are not coming true. In other words He has dared not to fit in the box we've relegated Him to.

I believe we should view disappointments as opportunities for looking at issues or situations we are faced with, and examining our attitudes – why has this affected me so badly, and so on.

Walking away from our disappointments or bottling them up smacks of pride, because we somehow believe that in ignoring what we're currently experiencing, we are being 'good Christians'. But we can go on trusting and believing Him whatever our experience because our faith is not based on quick fixes and easy answers. It's based on trust – no matter the cost or what we see or don't see.

Ecclesiastes 6

'I have seen another evil under the sun, and it weighs heavily on men ...' (v.1)

For prayer and reflection

Dear Lord, forgive my pride and refusal to acknowledge whatever I am going through. Help me to understand whatever You may be trying to teach me. Thank You for the liberty Your grace brings. In Jesus' name. Amen.

The **seed principle**

Ecclesiastes 11:1–6

'Sow your seed in the morning ...' (v.6)

There are biblical ways of dealing with disappointment. Today's reading talks about sowing our seeds. It also says that, 'If clouds are full of water, they pour rain upon the earth' (v.3). Translated thus, it means that whatever we give our heart to and feed on is what will be multiplied in our lives.

When we are disappointed in something or someone, it is only natural that we feel wronged, neglected and even hurt. Perhaps you have been believing God for a child but this hasn't happened yet and you're experiencing all the emotions I just described. I wonder if you have thought about praying for other women in your position. There is a particular spiritual strength and encouragement that is released when one does this and it pleases God.

And lastly but not least importantly, perhaps the road to healing/deliverance from disappointment is to acknowledge what we are feeling. Yes, we are Christians but that does not make us devoid of emotions. And no, the Lord will not love us any less for acknowledging what we feel. The road to healing starts with a truthful assessment of our situation. We could start by asking ourselves what lies behind our disappointment. Could it be that we are blaming others or have been let down by people who perhaps were not aware of the expectations we have of them?

So go on, admit your disappointments to God and start walking towards your healing.

For prayer and reflection

What are your current disappointments? Draw up a list and present it to the Lord. Next, draw up another list with your expectations and desires. Present both lists to the Lord and listen to what He has to say about them.

Not disappointed, **just awed**

T here is another side issue of disappointment that we have to examine. For many Christians, disappointment comes with a partner – guilt. Even though we have the intellectual knowledge that God gave us our feelings, we can still feel guilty when we experience them. We may think that we cannot articulate that we feel let down by people, God or our circumstances because it is unchristian to do so, so we stuff down our emotions and go about our daily lives. We've been told so many times not to allow ourselves to be dominated by our emotions that we're in danger of becoming congregational robots! Even those with a good support network find themselves with almost nowhere to go.

The end result is a stagnant Christian life, one that is imprisoned by guilt, grieved by disappointment and unable to move on. Which doesn't make for much Christian growth, does it?

This week, I pray that you have been emboldened to confront your feelings and deal with them truthfully. We should not be scared of our emotions otherwise they will rule over us. And although God already knows how we are feeling, the Bible encourages us to bring it all to Him. That is the joy of being a child of God. Remember that in all our challenges, He is there with us, using those difficult seasons to mould us and reveal Himself to us. If our faith journey were uneventful, without any incidents to challenge us, it is a guaranteed fact that we wouldn't grow as human beings, nor as Christians would we learn to appreciate the value of what was done at the cross.

Ecclesiastes 5:1

'Guard your steps when you go to the house of God.' (v.1)

For prayer and reflection

Thank You, Lord, for working in me by the power of Your Holy Spirit, and encouraging me to work through my disappointments this week. All glory be to Jesus. Amen.

WEEKEND

From disappointment to glory

For reflection: Psalm 121; Ecclesiastes 2:22–23

I pray the week's devotionals have been helpful in allowing you to get to grips with your hurts and disappointments and, finally, to prepare you for the great things that God has in store for you.

Emotions are outward expressions of what we are feeling inside. We should not be condemned or imprisoned by them. And neither should we allow them to rule over us. When we feel low or when we are going through periods of low self-esteem, one of the most practical things we can do is to align our minds with what the Bible says about us as God's children and how highly He esteems us.

Often, when we go through seasons of low self-esteem, it is because we believe we have fallen short of what is expected of us and we wonder if things can ever be made right. Whatever our feelings or situation, we have to believe the truth about God, namely that He is a loving Father who created us. He sees our weaknesses and has given us the firm assurance that nothing can ever change His love for us. That is the promise we have in Jesus Christ.

Spend some time reading Psalm 121 and take encouragement from God's promises to you as revealed in the psalm.

Even in **the wilderness**

As we approach the end of our reflections on Ecclesiastes, we will take this time to reflect on everything we've learnt about different difficult seasons and how God uses them to build our Christian character. The Christian life can be likened to our human growth. When we first dedicate our lives to the Lord, we are like newborn babies. Everything is new and exciting. Like babies, we have to be fed and nurtured in the Word. Slowly, as we begin to grow and develop, we encounter trials and challenges designed to develop our growth and knowledge of God. Suddenly, we realise that the easy life we thought we had signed on for is not what we are experiencing. *Where is the God of our youth?* we cry out.

Many Christians go through this stage. Today's exhortation for us to remember the Lord in the days of our youth is a call to remember the Lord's faithfulness to us in times past. When we do this, our faith is strengthened and our hope restored.

There is a popular saying that sometimes you can't see the wood for the trees. In our Christian walk, sometimes we can't see the Lord because of all our challenges. At times there are no easy answers but there are guidelines laid down in the Bible that we can follow when we don't know the way. Such as the times when our faith lacks direction, when we're just going through the motions.

Allow God to speak into these times. Let Him use the wilderness times to grab your attention and refocus on Him, His truth and His promises.

Ecclesiastes 12:1–5

'Remember your Creator in the days of your youth …'
(v.1)

For prayer and reflection

I might not understand this wilderness season, Lord, but I do know that You are in control of it. In Jesus' name. Amen.

A man **for all seasons**

**Ecclesiastes
12:6–8**

'Remember him
– before the silver
cord is severed …'
(v.6)

Seen in the light of eternity, our earthly life is rather short. Here today, gone tomorrow. Viewed thus, it makes sense for us to make use of the time we have on earth to do something worthwhile.

In today's verse, the Teacher tells us to remember the Lord before the silver cord is severed. Indeed, at first glance, this makes for depressing reading, until we read it again and realise it is an urgent plea from a man who has devoted his life to seeking wisdom, engaging in pleasure and, in general, looking for what the world calls 'the meaning of life'. Having done all these things, he can only proclaim that it is all meaningless.

It is not the cry of a man who has given up on life. Rather it is the cry of a man who, having sampled all that life has to offer, concludes that man is spirit and can indeed do nothing by himself. Today's verse is a sombre one. After all is said and done, in the event of our passing, the world will still function. The milkman will still deliver the milk; the postman will still deliver the post. Our mark on the world, visible to some but unremarkable to others might or might not be commented on. It makes sense to live it in light of eternity – by serving God and living a Christ-centred life.

Remember Him. A cry to the lost. *Remember Him.* A cry to Christians. *Remember Him.* A cry to us all. Whatever your season, remember the Lord even when you lack understanding about what you're going through. Remember Him because He remembers you.

For prayer and reflection

Autumn, spring, summer, winter. You are always there. May my life be a living testimony to Your goodness and Your mercy. In Jesus' name. Amen.

God's Word **stands forever**

I n the West we have access to so many books and translations of the Bible that we are spoilt for choice. You have a problem but don't know how to resolve it? It's not a problem. Someone, somewhere has written a book about it. It is a sad fact that many Christians today would rather read a book that tells them what the Bible says about something than read the Bible itself. I wonder, what does this say about us and Christianity today?

Many people I know do not like reading the Bible. They know they should read it but find it hard to do so. I am a fiction writer and my primary motivation for writing fiction was to bring God's Word to unbelievers in a way they would never have considered. To do this, I incorporate spiritual truths into what I write.

But we believers need so much to read God's Word – to ask His Holy Spirit to give us wisdom and understanding as we read it, to listen to good teaching on it, to learn it, to absorb it, to meditate on it, that its words might be actually 'written on our hearts'. I am constantly amazed by how the Holy Spirit flits Bible verses through my mind in my times of need. This is the power of the gospel and what the Holy Spirit does for us.

If you find it hard reading the Bible, set yourself a challenge. Read a paragraph a day. Psychologists say it only takes 21 days to develop a habit. In this new year nurture a love for the Word that will sustain you in all seasons. Remember, it stands forever and never loses its power.

Ecclesiastes 12:9–14

'Of making many books there is no end, and much study wearies the body.' (v.12)

For prayer and reflection

As I meditate on today's Bible verse and notes, Lord, I ask You through Your Holy Spirit, to kindle my spirit and fill me with a renewed love for the Bible. In Jesus' name. Amen.

A sense of **déjà vu**

**Ecclesiastes
1:1–11**

'… there is nothing
new under the
sun.' (v.9)

The Christian life is indeed like nature's seasons whose times God has ordained. In the UK, we have four seasons: autumn, winter, spring and summer. In Nigeria, where I grew up, there were just two: the rainy season and the harmattan (dry) season. In the same way we go through such seasons in our Christian lives.

I know that September heralds the start of autumn so I start making changes to my wardrobe in preparation for winter. In much the same way, our seasons of change do not suddenly creep up on us. Preparing for faith-challenges requires us to undergo faith-strengthening exercises; immersing ourselves deeper in the Word, surrounding ourselves with people who will encourage us and drawing ourselves into deep prayer. Those are the ways to build and strengthen our faith. Then we will not be taken aback when we are faced with challenges.

In addition, we ought to know by now that whatever situation we go through, God is in control and whatever happens, the fact that He's brought us out of previous challenges (although not always in ways we expected Him to) should encourage us. Such knowledge and simplicity of faith should keep us going.

For prayer and reflection

We can think that whatever we're going through, we're the first people it's happened to. But there is nothing new under the sun. You're not the first to experience what you are experiencing. If you're going through a particular challenge and you don't know which way to turn, seek the (godly) counsel of others who've endured the same thing and come out of it. They can counsel you in a way that others who haven't 'walked in your shoes' cannot. Above all, always remember the words of the Lord: *I am with you always*.

Thank You, God, for reassuring me that my situation is not unique. Grant me the freedom to minister to others so they too can be set free. Amen.

It all comes down to **one thing**

his verse though often quoted might seem strange to some, particularly in light of what we've been discussing about seasons. But it is very apt. The Teacher's exhortation for us to fear God can also be seen as wise words from a man whose mother not only committed adultery but whose lover then murdered her husband. He was also a man who'd witnessed much bloodshed and his family torn apart by greed and unfocused ambition. Solomon had untold wealth and later in life became self-indulgent (see 1 Kings 11:1–13). He was a man who had been through all life's seasons and lived to tell the tale. We can learn a lot from him.

If you have been wronged, take heart from today's reading. Jesus is a just judge and He will bring every evil deed against us to judgment. If you are having problems letting go of your hurt, pain and disappointment, then let today's verse encourage you to develop a healthy fear and trust in God even when everything within you screams the exact opposite.

As we draw near the weekend, take some time to revisit everything we've done this month. Have your own private slide show in your mind and endeavour to follow and obey God in this particular season of your life. This is our duty as Christians; to follow God regardless of the season.

The fear of the Lord is a healthy one. It is a fear borne out of love and respect for the One who created us and gave up His life so that we might live. Can we do any less for Him?

Ecclesiastes 12:13–14

'Fear God and keep his commandments, for this is the whole duty of man.' (v.13)

For prayer and reflection

I fear You, Lord. However, it is a fear propelled by love for You and what You did for me at the cross. Blessed be Your name.

WEEKEND

He has a plan for my life!

For reflection: Psalm 20

This weekend, we will look at the desires of our hearts.

Perhaps you have a desire or a goal you would like to fulfil this year. For example, I have a personal desire to run the London marathon.

Do you have such a desire – maybe something that burns inside of you that you think is too foolish for God to answer or anyone to understand? That's OK because that's why God gave us unique personalities and traits. As long as your desire is holy and focused righteously, I would encourage you to go for it. It might take you all year to fulfil. You might stumble more times than you care to remember in fulfilling it. But remember the words of the psalmist:

> If the LORD delights in a man's way,
>   he makes his steps firm;
> though he stumble, he will not fall,
>   for the LORD upholds him with his hand.
>
> (Psa. 37:23–24)

I pray and hope that this will be the year you fulfil your heart's desire. If you don't think you have a real goal or heart's desire, ask God to give you one.

Wisdom, freely given

I t is inevitable that in trying to make sense of what we're going through we will make mistakes. That is what makes us human. Some of us, and maybe it's women in particular, have the tendency to compare ourselves with others using the 'sinometer'. It's like a consolation exercise. *At least, I'm not as bad as x or y,* we mutter to ourselves when we come short. We do this because it makes us feel better. The thing is, the Bible does not tell us to measure ourselves against x or y. It tells us that Jesus is our model and the only one we should emulate. God in His infallibility is well aware of our human fallibility.

Yes, we do have the Holy Spirit within us, empowering and enabling us to make the right decisions, but the truth of the matter is that we will fall because we inhabit a fallen world and dwell in fallen bodies. This knowledge should not be given as an excuse for sinful behaviour but it should free us from the bondage of guilt after we have repented of our actions. We must not let it drag us down.

As we look back on everything we've learnt over the last few weeks, I pray that you have gained a better understanding of the various tough seasons of your life. The Christian life comes with its own set of unique challenges, not least because Christians live against society's rules and, for the most part, our actions and practices are not always understood. However, I hope this study of Ecclesiastes has enabled you to gain a better understanding of why these seasons occur and why we need them to grow the way the Lord wants us to.

Ecclesiastes 9:13–18

'So I said, "Wisdom is better than strength."'
(v.16)

For prayer and reflection

What particular lessons have you learnt this month about yourself and your relationship with God?

Moving on!

Psalm 100

'Know that the LORD is God. It is he who made us, and we are his ...' (v. 3)

Let us move on with thankful and expectant hearts for the great things the Lord will do. This year, endeavour to grow in your knowledge of God and learn how to apply to your life His panoramic view of it. Wisdom is not limited to a few seers of the kingdom. The Bible says it will be given freely to all who ask for it. Whatever situation, season or challenge you will go through this year, remember it is just that: a season. It won't last forever even if it does seem like that sometimes! That knowledge alone should spur you on in your faith as you seek to live it out to the best of your ability.

God hasn't left you alone without a definite guide or plan to help you. He has given us Himself in the Person of the Holy Spirit. He will give you the knowledge on how to proceed in every area of your life. He will give you the peace that surpasses all understanding and enable you to praise God in the most challenging seasons. That is why today's verse talks about us giving thanks to God and celebrating His faithfulness to us throughout all generations and all seasons.

The Christian life cannot be lived in isolation, by oneself. A relationship with the Lord will help and sustain you during your trials and joys this year. Cultivate this most important relationship. A simple request in the morning asking the Holy Spirit to guide you and be with you as you face the day is more than enough for God to reveal Himself and make Himself known to you.

For prayer and reflection

Lord God, through Your Holy Spirit, I invite You to be my friend, counsellor and guide, not just this year but for all time. In Jesus' name. Amen.

Onwards and upwards –

reflections on 1 Timothy

Christine Platt

Christine's passion for writing started in Ivory Coast, West Africa where she worked with The Navigators. She now lives in New Zealand and enjoys the freedom and opportunities that semi-retirement brings! As well as local ministry she also travels regularly with teams to East Timor to support the church there in its courageous witness to war-ravaged people. She has now learned one of the languages (Tetun) and is writing Bible studies and devotional notes in Tetun.

Onwards and upwards

1 Timothy 1:1–2

'Paul, an apostle of Christ Jesus by the command of God our Saviour ...' (v.1)

This conviction strengthened Paul during his tumultuous life; God had called him to be an apostle. It was not his own idea; God clearly commissioned him for this pioneering role (Acts 9). Paul knew from experience that God never gave him a job without supplying the necessary gifts and ability to do it (2 Cor. 3:4–6). Moses and Gideon both initially doubted God's enabling, but went on to prove that when God calls, He equips for the task. He helped them grow into their new responsibilities.

During these next few weeks we will explore Paul's first letter to Timothy. We'll see Paul's confidence in God for all that lay ahead for Timothy in his role as leader of the Ephesian church. Following in Paul's footsteps would have been daunting for Timothy. He was a younger man, possibly timid (2 Tim. 1:7), and frequently ill (1 Tim. 5:23). He may well have needed to be reminded that grace, mercy and peace were available to him from God the Father and Christ Jesus his Lord (1 Tim. 1:2). The specific challenge confronting Timothy was false teachers who were confusing the faithful (1:3–7).

For prayer and reflection

What are you facing today? Has God placed a responsibility on you at work, at home, at church, in the community? Treat this as a learning and growing opportunity. God will enable you and develop His gifts in you as you launch out with Him. Don't expect to be instant superwoman! One of the best pieces of advice I ever received is: Failure is never final. You will not sail through life on a puffy white cloud – that has never been the experience of any of God's people throughout the ages. But setbacks, difficulties and responsibilities need never swamp you, because God's grace, mercy and peace are yours in abundance.

Father God, I bring to You this challenge I'm facing. Thank You for it. Help me grow through it as I lean on You.

On the **right track**

Some people in Timothy's church were misusing the Scriptures to promote their own pet theories. The same can happen in our churches today. Those who build a doctrine on a few obscure verses are on shaky ground. Equally dangerous is taking verses out of context. We need to abandon our prejudices and preconceived ideas as much as possible when we come to the Bible. It is a precious gift and must be carefully and wisely used. God will not turn a blind eye when people misuse His Word, but reserves judgment for them (Rev. 22:18–19).

Paul urges Timothy to teach sound doctrine (1:10) and to refute those who were spreading false teachings (1:3), in order to protect the flock from these malignant viruses.

How can we ensure we are not led astray? A growing working knowledge of the Bible – Old and New Testaments – will act as a protection for us, especially if we follow the Bereans' example. They 'received the message with great eagerness and examined the Scriptures every day to see if what Paul said was true' (Acts 17:11). Let's not assume that a gifted communicator has got it all right. God expects us to use our brains and analyse what's being taught. The Holy Spirit also leads us into all truth (John 16:13).

We have a part to play and God, by His Holy Spirit, has His part. Are we growing in our knowledge, understanding and application of God's Word? Do we really think about what we hear at church, at homegroup, on the radio, on TV?

For those who have a spiritual responsibility for others, it is vital that we become 'a workman who does not need to be ashamed and who correctly handles the word of truth' (2 Tim. 2:15).

1 Timothy 1:3–11

'We know that the law is good if one uses it properly.'
(v.8)

For prayer and reflection

Father God, thank You for the Bible. Please give me understanding and 'Open my eyes that I may see wonderful things in your law' (Psa. 119:18).

God of **transformation**

**1 Timothy
1:12–20**

'… I was shown
mercy … the worst
of sinners …' (v.16)

P aul holds nothing back. He declares himself to have been a blasphemer, a persecutor and a violent man ... the worst of sinners. What a fantastic God we have who shows such mercy.

I was recently glued to a TV documentary of a heavily tattooed gang leader. He'd robbed, raped and peddled drugs. Violence was his everyday companion. Also on the programme was a woman, now in her 40s who, as a 15-year-old, had been gang-raped by this leader's group. This had so traumatised her that she'd turned to drugs and extreme promiscuity.

They both told their stories of how God had picked them up out of their 'pits' (Psa. 40:2) and brought them to Himself.

At the climax of the programme the woman faced the man who had so brutally damaged her and said, 'I forgive you,' and the man received her forgiveness. It was powerful stuff on primetime TV.

The ghastliness of their lives could not be denied, but the mercy of God proved sufficient for them to turn away from their past and grow towards their future. Both were now involved in counselling services for people in similar need. Truly God is able to bring good out of the most hideous situations (Rom. 8:28). It will probably not be evident immediately, but in the course of time, He can transform the deepest wounds in our lives so that 'a spring of living water' (John 4:14) will flow out to refresh others.

This was evidently true in Paul's life. His profound experience of God's mercy spurred him on to tell everyone he could about Jesus. He knew that no one was beyond the reach of God's forgiveness. Paul's contribution to the kingdom of God is incalculable.

**For prayer and
reflection**

**Use these
thoughts about
Paul, and the
gang leader and
his victim, as a
stimulus as you
pray for friends
and family to
come to Christ.**

WEEKEND

Amazing grace, how sweet the sound

For reflection: Luke 7:36–50

The dictionary defines grace as 'unmerited divine assistance given to human beings for their regeneration or sanctification'. In other words, God reaches out in kindness to undeserving people – like all of us – to give a new start in life and to make us better people.

Simon the Pharisee considered himself superior to the woman who poured perfume on Jesus' feet. The woman had no illusions about herself. She knew she was in big trouble. Simon thought he was doing OK. But it was the woman who received an unforgettable outpouring of God's grace that day. She left the house a changed woman. Simon appears to have remained in a state of self-satisfied smugness.

If we've been Christians for some years it's possible to 'get used to' being forgiven and to lose the thrill of being cleansed from all sin. We forget how heinous even 'little' sins are to God. Others can feel constantly defeated by sin and never receive full forgiveness.

Wherever you are on this continuum, use this woman's actions as a model.

Take time this weekend to pour out your love and gratitude to Jesus for His amazing grace to you, an undeserving sinner.

Too busy not to pray

1 Timothy 2:1–4

'I urge, then, first of all, that requests, prayers, intercession and thanksgiving be made ...' (v.1)

Paul had a lot on – sermons to preach, letters to write, journeys to make, thorny issues to resolve. If anyone didn't have time to pray, it was Paul. But prayer permeates his writings.

We can be tempted to shoot a quick prayer heavenwards at the beginning of the day, then get on with our work and other activities, hoping to get some more prayer time later, which may or may not happen.

Paul stresses prayer – 'first of all' – No. 1 priority. He knows that in the spiritual battle we face, nothing of significance will be accomplished without God's intervention in answer to prayer. Only as we stay close to God, listening to Him, being guided and empowered by Him, can we fully co-operate in His purposes for our lives, families, communities, world. His thoughts and His ways are so much higher than ours (Isa. 55:8–9; John 15:5). How can we expect to understand His plans for our days with a quick 'Hello, please bless my plans. Goodbye'?

Somewhere in our days we need to come aside to meet with God so we can make requests, prayers, intercessions, and give thanks. Praying with others can be a real stimulus. Try to get a prayer partner if you haven't already got one.

Another challenging aspect in this passage is the exhortation to pray for those in authority. The notorious godless emperor Nero was in charge when Paul wrote. It is so much easier to criticise than to pray. Even if we consider our politicians and leaders to be the lowest rats in the pack, making a complete hash of everything, we need to respect their position and pray for them. In fact, if they are that bad, they need our prayers more than ever!

For prayer and reflection

Lord, teach me to pray. Help me make this a priority in my life, just as it was in Yours (Luke 11:1).

Mediator par excellence

A s I write this there is yet another round of peace talks going on between Israel and Palestine. The mediator – 'the one who is intervening between parties in order to reconcile them' (*New Penguin English Dictionary*) – is the US Secretary of State.

In other conflicts also, mediators come and mediators go, but in many cases the violence, hatred and injustice remain. The mediators do their best but the problems are of gigabyte magnitude.

How much more huge was the problem facing Jesus! On one side Holy God, awesome in purity, and on the other side exceedingly sinful people. How was He to reconcile them? Our perfect mediator left the glory of heaven, came to share in our flawed humanity and offered Himself as a ransom for all people (v.6). And the deal was done! God accepted His offering. The veil in the Temple separating man from God was ripped apart (Matt. 27:51). Our sins could be forgiven. 'Jesus Christ, the Righteous One' speaks to the Father in our defence (1 John 2:1), and we could all be adopted into God's family (Eph. 1:5). Whoopee! Hallelujah!

No one else could have done the job. There truly is only one way to God and that is through Jesus, '... there is no other name under heaven given to men by which we must be saved' (Acts 4:12). Other religions and sects, however well-meaning, have missed the point.

No wonder Paul is so eager to get the truth out (2:7). Like Paul, we have magnificent news to share. Our friends, family, work colleagues, neighbours, in fact everybody, needs to hear it. Do you feel sometimes reluctant to speak of Christ? Maybe you've lost sight of all that Jesus has done for you. Paul was captivated by love for Jesus – that was his motivation (2 Cor. 5:14).

1 Timothy 2:5–8

'For there is one God and one mediator between God and men, the man Christ Jesus ...' (v.5)

For prayer and reflection

Take some time to thank Jesus for all He accomplished on the cross for you. Don't rush it. Ask Him for new insights.

41

What not **to wear**

1 Timothy 2:9–15

'I also want women to dress modestly, with decency and propriety … with good deeds …'
(vv.9–10)

For prayer and reflection

Lord, help me see any changes I need to make so that my life honours You in every way – inside and outside.

One of my favourite TV programmes is *What not to wear*. Two fashion-savvy women take style-challenged men and women, and we watch as beautiful creatures emerge! We, who are created in God's image (Gen. 1:27), need to reflect His beauty, and that includes our appearance.

It seems that the women in Ephesus, where Timothy was pastoring, were going overboard with elaborate hairdos and outfits, using external decoration to attract attention to themselves. Possibly the women in the church were tempted to follow suit. Paul emphasises that Christian beauty comes from within. Peter, his co-leader, echoes this: 'Your beauty should not come from outward adornment … Instead, it should be that of your inner self, the unfading beauty of a gentle and quiet spirit …' (1 Pet. 3:3–4).

Our first priority should be to fully co-operate with the Holy Spirit so His beautiful fruit – love, joy, peace … (Gal. 5:22–23) is increasingly evident in our lives. We need to apply ourselves to doing good deeds and serving others. Paul says this is: 'appropriate for women who profess to worship God' (2:10). Our bodies are the temple of the Holy Spirit (1 Cor. 6:19–20). He is within us so something of His glorious strength and beauty should show.

As a young Christian I went through an ascetic phase – no make-up, dowdy, sensible clothes, as I thought that was more spiritual. Later I realised that to neglect my outward appearance did not honour God, and therefore was not more spiritual. I may never win a beauty contest, but I'm sure God wants my life to reflect Him in every area which includes the care I take over my appearance.

A leader! Who me?

It is so much easier to sit back and let someone else take responsibility to exercise leadership – to be a passenger or a crew member, rather than the captain. Leadership in the Church has been a minefield for women – many mistakes have been made on both sides. Against all the odds some women have raised their heads above the parapet and demonstrated godly leadership in a womanly way.

Leadership is exercised at many levels. Most church traditions now encourage women to exercise their gifts within certain parameters. I often hear women say: 'I could never lead a Bible study group or a prayer group. I could never speak in public.' Do some of us place artificial limitations on ourselves?

Leadership at any level is a 'noble task', and somebody has to do it. Why couldn't it be you? Moses, Jeremiah and Gideon all felt inadequate for their roles, but eventually went forward in faith. Paul mentions several women by name in Romans 16 who were fellow-workers with him in a culture where women were significantly disempowered.

Paul stresses that leaders need to develop knowledge, skills and character. None of these is obtainable overnight. But if we keep close to God and pursue a greater knowledge and understanding of the Bible, as well as co-operate with the Holy Spirit as He transforms our character, we will be able to fully fulfil the role for which God has uniquely gifted us. There are many training courses available. Starting off as an assistant to someone in a leadership role is a helpful way of learning on the job as Joshua did with Moses.

How many Deborahs or Priscillas do we have in our midst who are hiding their lights under a bushel?

1 Timothy 3:1–7

'If anyone sets his heart on being an overseer, he desires a noble task.' (v.1)

For prayer and reflection

Father God, please make me the leader You want me to be. I commit myself to Your training programme to grow in knowledge, skills and character.

Sticks and stones

The Greek for the word 'wives' simply means 'the women'. The context refers to women who serve in the church. It's interesting to note the phrase 'not malicious talkers' is applied to women and not to the men in this chapter.

If you watch children playing together little girls chatter away to each other whereas little boys often play without many words passing between them. Women usually find social chit-chat easier than men and it's a wonderful gift to be able to put people at their ease, to provide the oil to smooth situations and promote friendships. A kind word cheers people up (Prov. 12:25), but harsh words stir up anger (Prov. 15:1).

I remember realising with great glee the power of words when I was a child. I was the youngest and smallest in the family. I could never win physical fights with my big sisters, so I refined and practised some choice insults which I hurled frequently as mighty missiles. It was gratifying to watch the effect when they hit their mark! Since coming to Christ I've had to learn a lot about using words in a more beneficial way!

It is not true that 'sticks and stones may break my bones, but words can never hurt me'. Words have dynamic power for good or evil (James 3:3–12).

We women, who generally have a more natural facility with words than men, have untold capabilities at our disposal. We can wound or heal. We can destroy or build up. We can be kind or malicious. We can gossip or keep confidences. As with any gift of God we have responsibility to use it wisely and well.

WEEKEND

Looking after leaders

For reflection: Hebrews 13:17

It's tragic when you hear of church leaders getting burned out, disillusioned or going off the rails. The church falls apart. No one escapes collateral damage. Unbelievers look on and shake their heads as if to say: 'That church is in a mess. Why would I want to go there?' They turn away, disappointed, wondering where they can go to find God.

How can we support our leaders to avoid such devastation? Hebrews 13:17 gives some clues:

> Obey your leaders and submit to their authority. They keep watch over you as men who must give an account. Obey them so that their work will be a joy, not a burden, for that would be of no advantage to you.

We should do all we can to make sure their work is a joy to them, not a burden. Send an encouraging email or card. We should strive to be load-lifters not drains. Do you know what your pastor's day off is? Do you refrain from calling on that day? Does your church budget enable your leaders to go on training/teaching conferences for personal refreshment?

Maybe if we looked after our leaders better our churches would be healthier and more attractive to onlookers.

Heaven, here we come!

1 Timothy 3:14–16

'He appeared in a body … was taken up in glory.' (v.16)

At Christmas we celebrate Jesus coming to earth. Later on in the Christian calendar we celebrate Easter – Jesus' death and resurrection into glory. There were 33 amazing years when God was among us in bodily form.

I often wonder whether I would have been a believer, a mocker or a doubter if I'd met Jesus during His earthly life. I'm so thankful that I've met Him now and one day I'll be with Him in heaven, in glory. Heaven is a mysterious and huge concept – let's unpack it a little.

I've just looked at a seashell and noticed its delicate shades of colour, its smoothness inside and roughness outside. Its intricate shape is ideally suited to its occupant. There are trillions of sea creatures and God provides each one with an ideal place to live.

Jesus promised to prepare a home in heaven for every believer (John 14:1–3). He sees us as individuals. His provision will never be sub-standard or 'one size fits all'. I picture Him choosing colours, designs and furnishings to delight each eagerly awaited new arrival.

For prayer and reflection

'My Jesus, My Saviour, Lord, there is none like You.' Use this song (by Michael W. Smith), or another worship song to praise Jesus. You're preparing for heaven!

As I get older I am increasingly thankful that part of the 'in glory' deal is a new body (1 Cor. 15:35–54) … an imperishable, glorious and powerful body, fit to live eternally with God.

A new body, a new home and new friends. We'll meet Elijah, Deborah, David, Hannah, Mary. How exciting to meet heroes of faith we've read about!

Most importantly we'll meet Jesus, not as a baby or mortal man, but as the Lamb upon the throne (Rev. 5:6), as King of kings and Lord of lords (Rev. 19:16). We'll fall at His feet and worship. However inadequate we feel our worship is today, when we see Him it will be full, sincere and worthy of Him.

Beware, false teachers about!

Thishis would be an interesting passage for Valentine's Day! God clearly wants people to marry. He instituted marriage in the first place. I'm sure He enjoys the celebration of love on Valentine's Day. Food is also good. Verse 4 says: 'For everything God created is good, and nothing is to be rejected if it is received with thanksgiving …' God is good and gives good things.

Paul warns us about religious people who are false teachers. They come up with rules and regulations which are not of God. Unfortunately these 'hypocritical liars' are often powerful, influential people who readily attract a following. Some liars excel at mind-games and mental and spiritual manipulation. People are drawn in and eventually seem to lose all power of objective reasoning. They do the most illogical things which in their right minds they would never consent to.

How can we avoid taking the first step on that slippery slope? God provides us with safeguards: The Word of God, the Spirit of God and the Church of God. If we are wise we will measure what we hear preached, we will listen to the Spirit's prompting, we will place ourselves under the authority of a Bible-believing church and develop supportive, accountable friendships with mature Christians.

Paul leaves us in no doubt as to why these liars act in this way. They are led by 'deceiving spirits … taught by demons' (v.1). Satan aims to destroy God's people. Let's not be 'unaware of his schemes' (2 Cor. 2:11). The danger is real. We can be sure there are just as many false teachers about today as they were in Paul's time. We need to be on our guard.

1 Timothy 4:1–5

'… hypocritical liars … forbid people to marry and … to abstain from certain foods …' (vv.2–3)

For prayer and reflection

Do you need to take more advantage of God's safeguards to make sure you're not led astray?

47

Spiritual life-savers

1 Timothy 4:6–10

'… train yourself to be godly … godliness has value for all things …'
(vv.7–8)

Yesterday I watched my local life-saving club doing training classes. Children from six years up to late teens had to grab their surfboard, run into the sea, paddle right out around a buoy, surf back to the beach, drop their board, run up around some markers on the beach and back out again. They puffed, panted, sweated and strained to build muscle, stamina, agility and confidence as they rode the waves. I was very thankful that if I needed to be rescued there would be strong people around to save me.

We know we need to take exercise and keep our bodies as fit as we can, but we are also called to be spiritual life-savers. Verse 10 talks of the living God who is the Saviour of all men. His salvation is offered to all and He chooses to use us as intermediaries.

Are we building our faith muscles by studying and applying God's Word (Rom. 10:17) and launching out into new endeavours for Him? As I watched the life-savers I realised that appearance does matter. I would not feel confident if a puny nine-year-old wearing water wings paddled out to rescue me. In the same way, does our character increasingly reflect Christ so as to give people confidence that we do know the Saviour? If we say God is loving and compassionate and yet display negative critical attitudes, people will turn away. If we claim God gives joy and peace and we walk around with doleful expressions, racked with guilt or anxiety, they will conclude: Christianity doesn't work.

The fact that you're reading this indicates you're serious about 'training yourself to be godly'. The life-savers constantly push themselves to the limits of their stamina preparing to 'rescue the perishing'. Can God's people do any less?

For prayer and reflection

How can you develop your spiritual fitness? Why not go for a prayer walk and combine spiritual and physical training?

Unwrap those **gifts!**

Christmas comes and goes. Gifts are opened and enjoyed or ignored; I doubt many are left unopened. God is so generous. By His Holy Spirit He gives gifts to everyone (1 Cor. 12:4–7). We are all gifted people. How exciting to think that each of us has a unique contribution to make!

All the gifts are of equal value. Some may be more visible or spectacular, but even the gifts that are expressed quietly behind the scenes are of immense value to the kingdom.

It would be nice if these gifts were given in a fully mature and developed state but, like most other things in life, they come in embryonic form. And, like an embryo, they need the right environment in which to grow.

Timothy's gifts were probably in leadership, pastoring and teaching. Even he needed to be reminded not to neglect them. Paul had nurtured his young colleague and encouraged the flowering of his gifts to the point where Timothy was able to take on greater responsibilities. We can all have a role in helping others discover their gifts. Look out for people who need a bit of encouragement to try new things – like helping with children's ministry, hospitality, administration, visiting the sick or housebound, giving, interceding.

Looking at the Church today it seems there are substantial quantities of gifts still firmly wrapped up. There are children's classes without teachers, young people without mentors, projects without managers or finances, mission opportunities passing us by. I'm not saying this to make us feel guilty or to take on extra roles and become exhausted. The answer is for us to fully develop our own gifting and also help others to identify their gifts, so we all work together.

1 Timothy 4:11–16

'Do not neglect your gift …' (v.14)

For prayer and reflection

Father God, thank You for my gifts. Please help me identify, develop and use them for Your glory and the extension of Your kingdom.

God is **our refuge**

'The widow who is really in need and left all alone puts her hope in God …' (v.5)

I n biblical times widows were extremely vulnerable – there was no pension, life assurance or State assistance. There was no one to call on for help except God. All the normal support systems were gone. With that background one can more fully appreciate Jesus' compassionate response to the widow who was burying her only son (Luke 7:11–15), and His heartfelt praise of the widow who gave all she had to the Temple offering (Mark 12:41–44). Widows were fairly low on the social scale in Jesus' time, but their plight was important to Him.

We may not be in the same circumstances as these widows, but we can at times feel similarly abandoned and without resources. God is our only hope. Even though adequately supplied materially, we may be spiritually bankrupt and in dire need of help.

'God is our refuge and strength, an ever-present help in trouble' (Psa. 46:1). Whatever situations you or your loved ones are facing, God is able to help. He may not change the circumstances, but He will give strength and ability to cope. He is not oblivious to your pain.

For prayer and reflection

But we need to 'put our hope in God' – trust Him completely. Paul says these widows continue 'night and day to pray and ask God for help' (1 Tim. 5:5).

'Trust in him at all times ... pour out your hearts to him, for God is our refuge' (Psa. 62:8). God wants to be your refuge today.

Trouble and stress can either bring us closer to God or drive a wedge between Him and us. It's our choice. We can either draw near to Him and pour out our hearts to Him, or we can run away in anger and disappointment, screaming *Why?* If we draw near He may well reveal new insights about situations which will give us a different perspective and enable us to cope. In any case He will certainly strengthen us and show us more of Himself.

WEEKEND

The power of one

For reflection: Micah 6:8

Like widows in Paul's time, today there are millions who are powerless and poor, languishing at the bottom of the pile. Images of AIDS orphans, refugees from war, tsunami and famine victims, flit across our TV screens. In developed countries too there are abused, neglected children, victims of family violence and drug abuse. So much pain and injustice. God says:

> 'Speak up for those who cannot speak for themselves, for the rights of all who are destitute. Speak up and judge fairly; defend the rights of the poor and needy.' (Prov. 31:8–9)

I recently watched *The Power of One* – a compelling film about a white boy growing up in South Africa in the apartheid era. I was inspired to see the difference one person could make to a whole community, despite almost insurmountable difficulties.

There is the power of one and also the power of community. Many individuals and groups are making heroic efforts to fight injustice and the relentless cycle of poverty.

How can you express your power of one or join your power to a community? God is inviting you to take action.

Good deed for the day

1 Timothy 5:9–16

'… well known for her good deeds … devoting herself to all kinds of good deeds.' (v.10)

D orcas came to mind when I read these verses. She was known as a disciple who was always doing good and helping the poor. One of her good deeds was making clothes for widows and they were evidently delighted with them (Acts 9:36–42).

We live in a world of much need – not only material and physical, but also emotional and spiritual. The marvellous thing about being surrounded by need is that it gives us a huge variety of ways we can contribute towards meeting those needs. Dorcas made clothes. Mother Teresa cared for the poorest of the poor. Others visit shut-in people, foster troubled children, provide respite care for families with special needs children, do shopping for the elderly or sick, or provide a listening ear for those who are hurt or grieving.

A friend of mine is a statistician. 'What use is a statistician in God's economy?' she wondered. God wasted no time in telling her. She is now a key person in a Leprosy Eradication and Treatment programme in Nepal. God can even use people who revel in columns of numbers!

We are urged to devote ourselves to all kinds of good deeds. This is a lifestyle choice. 'Devote' implies a settled decision, not just a whim. This woman has set her course to do good deeds. It's not just if it fits in with her schedule that week. 'Devoting herself' also implies that she has thought through which good deeds to devote herself to, rather than being tossed around by each need that comes up and not being faithful to carry out one good deed well. Those with the gift of mercy and help need to put clear boundaries around themselves. A burned-out, compassion-fatigued Christian is not an attractive specimen.

For prayer and reflection

Can you pray this? Lord, I choose to devote myself to good deeds. Please guide me to those good deeds You have chosen for me.

Honour **your leaders**

Good church leaders are worth their weight in gold. Unfortunately there are always some followers who, though not willing or equipped to take the leadership themselves, are very happy to try to direct affairs from the sidelines. They tend to do this by criticism and seeking to influence others to their way of thinking, thus creating a dissatisfied faction within the church community.

Moses had his fair share of criticism from his own brother and sister as well as the Israelites. What completely blows my mind is that even the most perfect leader that ever lived, Jesus, had a follower who didn't appreciate His leadership!

No one leadership style will appeal to everyone. All leaders are fallible. So, anyone looking for the perfect church with a perfect leadership team, is doomed to disappointment.

It follows then that there are bound to be problems ahead for anyone who accepts a leadership role.

Paul asserts that those who lead well, especially those who preach and teach, are worthy of double honour, and that includes suitable financial remuneration. How can we give double honour to those who serve by leading (Luke 22:24–27)? We should squash criticism and gossip as soon as we hear it. If there is a genuine concern then people should be strongly advised to go to the leadership about it, and not try to raise support for their views from others, or spread gossip.

Any positive affirmation would be appreciated by any leader. Leaders can become tired and spiritually drained. To honour them might involve enabling them to take time off to attend retreats and conferences for continued growth, refreshment and stimulation.

**1 Timothy
5:17–20**

'The elders who direct the affairs of the church well are worthy of double honour ...' (v.17)

For prayer and reflection

Pray for your leaders that they might experience the touch of God on their lives today.

53

Going **against the flow**

'Don't sin because others do, but stay close to God.'
(v.22, CEV)

I n this passage Paul warns Timothy not to accept unworthy people into leadership positions in the church even if others strongly recommend them. Their supporters may be motivated by favouritism (v.21), or be seeking to promote their own bandwagon. Timothy is not to join them in their sin.

This same principle applies in every other area of life. We need to do what is right and not just go along with the crowd. We recognise that peer pressure poses enormous problems for young people, but adults are not exempt. It's so much easier to go with the flow, but we are all to stay close to God even if that means battling against the tide of popular opinion.

Jesus demonstrated this many times in His dealings with the religious establishment. In His encounter with the woman caught in adultery He cut through the rhetoric with this incisive statement: 'If any one of you is without sin, let him be the first to throw a stone at her' (John 8:7). He didn't try to accommodate different points of view. He was direct and straightforward.

Staying close to God and doing what is right will sometimes reap disapproval or rejection, and that's never easy to cope with. However, we must make sure that we don't exacerbate situations by displaying an argumentative or superior attitude. The Lord's servant 'must be kind to everyone ... Those who oppose him he must gently instruct ...' (2 Tim. 2:24–25).

I've met very few mortals who enjoy conflict situations; the stress and tension involved don't usually bring out the best in us. But however strongly we feel about an issue we must always seek to display the fruit of the Holy Spirit, otherwise we are allowing the sin of others to lead us into sin.

For prayer and reflection

Is there an area where you are tempted to compromise? How can you 'gently instruct' your opponents?

Choose **your attitude**

The gospel brought a whole new status to slaves in the Roman Empire. The State considered them non-persons, but in Christ they were brought into freedom (Rom. 8:21), and had equal standing with all other believers as children of God (Gal. 3:28).

There is a level playing field at the foot of the cross. Presidents, celebrities, missionaries, church leaders and the newest baby Christian all stand together with equal access to the throne of grace (Heb. 4:16). The Christian community is truly a revolutionary concept!

However, it seems that some of the slaves in Timothy's church were taking their privileges too far. They were not serving their masters as they should. They needed to realise that their new-found spiritual freedom did not change their social position. They were still slaves in the legal and physical sense, even though spiritually they were liberated beyond their wildest dreams. Their spiritual freedom should in fact enhance their service as they should seek to bring honour to God's name in their attitudes and actions (1 Tim. 6:1).

The young Israelite girl who was taken captive by the Arameans and sent to serve Naaman's household was a shining example of this (2 Kings 5:1–19). By her service and her speech she pointed her masters to the one true God. She had every reason to be resentful and angry but she chose to honour her masters and seek their best.

Most of us work in secular contexts. Some of us may feel powerless, like slaves, but we are all totally free to choose our attitude to life, to work, to others. In whatever situation we find ourselves, let's strive to be 'the salt of the earth' and 'the light of the world' (Matt. 5:13–14).

1 Timothy 6:1–2

'All who are under the yoke of slavery should consider their masters worthy of full respect …' (v.1)

For prayer and reflection

Lord Jesus, thank You for the freedom You've brought me into. Grant me grace and strength to honour You today in all I do.

Get rich quick?

1 Timothy 6:3–10

'People who want to get rich fall into temptation and a trap and … harmful desires …' (v.9)

Are you as sick as I am of game shows on TV where people strive to win tons of money; or of the Lottery, scratchcards, or adverts which scream 'Buy now, don't wait'? These all foster the natural greed that is in all of us. Gaming machines hold out the same false hope. You might win – but you most probably won't and you'll have lost your money in the process.

Paul warns about the inevitable outcome of those who want to be rich: they are plunged into 'ruin and destruction' (v.9).

Sure it seems like it would be great to get rich quick and not have to put in the hard grind to meet our basic financial needs, but some of the ways we go about getting rich are foolish and destructive. Credit card debt is a noose around many necks.

This passage also speaks about being content. This doesn't necessarily mean sitting at the bottom of the employment ladder contentedly earning a low wage. The Bible encourages us to use our gifts, work hard and fulfil our potential (Prov. 12:24; Col. 3:23). Contentment doesn't relate to our bank balance. We can be content with little money or with untold wealth (Phil. 4:11–12). It's an attitude of heart. Rich people who love money run the same risks as poor people who love money. Both are hurtling towards pain, trouble and destruction. The poor may just get there sooner than the rich.

Western culture influences us to think that money can solve all our problems. One only has to look at the lives of some rich people to realise that is not true.

Money is a fantastic servant, but a ghastly destructive master.

For prayer and reflection

Lord God, thank You for the money You give me. Please help me use it as my servant and not allow it to become my master.

WEEKEND

Generous Jesus

For reflection: Philippians 2:5–11

Jesus was Lord in a kingdom of unutterable joy, inexpressible love and incomprehensible peace, yet for our sakes, He gave it all up. He came to our world of pain and injustice. He suffered more than we can ever contemplate, and then died, so that we could inherit kingdom blessings.

> For you know the grace of our Lord Jesus Christ, that though he was rich, yet for your sakes he became poor, so that you through his poverty might become rich. (2 Cor. 8:9)

This is why we are to be generous to others in need – out of gratitude for Jesus' awesome generosity to us. It is not to earn extra brownie points; we are already top of Jesus' hit parade (Eph. 1:4–6)! It is not out of guilt that many of us in the Western world have such abundance when countless millions starve. These are unworthy motivations.

We are generous because we follow the example of Jesus who poured out His life for ungrateful, unworthy wretches like us.

This weekend, take some time to focus on the cross and allow gratitude to well up in your heart and spill over into praise to Jesus.

Unapproachable light

**1 Timothy
6:11–16**

'… King of kings
and Lord of lords
… immortal
and who lives in
unapproachable
light …' (v.15–16)

I n Paul's letter to Timothy there are strong
encouragements, hard words and firm instructions
– quite a daunting list for Timothy, and for us as
we take these teachings on board.

The Christian life can seem tough if we lose sight of
the One who is at the centre of it all – our mighty King
and highest Lord 'who lives in unapproachable light'.
He is utterly stupendous, incomprehensibly glorious
and majestic in power. Living in unapproachable light
speaks of God's holiness. His intense purity cannot allow
even the tiniest sin near Him. His holy heart even had
to turn away in disgust from His beloved Son when all
the rottenness of our sin was piled on Him on the cross.
Jesus deeply felt that abandonment (Mark 15:34).

In Old Testament times the high priest had to make
the prescribed animal sacrifice and could only go in
once a year to the Most Holy Place in the Temple where
God dwelt. The common people had no personal access
at all (Lev. 16).

**For prayer and
reflection**

**Father, I praise
You for all
that Jesus
accomplished
on the cross for
me, that I can
be forgiven and
approach Your
holy presence
with confidence
and joy.**

When God came down on the mountain in fire and
smoke with the deafening sound of trumpets, the Israelites
were terrified and begged Moses to talk to God for them.
This mighty God was too awesome for them to even think
about drawing near (Exod. 20:18–21).

We have to balance the truths of God's awesomeness
and unapproachability with His invitation to draw near
through Christ, our great High Priest (Heb. 4:14–16).
This means not holding back in fear, but approaching
confidently, yet not abusing this immense privilege. All
sin needs to be confessed and repented of before we
venture to place a foot on the threshold of His presence
so that we come to God with a cleansed heart, ready to
worship, honour and obey.

You can't take it with you!

aul echoes Jesus' words from Matthew 6:19–21: 'Do not store up for yourselves treasures on earth, where moth and rust destroy ... But store up for yourselves treasures in heaven ...' Storing up treasures in heaven involves using our present riches of time, energy, gifts, talents, material possessions and money for the benefit of others, and not letting anything lie fallow, gathering dust.

'You can't take it with you when you go' applies to all our present riches. What we send on ahead of us is our contribution to building God's kingdom, which we'll lay at Jesus' feet when we meet Him face to face. Don't we want our contribution to be as big as possible to honour our Mighty Saviour?

The apostle Paul gloried in the knowledge that when he met Jesus he would present to Him the people he'd influenced for His kingdom (1 Thess. 2:19).

I recently helped clear out an elderly lady's home. For years she'd bought material, zips, buttons and sewing cotton to make clothes, but had never got around to doing anything with it. Her rooms were full to the brim with stuff. Some of it was still useable, but much had gone mouldy. What a waste!

This, to me, was a picture of life. Are there bits of our lives which are unused and going mouldy? On a practical level, are there items in our cupboards and wardrobes that we never use and that are just gathering dust? Why not have a clear out, take them to a charity shop or have a car boot sale and give the money to charity?

Or what about time? Are there fallow hours? Can we rearrange our timetables and create some more space to serve God's kingdom?

1 Timothy 6:17–21

'... they will lay up treasure for themselves as a firm foundation for the coming age ...' (v.19)

For prayer and reflection

Do a spiritual assessment of your life. Are there earthly 'treasures' you can dispose of in order to send spiritual treasures ahead of you to gladden God's heart?

Living a life
of wisdom

Ruth Valerio

Dr Ruth Valerio is Churches and Theology Director of A Rocha
UK. She lives with her husband and two daughters in Chichester
and writes and speaks regularly on the Bible, in particular on
issues around justice and caring for God's world. She is the
author of *L is for Lifestyle: Christian living that doesn't cost
the earth* (IVP, 2008). Concerned with 'practising what she
preaches', Ruth has an allotment, is actively involved with her
local community and keeps pigs with friends.

Living a life of wisdom

Proverbs 1:1–9

'The fear of the LORD is the beginning of knowledge, but fools despise wisdom and discipline.' (v.7)

A t lunchtime I listen to a topical chat show. Each day it takes an item for debate that is in the news, has one or two 'experts' to comment on it and then opens the discussion up to the listening public. Just this week there have been discussions on the rights of a person to die how they want, teenage pregnancies, nuclear fuel versus wind power and how to solve poverty in Africa. None of these issues is simple and none of them has a clear-cut answer. It takes wisdom to know how to deal with these – and other – issues. In particular it takes wisdom to know how, as followers of Jesus, we can steer a straight course through life's choppy waters.

Can you remember the last time your church had a teaching series on the book of Proverbs? If your answer is no, then that is sad, because Proverbs is written precisely to help the people of God remain true to Him in a complicated world. For that to happen we need discipline, insight, prudence, knowledge and discernment and Proverbs promises us that these things can be ours if we take care to listen to and not forsake the teaching that is found in this book.

The key to Proverbs is in the phrase 'fear of the LORD' (1:7). This does not, of course, mean being terrified of God, but rather is about knowing and understanding the character of God and wanting to live our lives in ways that honour Him. In this sense, then, the 'fear of the LORD' is both the starting point for us gaining wisdom, and the foundation, in that all knowledge and understanding must be based on knowing God and wanting to live our lives for Him.

For prayer and reflection

Make a list of all the things that are promised to us if we take on board the wisdom of these proverbs (vv.2–6). Ask God that this might become a reality in your life.

The carrot and the stick

For most of the time my children and I exist in harmony together! However, sometimes I need them to do something and they stubbornly refuse all my efforts of persuasion. As with all discipline, there is the time for the carrot and the time for the stick. Yesterday we saw the carrot – the reward. If you listen to Proverbs' teaching and follow God's ways you will be richly blessed, with a 'garland to grace your head and a chain to adorn your neck' (v.9). Today we see the stick – the consequence of disobedience. If you reject wisdom's advice then you will only follow a way that leads to death and God will not be found (vv.19,28).

It is helpful to hear the strong warning against living in a way that goes against God; to have it clearly stated that the consequences of ignoring what we will read these next few weeks are dire. Despite these hard words, though, what we do not see here is a 'Victorian schoolmaster God' with stick in hand, ready to punish at the slightest failure. Here is a loving Father God, desperate to pour out His heart to us and have a deep relationship with us (v.23).

We had a young man living with us who was determined to demonstrate that he needed nothing and nobody to help him. Gradually his life started to fall apart. He began drinking heavily, got into trouble with the police, accrued debts and lost his friends. Despite numerous attempts to warn him of where he was headed and to help him, he refused to listen to what we were saying and eventually we had to let him go on his way and reap the consequences. His life is a parable to us to listen to Wisdom's call.

Proverbs 1:10–33

'… if sinners entice you, do not give in to them.' (v.10)

For prayer and reflection

It can be easy to ignore God if He is saying something that we do not like. Ask Him to be honest with you now. Hear Him and respond.

The benefits of wisdom

Proverbs 2:1–22

'… if you accept
my words and store
up my commands
within you …' (v.1)

W isdom is something that we do not tend to talk about much in our culture today, at least coming from the United Kingdom. We might talk about being clever, or knowledgeable or learned, but being *wise* is not a common concept. According to the book of Proverbs, wisdom encompasses cleverness, knowledge and learning (v.6), but goes further than that as, being rooted in the fear of the Lord, it goes beyond the world of academia and books into the everyday lives that we live.

Thus, as we shall see further on, wisdom is immensely practical and has immensely practical results. It brings with it many benefits. If we accept the words of Proverbs and apply our hearts to what is said (v.1), we will understand the fear of the Lord and find the knowledge of God (v.5); we will be given victory and protection (vv.7–8); we will grow in moral discernment (v.9) and we will be true inheritors of God's promises (v.21). Protection is an important theme of today's chapter, as gaining wisdom will protect us from leaving the straight paths of God and walking in dark ways (v.13). There is so much temptation around us in our culture and this chapter gives us great encouragement to know that, as we follow wisdom, so we will be kept from straying into ungodly territory.

How does your life match up with these descriptions? Are you an illustration of how searching after wisdom and calling out for insight has led to a deeper knowledge of God? Have you had periods when you have known that God has been protecting you and watching over your ways? Can you think of times when He has rescued you and given you the strength to resist temptation? What a merciful God we have!

For prayer and reflection

Dear God, as I see the benefits that wisdom brings and read about the dangers that it protects me from, please may this be the case in my own life's experience.

WEEKEND

Strong love

For reflection: Proverbs 4:23
'Above all else, guard your heart, for it is the wellspring of life.'

In February we have St Valentine's Day, a time when we are surrounded by hearts and flowers. As with so much in our society, commercialisation means that the symbol of the heart has been overdone and corrupted; turned into a marketing ploy. The heart, for many people, symbolises slushy love and romanticism, leading to relationships that are too easily broken.

In the Old Testament, however, the heart was the seat of the emotions and symbolised strength rather than sentimentalism. Along with the mind, it is vitally important in our relationship with God and in our ability to live for Him. As women, we know that our hearts face many pressures and many attacks. Perhaps you know particular pressures that are heavy on your heart at the moment.

Take this weekend to focus on guarding your heart and keeping it strong and pure for God.

Maybe you need to go for a walk to find some space for yourself.
Maybe there is a conversation you need to initiate.
How will you ensure that your heart is guarded?

Reflecting God

Proverbs 3:1–26

'Let love and faithfulness never leave you; bind them around your neck …' (v.3)

What beautiful words are contained in this chapter! Love and faithfulness are two words used to describe God throughout the Old Testament (eg Exod. 34:6, Psa. 138:2). They are based on the events of the Exodus, when God heard the cries of His people, remembered His promise to them and, out of love for them, acted to deliver them from oppression and injustice in Egypt (Exod. 3:7–9, 16–17).

God is known as a God of love and faithfulness and we too, as His people, are called to demonstrate those characteristics in our own lives.

What is love? Love is about my relationship with another; it is about putting that other's needs before my own; it is being willing to go out of my way for another, to do something inconvenient and time-consuming for the sake of another. Love recognises that I am not right all the time and makes me look always for reconciliation.

What is faithfulness? Faithfulness means I will stick like glue to my promises. It means that I will be constant in my friendship whatever obstacles come in our path, whether they be geography or health or other circumstances.

So much of the 'right living' that we will see in Proverbs comes from this foundation of love and faithfulness, whether between ourselves and God or ourselves and other people and so it is worth taking time at this stage to consider these two characteristics and contemplate how they apply to us.

Where do I demonstrate love and faithfulness in my life? Are there relationships or situations in which they need to be bound tighter around my neck and written more clearly on my heart? We know that good comes to those who have these foundations secure (v.4).

For prayer and reflection

Father God, please may my life be one in which Your love and faithfulness are clearly seen.

The pain of **unfaithfulness**

Proverbs 5

'… a man's ways are in full view of the LORD, and he examines all his paths.' (v.21)

Until the very end chapter, women get a pretty raw deal in the book of Proverbs; they are mostly depicted as nagging wives or adulterous women, out to seduce the young man being addressed here (on the positive, of course, Wisdom herself is a woman). We may wish to let the father of Proverbs know that not all women are like this! However, the sad fact is that these words are as relevant today as they ever were then, as adultery is rife in our society and, heartbreakingly, not uncommon in our churches too.

Writing these notes to such a diverse audience I am aware that this chapter of Proverbs will be looked at through so many different eyes. Perhaps you have experienced unfaithfulness yourself from your husband and are in the process of rebuilding your life. Perhaps you are supporting a friend through something similar. Perhaps you find yourself 20, 30 … years into your marriage, with your children leaving home and with a new lease of life, wondering if you still have a relationship with your husband, tempted towards another man who seems more interested in who you are. Perhaps you are single and find your thoughts drawn towards an attractive married man in your church. Perhaps you are a newlywed and can't imagine how you could possibly find another man attractive or that your relationship might ever cause your husband to stray.

Whatever situation you are in, remember that all your ways 'are in full view of the LORD' (v.21). This isn't a threat, but a promise. God is with us at all times and sees everything, so don't be afraid to talk with Him about your innermost needs and feelings.

For prayer and reflection

Maybe today has stirred up many emotions. If so, ask God to show you how best to process them. You may need to talk this through more fully with someone. Or you may want simply to bring your feelings and concerns to God in silence.

Wisdom **in the whole body**

Proverbs 6:1–11, 16–19

'There are six things the LORD hates, seven that are detestable to him ...' (v.16)

What a contrast to Proverbs 3 is Proverbs 6 – there are no nice words here! Having set the scene in the first four chapters, urging his son to go after wisdom with everything he has and describing the benefits of so doing, the father now goes in hard (starting in 5:3) with his advice. You can almost picture his frustration in verse 9 as he looks at his young son's inability to get up in the morning and penchant for lying around. Maybe you can identify with the father here!

Verses 16–19 are a good list of things to consider. First, 'haughty eyes' asks us to think about our attitude to other people. Do we look down on people or do we demonstrate humility in our relationships?

Second, 'a lying tongue' reminds us of the importance of telling the truth and living lives of integrity, as does the description of a 'false witness who pours out lies' (v.19).

Third, 'hands that shed innocent blood' might sound far removed from us, but perhaps we can use this as an opportunity to consider the way we are all complicit in the terrible inequalities that are in our world today. What do we do to help?

Fourth, 'a heart that devises wicked schemes' brings us back to our weekend reading and encourages us to set our hearts on following the way of wisdom alone.

Fifth, feet are only 'quick to rush into evil' when they belong to a person who is foolish.

Finally we come to how all of this outworks itself in our relationships with others. The words here sound dramatic, but they come down to very simple concepts of speaking well of people and not stirring up trouble.

For prayer and reflection

Dear God, please test my life in the light of verses 16–19. How do I do? Show me where I need Your help to improve.

Jesus **the wisdom of God**

We have been hearing a lot about Wisdom over the last week and what has come through in all our readings is the urgency of listening to her words. There is no middle ground with Wisdom; no laid back approach in Proverbs; no sense of 'well, listen to me if you like, but don't worry if you decide not to ...' Wisdom's words are strong and clear: 'I am worth more than all the gold in the world, and you must do everything you can to get me, even if it costs you all you have.'

Why is there this sense of urgency?

Today's passage gives us the answer to this as we see Wisdom's relationship with God. Wisdom goes right to the very heart of who God is; she exists in communion with Him. Indeed, Wisdom is so foundational that she was there at the creation of the world and played a crucial role.

Verses 22–31 are a beautiful reflection on the creation narratives in Genesis 1 and show the creativity and joy of God as, with Wisdom by His side, He designs the world and puts everything in its place. The culmination is verse 31 which mirrors Genesis 1:31 and demonstrates conclusively God's attitude to His world; that He rejoices in it and loves it, with particular notice being made of humanity.

As Christians we cannot help but see the Person of Jesus reflected in these words. He, too, existed from the beginning (John 17:5); played an integral role in the creation of the world (Col. 1:15–17) and is in communion with God (John 1:1–3). Jesus is the true wisdom of God (1 Cor. 1:24): no wonder we are told, 'whoever finds me finds life' (Prov. 8:35)!

Proverbs 8:12–36

'... whoever finds me finds life and receives favour from the LORD.' (v.35)

For prayer and reflection

Dear Father, Creator of the world, thank You that through Your Son I have found life in You.

Which banquet **will you choose?**

Proverbs 9

'"Let all who are simple come in here!" she says to those who lack judgment.' (vv.4,16)

I love food, to the point that it might almost be called an obsession! My favourite way of relaxing is to sit and read a food magazine and I can talk about food and related issues endlessly. There is a lot in this chapter, therefore, that I can relate to, as it describes two different sorts of banquets.

The first is that offered by Wisdom; here again personified as a woman. I love having people round for dinner and seeing how it acts as a catalyst for good conversation and deepening friendships and enjoy it when I have the space to put a lot of time into preparing the food. This is exactly what Wisdom has done (v.2) and we are to imagine a sumptuous banquet with the choicest of foods, laid out for those who accept her invitation (v.5). As the freshest, best quality foods lead to the healthiest bodies, so Wisdom's food leads to the most godly lives.

The second is that offered by the woman Folly. Her invitation (v.16) is very similar to that of Wisdom's (v.4) and, at first sight, it might be hard to discern between the two. However, the banquet offered by Folly could not be more different to that of Wisdom. The fare at her table is 'stolen' and her guests have to eat 'in secret' (v.17). Like the poorest quality food, there is nothing nutritious here and it leads only to death.

This chapter concludes the opening introductory chapters of Proverbs and provides us with another opportunity to ask the question: in the choices that you have to make in your everyday life, which woman will you listen to? How, practically, will you accept Wisdom's invitation and eat the food at her table?

For prayer and reflection

Dear God, I am simple, but I want to gain understanding. Please help me to eat at Wisdom's table each day. Please keep me from listening to Folly.

WEEKEND

Prospects of joy

For reflection: Philippians 4:12–13

I f someone were to ask you 'what are your prospects?', how would you answer them? Would you say your prospects are good? Your career is going well? Your relationships are flourishing? Your bank account expanding? Or, is it hard to have a positive outlook for the future? Are you lonely? Are you struggling at home with young children? Are you in a difficult situation with no hope of relief?

Proverbs 10:28 tells us that 'the prospect of the righteous is joy, but the hopes of the wicked come to nothing'. Joy is not a 'grit my teeth and pretend everything is OK really' kind of attitude. Joy comes from knowing Jesus and from having His presence with us in all our circumstances, whether good or bad.

Paul tells us that he has 'learnt the secret of being content in any and every situation' because 'I can do everything through him who gives me strength' (Phil. 4:12–13). As Paul learnt, this didn't always mean that God would rescue him *out* of a situation, but that God would give him the strength to bear it.

What does it mean for you to have 'prospects of joy'?

Feasting at Wisdom's table

....

Proverbs 9:1–6

....

'Come, eat my food and drink the wine I have mixed.' (v.5)

On Friday, we considered the invitation to eat at Wisdom's banqueting table. We are going to start this week by taking this further in the form of a meditation.

Begin by settling yourself down. Bring to God all the things that are distracting you from focusing on Him. Ask Him to speak to you. Now read through Proverbs 9:1–6 again, slowly, with an open mind and without trying to anticipate what God wants to say to you. Close your eyes and picture yourself walking down the street/at the supermarket/at work/at home (wherever feels most natural) and hearing Wisdom's invitation. You listen to it and decide to accept it.

Imagine yourself walking to her magnificent house with its pillars, going in and finding the banqueting hall. Wisdom comes to greet you and leads you to the table. Spend time picturing that table scene with all the wonderful food laid out on it. What do you see on the table? Now enjoy seeing yourself sitting and eating all that is there. Again, as you do this, don't try to force an explanation for what you think God is saying to you; take the time to enter into this fully and allow Him to move in you by His Holy Spirit.

As you feel yourself being touched by God, tell Him what is happening. Perhaps you feel an encouragement to take more time to feast on Him. Perhaps there are particular good things that God is filling you with. Maybe you feel unworthy to eat there and need to express that to God. Maybe you are simply enjoying having the space to be with Him. When you feel the picture finishing, bring your time to a close by a simple prayer or by reciting the Lord's Prayer.

....

For prayer and reflection

....

Thank You, God, for speaking to me today as I have eaten at Wisdom's table. Please help me to hold on to the work You have been doing.

Looking at **our attitude**

From Proverbs 10 onwards, we have the main section of the book, consisting of a whole range of sayings. They have been collected over a long period of time and finally arranged into the form we have them in today. They are a strange collection and there seems little reason as to why they have been put together in the way they have. They do not follow any logical progression and the many subjects that they deal with (eg diligence versus laziness) are dotted throughout the collection, rather than put together in one section. It is also true to say that they represent a culture and era far removed from ours and hence can sometimes appear almost offensive to our modern ears (eg 19:25, advocating corporal punishment).

Nonetheless, a read through of any of the chapters will show immediately how utterly full of wisdom (some might say, common sense) they are and one realises that, were we to live by its precepts, we would be more contented individuals living in a better society. As we see in today's reading, so much of Proverb's wise advice is about the attitude of our hearts, and here the focus is on generosity.

Verse 16 sums it up and shows the contrast with the attitude of our society. This verse is utterly disparaging towards wealth! I have a friend who is so big-hearted and generous. She never tires of helping people and will give of her material possessions without a moment's thought when she sees a need. She is a constant challenge to me because I know that I hold on to things more tightly than she does. As we follow Wisdom's advice over the next couple of weeks, let's remember that the focus is not on laws but on our attitude.

Proverbs 11

'A kind-hearted woman gains respect, but ruthless men gain only wealth.' (v.16)

For prayer and reflection

Would you be described as kind-hearted? Ask God increasingly to soften your heart and your attitude towards others.

Paths of **righteousness and evil**

'In the way of righteousness there is life …' (v.28)

Proverbs 10–15 sets out a series of contrasts, focusing on the difference between 'the righteous' and 'the wicked'. This follows on from the groundwork laid in the first nine chapters of Proverbs, culminating (as we have seen) in the contrast between Wisdom and Folly.

What do we learn from today's series of antitheses? We learn that those who are evil are deceitful (vv.2,5); are blood-thirsty (v.6); are destroyed (v.7); are despised (v.8); are cruel to animals (v.10); are envious of other people (v.12); become trapped by their own talk (v.13); tell lies (v.17) and have continual trouble (v.21). In direct opposition to this is those who are righteous. They are favoured by God (v.2); are enabled to stand firm in life (vv.3,7); are praised by others (v.8); take care of animals (v.10); are saved from trouble (v.13); promote peace (v.20); speak the truth (v.22); are helpful to their neighbours (v.26) and find life (v.28).

This is a remarkable list and serves as a helpful antidote to our 'politically correct', tolerant society that allows for few clear-cut statements to be made on issues of lifestyle and morality. Of course, we might want to take issue with some of the assertions made here; not least the assumption that it always goes well for the righteous, who prosper, and badly for the wicked, who end in poverty (and it should be stated that Proverbs, too, is not as naïve as it looks – see, for example, 15:16–17 and 16:19). However, this is surely missing the point, which is to set before us every possible motivation to make sure that *we* do not become fools who chase after evil, but instead ensure that *our* feet are firmly planted on the road of righteousness that leads to life.

For prayer and reflection

Think through how the contrasts in this chapter apply to your life. Bring these thoughts to God.

Accepting **discipline**

O ne theme that comes out again and again throughout Proverbs is the importance of listening to advice and accepting correction. If we – the simple – are going to gain understanding (9:4–6), then inevitably there will be areas in our lives that are going to have to change. Discipline is not always a word that goes down terribly well in our society: 'Who are you to tell me what to do?' is the general attitude. And yet, if we are to learn how to follow Wisdom, then we have to be prepared to let others tell us where we are going wrong. As this chapter tells us, only a mocker refuses to 'listen to rebuke' (v.1) and 'He who scorns instruction will pay for it, but he who respects a command is rewarded' and it is a wise son who 'heeds his father's instruction' (vv.1,13). Does that challenge any underlying arrogance or sense of independence in you?

Where are we to get this instruction from? Proverbs 13 makes it clear that 'He who walks with the wise grows wise, but a companion of fools suffers harm' (v.20). In other words, we should choose our travelling companions with care! These verses do not tell us to open up our lives to everybody and receive advice from everyone. No, the rebukes, disciplines and instructions come from those we know who are wise. The Celtic Christians talked about having an *anamchara* – a soul friend. Each of us needs someone with whom we can be completely open; who will rebuke us and correct us when needed; give us advice when needed, and sometimes just sit in silence when that is what is needed.

This sounds lovely on paper, but the hardest thing is when you actually receive a rebuke. How do you respond?

....
Proverbs 13
....

'He who ignores discipline comes to poverty and shame, but whoever heeds correction is honoured.' (v.18)

....
For prayer and reflection
....

Father, I know You discipline me because I am Your child whom You love (Heb. 12:7–11). Please give me the grace and humility to accept Your words and to live by them.

The **power of the tongue**

Proverbs 15

'A gentle answer turns away wrath, but a harsh word stirs up anger.' (v.1)

Some while ago I was involved in an unpleasant situation within my circle of friends. Two people committed an offence and soon everyone was talking about it, giving their opinions and taking sides. No one had the sense to break the circle of gossip and stop talking and no one had the sense to talk with someone from 'the other side' and bring about reconciliation. It was a good lesson on the power of the tongue.

The book of Proverbs is immensely practical and nowhere is this seen more than in its advice on speech, as illustrated by this chapter. It warns us against speaking without thinking (vv.2,28); gossiping (see 16:28; 17:4); speaking bad-temperedly (v.18; 14:17); provoking quarrels (v.1; 17:19) and lying (v.4; 26:28). In the New Testament, James describes the tongue as like a small spark that can create a fire (3:5). In his characteristically colourful language, he warns that it is very hard to tame and is 'full of deadly poison' (3:8). Conversely, the tongue can do a tremendous amount of good and Proverbs instructs us to use it to speak the truth and bring peace (15:1). We might never know what blessing we bring by a simple positive word spoken to someone at a particular moment.

For prayer and reflection

Do you use your tongue to do good or damage? Are you quick to react to an offence or do you know when to keep silent?

Are you too easily drawn in to talking negatively about someone or are you brave enough to point out when people are gossiping?

Dear God, please help me to remember the power that is in my tongue. May I use that power to bring peace, truth and healing to those around me.

Does your tongue let you down when you are grumpy or can you control it?

What does how you speak say about your character?

WEEKEND

'In God we trust'

For reflection: Matthew 6:24

I n my church we used to be forced to sing the song, 'Blessed be the name of the Lord' – or rather, we were forced to do the actions that accompanied the words, 'The name of the Lord is a strong tower, the righteous run into it and they are saved'! Strangely, we never sang the next verse: 'The wealth of the rich is their fortified city; they imagine it an unscalable wall' (Prov. 18:10–11).

In a similar manner to Jesus in Matthew 6:24, faith in God is contrasted with faith in money/riches and the gauntlet is thrown down.

In whom or what will you put your trust?

Which option really is the secure one: the strong tower of God or the fortified city of wealth?

My husband and I went through an unsettling period a while ago when it looked as though we might lose all our financial security. It was a horrible time, but it showed me that wealth is not 'an unscalable wall' and it strengthened my determination that, whatever happened, my faith would be in God and not in money.

Dear God, thank You that I am safe in You.

The God of the **dead ends**

'Commit to the LORD whatever you do, and your plans will succeed.' (v.3)

If you have been a Christian for some time, it is likely that you will be familiar with 16:3. It is the sort of verse that finds its way onto posters with pictures of beautiful scenery on them. It is certainly the sort of verse that people like to quote when embarking on a new church project!

How do we respond, though, when our church project does not succeed in the way we were hoping, or when our life does not look like beautiful poster scenery? A significant part of the answer lies in the next verse: 'The LORD works out everything for his own ends' (v.4). The problem is that sometimes the Lord's own ends are very different to ours.

Look at that remarkable statement from Joseph when he says to his brothers, 'You intended to harm me, but God intended it for good to accomplish ... the saving of many lives' (Gen. 50:20). When Joseph was taken into slavery it looked like a dead-end, both for himself personally and for the promises made to the nation of Israel. God, however, had other plans and He worked in that dead-end in order to save many lives.

For prayer and reflection

Lord, I give You the areas of my life that seem to be dead-ends. Please give me faith that You are with me and are using those areas for good.

Through so many instances in the Bible – and supremely in the death of Christ – God shows us that He works in the dark times to bring His purposes about. He may not work to our timetable (v.9). He may never actually rescue us out of a particular situation. But we can be confident – and Romans 8:28 assures us – both that God will be with us in those times and that He will be using those situations to bring about good. When life seems little more than a game of chance, still we can be sure that 'every decision is from the LORD' (v.33).

Developing **caring families**

Proverbs 17:1–25

I am staying at my parents' house with my two young daughters whilst writing this. Jemba – the youngest – was up all evening with a temperature and throughout last night too, resulting in some rather tired and grumpy grandparents this morning (not to mention a tired and grumpy mum!). I have just read Proverbs 17:6 to them and reminded them what a joy their grandchildren are ...!

'Children's children are a crown to the aged, and parents are the pride of their children.' (v.6)

As we know, Proverbs is purportedly the words of a father advising his son and so all we have been reading takes place within the context of family. Indeed family issues are an important part of the themes that run throughout Proverbs (we have already seen some in, for example: 5:18ff; 10:1; 11:29; 13:22; 14:1; 15:20). What we read here reflects a culture very different from our own. Whereas Western society encourages individualism and independence and hence works with a very mobile society that leads to family ties being weakened, the culture of Proverbs is one in which older people were honoured and parents and children maintained strong links. The description of adults being the pride of their children, in 17:6, is an interesting twist that makes us think more about our parents than ourselves.

Verse 17 is a beautiful proverb, demonstrating that we are in family units to care for one another, leading to the commentator David Atkinson describing families as 'covenants of care'. 'Family' means so many different things: the small unit of parents and children, or two families combined through re-marriage, or single parenthood and so on. Whatever 'family' means to you, verse 1 is a good summary of our aim: to be developing families where our focus is on peace rather than material gain.

For prayer and reflection

Who is in your family? Bring each one before God and pray that your family will be one of peace and care.

Working for God

Proverbs 20:1–25

'Do not love sleep or you will grow poor; stay awake and you will have food to spare.' (v.13)

It is the middle of the week and how are you feeling? Bogged down in a pile of work? Relieved that you are halfway there and by the end of the day it will only be two days till the weekend? Do you get out of bed in the mornings excited by the prospect of the day ahead (whether you are working in or out of your home) or do you dread another day of boring routine? What is your attitude to the work that you do?

Proverbs has no time for the person who is lazy and wants to sit around or lie in bed all day, and we saw earlier in the month the father's frustration with his son (in chapter 6). Proverbs comes from a society where, if a person did not work, they literally would have nothing to eat and so would become a burden on other people (most notably on their families, linking in with yesterday's reading).

For Proverbs, then, work is a matter of taking responsibility for one's life. It is also a matter of how one goes about one's work. The wise person is one who works hard at what he or she is doing (v.21), who plans ahead (v.4) and who works honestly and with integrity (vv.10,17,23). Work is clearly seen as something good that God has given us to do and hence to be undertaken appropriately.

For prayer and reflection

Heavenly Father, thank You that You have given me creativity and gifts to be outworked in and out of my home. Please may Wisdom be my guide each day.

Think about your work, whether it be a profession of some sort, a caring role in the house, a voluntary job, or whatever it is. Do you feel that it is something God has called you to do or something that you undertake grudgingly? How might you apply all you have been learning about wisdom into this situation?

That your **trust may be in God**

Today's reading forms part of a little collection of proverbs called, 'the Sayings of the Wise' (22:17–24:34). They operate almost as a summary of what has been said so far, and if you have the time to read 22:17–29 and the rest of chapter 23 as well, then you will appreciate them even more. The reason for them is given in 22:19: 'So that your trust may be in the LORD.'

What, then, must we do if *our* trust is to be in the Lord? We should not only pay attention and listen to all that we have been reading this past month, but we should be ready to put it into action (22:17–18).

We should take care not to exploit the poor or be friends with someone who is bad-tempered or get ourselves into unwise debts (22:22–27). We should not take another person's property or means of livelihood (22:28). We should be wise in our attitude towards money: not craving it or the luxuries it brings (23:1–8). We should be wise in who we give advice to, but we should be careful to discipline our children.

Above all, the focus of this passage is – again – on our hearts. If our hearts are consumed with zeal for God, then they will be kept on the right path; we will not drink too much alcohol or over-indulge in our eating, but will instead be wise and righteous, disciplined and full of understanding and a delight to our parents (vv.17–25).

What sensible and practical words to help us as we try to live God's way in our society! Why not go through each instruction in today's reading as a 'spiritual health check' to ensure that your trust might be in the Lord?

Proverbs 23:1–28

'Apply your heart to instruction and your ears to words of knowledge.' (v.12)

For prayer and reflection

Dear God, please may my heart be consumed with zeal for You. Show me where it hankers after other things and bring it back to You.

Compost and weeds

Proverbs 24

'I applied my heart to what I observed and learned a lesson from what I saw ...' (v.32)

The 'Sayings of the Wise' continue in this chapter, taking us further into what we must do if our trust is to be in the Lord (22:19). As I read this chapter, I am particularly struck with the final observation by the wise person looking at the 'field of the sluggard'. These verses resonate with me because I am a keen gardener, both at home in my garden and with my friends in our allotment.

Each March, I plan what will be grown that year, anticipating both the harvest to be reaped and the weeds that will grow up if I do not go down there often enough.

Any gardener knows that the best results come when we are prepared to work hard and be thorough. If we are not then we will not get an abundance of fruit and vegetables. How much more then is this the case for our relationship with God! I will spend hours in my allotment – growing seeds, transplanting, watering, weeding ... I wonder how much time I will spend on my relationship with God.

What seeds are being sown in my life? What 'compost' am I putting on them to make them grow? What sort of weeds am I allowing to grow in my life; things that might choke and overpower my relationship with God?

It can be easy to take shortcuts with God, giving Him the last bits of our time and – if we are honest – focusing our lives on other things. Instead, the book of Proverbs shows us how to focus ourselves on wisdom. By its very nature, wisdom takes time to develop and mature. If we are to gain wisdom and see God's fruit in our lives there can be no short cuts!

For prayer and reflection

Take some time to think through this analogy of the field/allotment as being your relationship with God. What might God be saying to you in this?

WEEKEND

Don't be a fool!

For reflection: Matthew 7:24–27

Throughout this month's readings we have been looking at the contrast between Wisdom and Folly and those who follow them – the wise or the fools.

Read through Proverbs 26:1–12. It is a sustained attack once again on fools; sarcastic and disparaging in its tone. It is almost as if the book as a whole is saying, 'If you haven't quite got the message, let me give it to you one last time …'

Jesus had much to say about fools. They are the ones who hear His words but do not put them into practice (Matt. 7:26). Fools are those who do not prepare for the coming kingdom of God (Matt. 25:2). They are the people who are more concerned about religious trappings than the heart (Luke 11:40) and present security than the future (Luke 12:20).

This weekend, look again at our very first reading together and the statement that,

'The fear of the LORD is the beginning of knowledge, but fools despise wisdom and discipline' (Prov. 1:7).

Consider all that you have learnt this month. Reflect on these differences between the wise and the fools and bring these thoughts to God, asking Him to work in you.

Go and **be that neighbour**

'A word aptly spoken is like apples of gold in settings of silver.' (v.11)

When I was growing up, everyone in our road knew each other. Front doors were left open, the milk money could be put out the night before and the children were in and out of each other's houses. Such a contrast to how so many of us live today, where we hardly know our neighbours' names, let alone feel free to pop in to their homes!

Proverbs envisages a society where people know their neighbours well and it applies its wisdom, as practically as ever, to teaching us about good neighbourliness. Emphasising what we have seen elsewhere, this chapter encourages us not to lie about our neighbours (v.18); not to gossip about private things (vv.9–10) and not to get into legal disputes with our neighbours (vv.7–8). Overall, Proverbs teaches us that we should live with our neighbours in peace and blessing (3:29; 11:9; 24:28; 26:19).

Jesus teaches about the idea of neighbourliness in His story about the good Samaritan (Luke 10:25–37). In answer to the question, 'Who is my neighbour?' Jesus cleverly turns it round and, in effect, answers, '*You* are that neighbour, so go and do likewise' (v.37). Wisdom asks *us* to be that neighbour today. What does that mean for you?

Are there things you could do to bring a demonstration of the good news of Jesus into your neighbours' lives? Are there particular people in your street who have been beaten up by life and need you to look after their wounds? Are there perhaps more broader community matters that you could get involved in through, for example, being on a residents' association?

Bring to God your community and the people who live near you; pray for opportunities to bless them and bring peace into their lives.

For prayer and reflection

Dear Father, whose Son came to live in 'my neighbourhood', please may I follow Jesus' example of bringing blessing to everyone I meet.

Responding to poverty

W hen he was a student at Bible college, Jim Wallis – the American writer and social activist – pulled out of a Bible all the pages that had references to the poor on them. What he was left with was not much of a Bible and He used to travel round churches showing them this Bible and asking them, 'Is your holy Bible full of holes?'! I wonder what would happen if we did the same to Proverbs and crossed out all the proverbs that had in them references to the poor and needy and to justice. We would lose a lot of what Proverbs has to say to us.

It is remarkable how, throughout the whole book (and especially in these final few chapters), caring for the poor and ensuring justice is done is such an important theme and hence such an important part of what it means to be wise.

We live in a world of terrible inequalities, both between countries and within countries (for example, in the USA the top 10% of the population has six times the income of the lowest 20%). Despite encouraging advances in East and South Asia, we are still in the situation in which the basic needs of many are not being met. It is estimated that there are around 840 million people who are chronically undernourished. In a world such as ours, Proverbs speaks loudly, telling us to 'understand justice' (v.5); 'be kind to the poor' (v.8) and give to the poor (v.27). What can we do? We can pray. We can support organisations working on the frontline of these situations and we can seek to live our own lives in ways that do as little damage as possible to God's world and the people who live in it.

Proverbs 28

'He who gives to the poor will lack nothing ...' (v.27)

For prayer and reflection

Father of all, I hear these words of wisdom. Please help me to carry them out in my own life.

85

Called **to serve**

Proverbs 29:1–20

'By justice a king gives a country stability …' (v.4)

Yesterday, we saw how Proverbs brings its wisdom to speak to the horrendous inequalities that are in our world today. Today, we consider the advice dotted throughout this chapter on how rulers should rule; a fitting subject since our nations' leaders have such a role in either perpetuating poverty or eradicating it. Their concern should be for justice and not corruption (v.4); they should be righteous and wise (vv.2,8); they should not listen to lies (v.12); they should judge impartially, not being biased against people who are poor (v.14); and they should maintain a good relationship with God (by keeping the law) and provide vision for those they are leading (v.18). Before reading on, take time now to pray for our nations' leaders, asking God that they might exhibit the qualities that Proverbs extols.

Although written for Israel's king, these words can also speak to all of us who are in some form of leadership: whether that be at work, in our communities, in the home or in church. We, too, are called by God to lead in such a way that is morally exemplary (see also Prov. 31:1–4). We are to lead in a manner that is fair, upright, wise, full of integrity and, above all, that leads to justice (again see how, in Proverbs 31:8–9, the primary call of the king is to 'speak up for those who cannot speak for themselves' and to 'defend the rights of the poor and needy').

Verse 18 is a challenging one for all of us involved in leadership in whatever sphere. Whether translated 'vision' or 'revelation', the point would seem to be the same: our focus should be on God. When it is then we can be confident that we are following His vision and leading by His guidance.

For prayer and reflection

Heavenly Father, whose Son came to serve, may I too follow His example in the roles and responsibilities that You have given me.

The wisdom **of the earth**

Proverbs 30 is a rather idiosyncratic part of the book of Proverbs. The word in verse 1 translated 'oracle' could mean simply the place where Agur comes from or that this is a word from a prophet. It could record a conversation between a sceptic Agur (vv.1–4) and Ithiel and Ucal, firm believers in Yahweh (vv.5–6), or it might all be the words of Agur.[1]

However this might be, what we see here is a clear demonstration of how much we humans have to learn from the world of nature. Verses 2–4 are an awesome description of the difference between humanity and God, reminiscent of Job 28:12–28. They show the power and immensity of God as He was able simply to have 'gathered up the wind in the hollow of his hands' and 'wrapped up the waters in his cloak' (v.4). Creation, therefore, bears God's fingerprints and has much to teach us of God's character. Agur is not alone in drawing out some of those lessons. Jesus, too, used the natural world in His teaching, using everyday pictures from the world around Him that would have been very familiar to those listening (eg mustard seeds, yeast and fig trees: Luke 13:18–20; Matt. 21:18–22). Most notably Jesus talked about the birds of the air and the flowers and grass in the field to teach that we should not worry about how we will eat or get clothes because God will look after us. Our main focus should be on God's kingdom and on His justice and righteousness (Matt. 6:25–34).

This brings us back to the remarkable prayer of Proverbs 30:8–9. In our society that wants continually to have more and more, what a challenging prayer! Can you pray it with conviction?

1. D. Atkinson, *The Message of Proverbs* (IVP, 1996), pp.161–162.

Proverbs 30

'Four things on earth are small, yet they are extremely wise ...' (v.24)

For prayer and reflection

Dear God, please give me the wisdom to be able to pray verses 8–9 and mean them. Thank You for all that You have made: show me how I can look after it.

True **beauty**

Proverbs 31:10–31

'… beauty is fleeting; but a woman who fears the LORD is to be praised.' (v.30)

Our society has a confused vision of what women should be like. On the one hand, we are told that we should be 'true to ourselves' and that size and looks do not matter. On the other hand, magazines focus on the women who are physically beautiful, with big breasts and no cellulite, and TV shows concentrate on helping us wear the right clothes and looking 'ten years younger'. Some aspects of our culture encourage women to find fulfilment in staying at home, nurturing the next generation, while others want the next generation to be in childcare, so women can find fulfilment in their career. As specifically *Christian* women, where do we fit into all of this?

This poem about the 'wife of noble character' is a wonderful way for us to end our month's readings together. It brings together what we have learnt about wisdom and helps us – women seeking to outwork the 'fear of the LORD' (v.30) – see how to apply it to our lives. It shows us that wisdom is not for hermit-like old men with long grey beards, but is for *us* as we try to juggle work, childcare arrangements, financial responsibilities, relationships and church commitments.

This is one remarkable woman: equally comfortable at home (v.27) or in society (v.31); with sharp business acumen (v.18) and compassion for the poor (v.20); faithful (v.12), wise (v.26) … the list goes on! She is a demonstration of how wisdom is not restricted to the more 'religious' matters, but is concerned with every aspect of our lives. The woman in Proverbs 31 has been described as 'a wonderful illustration … of Wisdom embodied, Wisdom lived out, Wisdom at home!'[1] May we women, too, be such an illustration.

1. D. Atkinson, *The Message of Proverbs* (IVP, 1996), p.196.

For prayer and reflection

Heavenly Father, please seal within me what I have learnt this month. Please may I carry these lessons out in my life. May I be an illustration of 'wisdom lived out'.

Angels on standby

Christine Orme

Chris's childhood ambitions were twofold – to write and to teach. With various diversions en route she's managed both. An Anglican lay-reader, she and her vicar husband, Eddie, are part of the ministry team in a Reading parish. They have four adult daughters and nine young grandchildren – an endless source of joy – and an allotment which keeps them active! A cochlear implant in 2013 made life as a deafened person simpler for Chris who feels her major challenge now is to grow older graciously and with an undiminished sense of humour.

WEEKEND

Angels on standby

For reflection: Psalm 34:1–20

Our topic this month is angels, and we shall be looking at some of the 300 biblical references to them. This lovely psalm is full of assurances that God actively protects and cares for his children. Verse 7 speaks of 'the angel of the LORD' surrounding those who fear God and delivering them.

Not many people have seen angels but we can be sure they exist – God's agents to help us in time of need. There is a wonderful illustration of this in 2 Kings 6. The prophet Elisha, besieged in Dothan by enemy soldiers, prayed for his panicking servant, 'O LORD, open his eyes …' (v.17). The servant was miraculously enabled to see 'the hills full of horses and chariots of fire all around Elisha'. The heavenly hosts were far more powerful than the enemy!

As you read and reflect on this psalm, ask God to open your spiritual eyes this month to understand more about the heavenly forces ranged on the side of believers.

The hosts of God encamp around
The dwellings of the just:
Deliverance He affords to all
Who on His succour trust.

Nahum Tate and Nicholas Brady 1696

Angels **guide**

A fter his wife Sarah's death, Abraham, now an old man, wishes to see their son Isaac married to someone from their own extended family. So he instructs his servant to return to his (Abraham's) homeland and find a wife for Isaac from amongst Abraham's relatives. The servant is understandably anxious at such a difficult assignment and nervously asks (as we often do) 'What if ...?'

Abraham, however, has come a long way – both literally and figuratively – in his journey with God since God called him to leave all that he knew and loved and to set out for a land that God would show him. He has proved God's faithfulness many times over and knows that He can and does guide those who seek to follow Him. So he assures his servant that God will provide him with an angel to 'go before' him (v.7).

In retelling the story, the servant speaks of the angel going 'with' him to make the 'journey a success' (v.40).

Abraham's confidence in God and the servant's obedience are rewarded in a series of amazing 'coincidences' and answers to prayer. Rebekah, Abraham's great-niece, gladly consents to return with the servant to become Isaac's wife, and her father and brother acknowledge God's hand in it all.

The Bible is full of promises for us, God's people, whom He has called to journey with Him in faith, like Abraham. When faced with a hazardous journey, or a difficult assignment, do we get bogged down in fearful imaginings: 'What if this happens?' 'What if that goes wrong?' 'What if such and such a complication occurs?' Perhaps instead we should take our cue from Abraham and ask specifically for angels to direct, accompany and guide us.

In what area do you need angelic guidance today?

Genesis 24:34–53

'The LORD … will send his angel with you and make your journey a success …' (v.40)

For prayer and reflection

'For this God is our God for ever and ever; he will be our guide even to the end' (Psa. 48:14).

Angels **commission**

Judges 13:2–20, 24

'The angel ... said, "You are sterile and childless, but you are going to ... have a son."' (v.3)

O ccasionally in the Old Testament God Himself seems to have appeared in human form. The phrase 'the angel of the LORD' is often a clue to such appearances and today's reading may describe one of them. At any rate, it illustrates well another angelic role – that of commissioning individuals to perform a specific task for God. Others so commissioned include Moses (Exod. 3) and Isaiah (Isa. 6).

The unnamed woman in this passage seems an unlikely candidate to do great things for God. Her status would have been low for she was 'sterile and remained childless' (v.2), but our God delights in choosing and using those whom the world ignores or looks down on.

The angel tells her that she will have a son who must be set apart for God, not just from his birth, but from the moment of conception, so she must watch her diet carefully. The spiritually perceptive woman reports the encounter to her husband, Manoah, describing the angel as 'a man of God' and Manoah requests a second visit so that they may be instructed in how to bring up such a special child.

Once more the angel appears, again to the wife, this time staying long enough for Manoah to speak to him. Manoah's question goes unanswered; the *woman* must do as the angel previously instructed. Manoah fails to recognise the true nature of their visitor until he 'did an amazing thing' and 'ascended in the flame'.

That child was Samson, a great (albeit wayward) deliverer of Israel.

Few people today are commissioned by angels but the story reminds us that our awesome God has a specific role for each of us from the moment of conception, however insignificant we may feel. And those whom God commissions He equips to serve Him.

For prayer and reflection

'But God chose the foolish things of the world ... the weak things ... the lowly ... and the despised ...' (1 Cor. 1:27–8).

Angels **encourage and nurture**

I n the chapter before this we can read the dramatic account of Elijah's single-handed contest with, and victory over, 450 prophets of Baal. This vindication of the God of Israel ended the three-year drought. However, Jezebel, Ahab's evil queen, vowed to take revenge and kill Elijah. He fled to the wilderness – an appropriate environment for he is emotionally, spiritually and physically in a desert place.

Falling into an exhausted sleep he is suddenly awoken – by an angel's touch. God provided, by means of the angel, *exactly* what Elijah needed: someone to touch him, a voice to cheer and encourage him in that lonely place and food to energise him.

Elijah ate and drank and lay down again. Once more the angel woke him (had he been watching over him as he slept?) and told him to eat again in preparation for the long journey ahead. That must have been 'angels' food' indeed, for it sustained Elijah for 40 days.

The rest of the story is well known: the still, small voice, God's reassurance and the commissioning of Elijah's successor, Elisha.

Like Elijah, we all have times when we feel depressed, discouraged, totally alone, even – perhaps especially – when we seem to be flourishing spiritually or are engaging in spiritual battles. But however we may feel, God's loving, fatherly eye is upon us and He will provide exactly what we need, as He did for Elijah. Sometimes God's agents in this process of encouragement and strengthening are other human beings – Christian friends, perhaps – but that sudden lifting of our spirits, or the renewed experience of the warmth of God's love, can, I believe, be a direct result of angelic intervention.

1 Kings 19:1–21

'… he … fell asleep. All at once an angel touched him and said, "Get up and eat".' (v.5)

For prayer and reflection

'May our Lord Jesus Christ himself and God our Father, who loved us … encourage … and strengthen you …' (2 Thess. 2:16–17).

93

Angels **execute God's judgment**

**2 Chronicles
32:1–22**

'… the LORD sent
an angel, who
annihilated all the
fighting men … of
the Assyrian king.'
(v.21)

**For prayer and
reflection**

'Ascribe to the
LORD the glory
due to his name;
bring an offering
and come into his
courts. Worship
the LORD in the
splendour of his
holiness …'
(Psa. 96:8–9).

Hezekiah, king of Judah, sought to follow God and encouraged his subjects to do so. He cleansed and repaired the Temple, reinstated the Passover and oversaw the destruction of pagan shrines throughout the land. Then Sennacherib, king of Assyria, a massive 'superpower' of the time, invaded Judah. Realising Sennacherib had his eye on Jerusalem, Hezekiah took practical steps to make it difficult to seize the city: blocking water supplies, repairing Jerusalem's wall and building a second wall.

Hezekiah urged his people to trust God for deliverance but Sennacherib initiated a propaganda war directed at all levels of Judaean society, pointing out that the gods of all the nations conquered so far had proved powerless against him – so why should *their* God prove different.

The second part of the passage reveals several examples of Sennacherib 'speaking about the God of Jerusalem as … the work of men's hands' (v.19). It was *this* – the grave dishonouring of the name of the true God – that caused Hezekiah and Isaiah to 'cry out' in prayer. As a result, God sent His angel to execute judgment. The Assyrian forces were destroyed (the parallel account in 2 Kings says 185,000 died), God's holy name was vindicated and His people delivered from an apparently invincible enemy.

We hesitate today to think of God executing judgment but He says, 'I am the LORD; that is my name. I will not give my glory to another or my praise to idols.' God's name stands for His character. We know Him only in grace or in judgment. Pray today for Christians in places where God's name is defiled and where it is costly to bear Christ's name.

Angels **protect and deliver**

D aniel, as faithful in captivity to his earthly ruler as to his God, is about to be given the highest position in the land, but his jealous rivals trick the king into issuing a blasphemous edict. Daniel quietly but openly refuses to compromise his loyalty to the one true God: 'when Daniel learned that the decree had been published, he went home to his upstairs room ... Three times a day he got down on his knees and prayed ... just as he had done before' (v.10).

His enemies find Daniel 'asking God for help' – he was obviously aware of the potential consequences of putting God first. Triumphantly the conspirators report to the king, who realises too late the trap he has fallen into. Daniel is thrown into the lions' den – and the king can't sleep (perhaps there is an angel of insomnia!).

At first light the king is overjoyed to discover Daniel alive. Daniel is quite clear (v.22) about who saved his life – did he see the angel? The king issues a further decree to the whole kingdom that Daniel's God is to be feared and reverenced (vv.26–27).

Daniel's story reminds us that God's angels protect and deliver His children – especially when they refuse to compromise and are prepared, if necessary, to lay down their lives rather than deny their God.

Perhaps you are 'out on a limb' at the moment because of your faith or your refusal to compromise your Christian beliefs. Peter calls the devil a 'roaring lion' (1 Pet. 5: 8). Maybe you face some kind of satanic opposition – a 'lions' den' – at work, or in some other situation. Trust God. He can send an angel to 'stop the lions' mouths', as He did for Daniel. Pray for courage graciously to stand firm to the end.

Daniel 6:1–23

'My God sent his angel, and he shut the mouths of the lions. They have not hurt me ...'
(v.22)

For prayer and reflection

'... the God we serve is able to save us ... and he will rescue us ... even if he does not ... we will not serve your gods ...' (Dan. 3:17–18).

WEEKEND

True security

For reflection: Psalm 91:1–16

Where, in today's terror-stalked world, can we find security? As usual, the Bible has the answer to this modern and yet most ancient question. True security can be found only under the shelter of God's wings (v.4).

Later, safety is promised to those who trust God and make their home in Him. Especially relevant to this month's topic is the promise of angelic protection for believers (vv.11–12) that Satan used to tempt Jesus to throw Himself from the Temple.

The book that inspired me most as a teenager took its title from the first verse of this psalm: *Shadow of the Almighty*. It told the story of five young American missionaries massacred by Auca Indians to whom they had gone with the gospel. How do we square this promise of protection with that? I believe that as Christians we can be absolutely confident that no *accidental* or *lasting* harm can come to us. God is working out His eternal purposes in and for us.

Reflect this weekend on the images and promises of this psalm and ask God to deal with any fears you have in these areas.

Attendant angles

After the glory of the opened heavens, with the Spirit descending like a dove and settling on Him after His Father's affirming declaration, Jesus goes from His baptism – in triumph to begin His ministry? No! He is taken by the same Spirit into the bleakness of the Judaean desert, there to wrestle – not as 'superman' but as a real human being – with extremes of temperature, hunger, loneliness, self-doubt – and the tempter. Satan apparently knew the circumstances of Jesus' baptism as well as he knew the Scriptures, for he cleverly begins the first two temptations with, 'If you are the Son of God ...', using the words Jesus had heard at His baptism: 'This is my Son.' We should not be surprised if the enemy tempts us to doubt what God has said, especially at the beginning of some new enterprise to which God has called us.

The devil is no gentleman! He tested Jesus at a time when He was pushed to the limit of human endurance, physically, mentally and spiritually, offering Him apparent shortcuts to spiritual goals, and backing his offers by plausibly quoted Scripture. Jesus countered Satan's suggestions with His own knowledge of Scripture and finally sent him away.

Only as the tempter departs do we read, 'angels attended' Jesus (v.11). Where were they earlier? Didn't Jesus need them when He was being tested to the limit?

Perhaps we should understand from this that angels are at *God's* beck and call, not ours! Like Jesus, we must learn, by God's grace, to fight our own spiritual battles, to resist everyday temptations like being irritable because we've had a broken night, or short-tempered because we are anxious. When God sees we need angelic help, we can be sure that we'll get it – for His timing is perfect!

Matthew 3:13–4:11

'Then the devil left him, and angels came and attended him.' (4:11)

For prayer and reflection

'**Submit yourselves, then, to God. Resist the devil, and he will flee from you'** (James 4:7).

Joyful angles

Luke 15:1–10

'… there is rejoicing in the presence of the angels of God over one sinner who repents.' (v.10)

Heavenly parties! Angels clearly have emotions, for we read here that they rejoice when any one of God's lost children is brought home. Jesus repeats this twice, at the end of the first two parables in today's reading.

These stories were prompted by the mutterings of the 'Pharisees and teachers of the law' – the religious establishment of the time – who were disdainful of the kind of 'disreputable' people Jesus was welcoming! So Jesus directs these parables at His critics, underlining the fact that angels cheer when 'sinners' come home to God! As usual, He uses homely pictures everyone would understand and here gives them extra point by having as their subjects people despised by the religious establishment: shepherds were not well thought of, women were beneath notice and the younger son (in the third story) does all the wrong things and certainly didn't deserve even to be welcomed back, let alone reinstated!

Jesus drove His message home: God loves the 'untouchables', the 'undesirables', the 'dying thieves' in any society – and heaven parties over them more than over those who 'don't need' to repent – who think they're OK. The shepherd continues searching until he finds the lost sheep, calling friends to share his joy, like the woman who finally finds the lost coin from her wedding headdress. So the angels share God's joy when He finds His lost children.

If the angels rejoice over repentant sinners, then no doubt they rejoice too when we gain spiritual victories, when we stop trying to live independently of God, when we trust Him with things that bother us. How will you make the angels cheer today?

For prayer and reflection

'… you have come to Mount Zion … the city of the living God. You have come to thousands upon thousands of angels in joyful assembly …' (Heb. 12:22).

Guardian angels

The Gospels show us the disciples, 'warts and all' – ordinary, fallible human beings whom Jesus chose to accompany and learn from Him, before entrusting to them the task of spreading the good news. In this passage the disciples have again 'lost the plot'. They have evidently been discussing rank, for they ask Jesus who is the greatest in the kingdom of heaven.

In response, Jesus uses a child as a visual aid. The kingdom of God, He says, unlike earthly kingdoms, is not about rank, privilege and 'pecking order' but about uncomplicated faith in a heavenly Father – the kind of trust a small child, dependent on powerful adults for every need, exhibits all the time. In another reversal of accepted wisdom Jesus points out that childlike humility is the distinguishing mark of the 'greatest' in God's kingdom, and that as we welcome children we welcome Him. He utters very solemn warnings about those who abuse a child's trust.

The theme of children continues (v.10) in a saying which has given rise to many ideas (not all of them biblical!) about guardian angels. Children, Jesus says, have angels who are in the presence of God and can look on Him without perishing (the seraphim in Isaiah's vision, remember, covered their faces). Little ones, says Jesus, are *that* important to God. This must surely mean that there are angels assigned to watch over children and (by inference) the weak. Although we know that children and vulnerable adults do suffer abuse and worse, God has not forgotten them. Instead of discounting Jesus' words because of our awareness of evil, let's pray more earnestly for angelic protection for the weak, and work and pray to end abuse of children worldwide.

Matthew 18:1–14

'… do not look down on … these little ones … their angels … see the face of my Father …' (v.10)

For prayer and reflection

'Let the little children come to me … anyone who will not receive the kingdom of God like a little child will never enter it' (Luke 18:16–17).

A strengthening angel

'An angel from heaven appeared to him and strengthened him.' (v.43)

For prayer and reflection

'... we do not have a high priest ... unable to sympathise with our weaknesses, but ... one who has been tempted in every way, just as we are – yet was without sin' (Heb. 4:15).

Jesus' earthly life draws swiftly to its close. The Gospels devote much space to the events of that final week, starting with the triumphal entry into Jerusalem and culminating in the resurrection – but first the cross.

Crucifixion in many forms was the Romans' favoured means of execution. The horrific, public punishment was a stark warning to onlookers of the cost of defying the might of Rome. Jesus would have seen many crucifixions and knew what they entailed. He understood the cost, not just of defying Rome, but of bearing your sin and mine, and being cut off from His Father in the process. No wonder He agonised in Gethsemane.

Significantly He says to His disciples, 'Pray that you will not fall into temptation', for He was about to wrestle in prayer to overcome the greatest temptation He had ever faced – the temptation to avoid the cross. Jesus had demonstrated throughout His ministry His 'oneness' with His Father. His 'food', He said, was to do God's will. Yet here, in that quiet garden, Jesus longed, perhaps for the first time in His life, *not* to do His Father's will. Tempted to go His own way, to shrink from the cross, He knew that He must submit to His Father and be crucified.

He makes His decision, bowing to His Father's will, fully aware of the immense and terrible personal cost involved. And at that point, the victory over Himself won, 'An angel from heaven appeared to him and strengthened him' (v.43). Only Luke's Gospel has this detail. The battle of wills has been won. Jesus, physically and emotionally exhausted, is granted angelic aid and strengthening.

As we submit our wills to His, we too shall be strengthened.

Warrior angels

S till in the Garden of Gethsemane, today's passage from Matthew takes up the story where we left it yesterday in Luke. An armed gang sent by the chief priests arrives with Judas, who identifies Jesus by a prearranged sign.

As his Master is seized and arrested, Peter (named in John's Gospel) attacks the high priest's servant. Jesus prevents him doing further damage with a warning that violence begets violence and a reminder that this is no ordinary tussle with authorities. He remarks, matter of factly, that He has only to ask and His Father would put 12 legions of angels at His disposal. (A Roman legion had 6,000 soldiers, so Jesus was talking about *72,000* angelic beings coming to His assistance!) Peter's one clumsy sword thrust and that armed rabble are contrasted with thousands of angelic warriors just waiting for the Father's word of command. 'But,' Jesus continues, 'how then would the Scriptures be fulfilled?' – those Old Testament prophecies of the suffering servant, who was 'wounded for our transgressions, bruised for our iniquities' (Isa. 53:5, AV).

So Jesus chose *not* to ask for angelic reinforcements. He had just won the battle to submit to the Father's will and He goes through with that decision, not resisting arrest, not reproaching Judas, healing the injured man (Luke 22:51), and standing trial alone before the Sanhedrin, since His 'disciples deserted him and fled' (v.56).

The 12 legions of angels recall the heavenly armies seen by Elisha's servant, and we should be encouraged that there are indeed immense and powerful heavenly hosts arrayed on the side of God's children. If Jesus could ask His Father for angelic help then surely we can do so too?

Matthew 26:47–68

'… my Father… will at once put at my disposal more than twelve legions of angels?' (v.53)

For prayer and reflection

'Don't be afraid … Those who are with us are more than those who are with them' (2 Kings 6:16). Reflect on these words today.

WEEKEND

Alleluia! The Lord is risen!

For reflection: Matthew 28:1–10

Angels figure rather intermittently in the Gospels, appearing in Matthew's and Luke's stories of Christ's birth, Mark's and Matthew's accounts of the temptation and Luke's of the agony in Gethsemane. All four, however, have angels in their resurrection stories!

Sometimes angels in the Old Testament were 'disguised' as human beings, but not on this New Testament occasion! This is so important that God's agents appear in all their dazzling glory to tell the demoralised disciples, 'He is not here; he has risen'!

Read today's passage (and if possible, the other three resurrection stories) focusing on the angels – you may find details you haven't noticed before, for example the earthquake (what power!), the effortless rolling back of the stone sealing the tomb. Then comes the detail I love: the angel 'sat on it'. The angel *sat* on the stone – waiting to announce the best news ever heard on earth:

Vain the stone, the watch the seal; Alleluia!
Christ has burst the gates of hell; Alleluia!
Death in vain forbids him rise; Alleluia!
Christ has opened paradise! Alleluia!

He is risen indeed! Alleluia!

Ascension angels

We have seen how key events in Jesus' life were marked by the presence of angels, and His 'ascension' – His return to heaven – was no exception. Apart from a brief reference at the end of Mark, only Luke tells us about this. Many Christians ignore Ascension Day but Jesus' ascension was very significant. We see from the Gospels that on rising from death He had a different kind of body, one that could pass through doors, for example, though it was recognisably human.

Between His resurrection and returning to His Father, Jesus appeared on certain occasions to those who had known and loved Him. Where was He between those appearances? He was probably 'visiting' heaven, and when He finally returned there, His earthly work complete, the age of the Spirit about to begin, the disciples were witnesses to the event so that there could be no doubt whatsoever in their minds that Jesus was indeed God. That's why, as our key verse says, they 'worshipped' Him – I believe that as He ascended, they were granted a glimpse of their glorified Saviour in all His heavenly splendour – and that's partly why they 'returned to Jerusalem with great joy'.

The other reason for their joy was, I believe, the message that the 'two men dressed in white' – angels – gave them (v.10). They promised that Jesus would return to earth in the same manner as He had left. The Early Church, hounded and persecuted, lived in daily expectation of Jesus' return, which was so important to them that it became known just as 'the Day' – the big day!

We still await that glorious day when Jesus will return. May the hope of His coming motivate all that you do today as it motivated and inspired the first Christians!

**Luke 24:50–53;
Acts 1:1–11**

'While he was blessing them, he … was taken up into heaven … they worshipped him …' (vv.51–52)

'… we wait for the blessed hope – the glorious appearing of our great God and Saviour, Jesus Christ, who gave himself for us …' (Titus 2:13–14).

An angelic **commission**

Acts 8:4–8,
26–40

'… an angel …
said … "Go south
to the road –
the desert road
… down from
Jerusalem …"'
(v.26)

**'Those who obey
his commands live
in him, and he in
them. And … we
know that he lives
in us … by the
Spirit he gave us'
(1 John 3: 24).**

Acts tells the story of the young Church in the era immediately after Jesus' ascension and the promised outpouring of the Holy Spirit. That period might almost be described as an 'overlap' between the time when the Man Jesus taught, worked and healed on earth and the time when the Holy Spirit came to lead and guide His disciples as they sought to fulfil the great commission.

It's perhaps not surprising, therefore, that in Acts we find references not just to the work of the Holy Spirit but also to angelic intervention and operation. It's also interesting to see that the angels fulfil very similar roles to those in the Old Testament incidents that we considered in the first week.

In today's story Philip, one of the Seven (Acts 6) is in Samaria, preaching and performing miracles with such astonishing results that Peter and John are sent as reinforcements. In the midst of this successful preaching and healing campaign, Philip is commissioned by an angel to go … to the desert! It must have seemed ludicrous to leave Samaria when so much was happening. Maybe that's why the angel was sent with the message, so that Philip couldn't ignore it.

God's strategy is often different from ours! God knew that travelling on that desert road was someone who was seeking God … and Philip was the one to explain the gospel to him! That Ethiopian chancellor of the exchequer must have been a key figure in northeast Africa at the time and Philip's obedience to his angelic commission resulted in probably the first convert in that area.

We may not see such obvious or immediate results of our obedience, but God will bless us and honour our faith as we respond to the promptings of His Spirit today.

An angelic **deliverance**

Herod Agrippa (grandson of the Herod visited by the wise men, and nephew of the Herod who had John the Baptist beheaded) was brought up in Rome and owed his power to his friendship with the emperor Caligula. One way of currying favour with Jewish leaders was by persecuting the Church.

So Herod had John beheaded and seeing 'this pleased the Jews' had Peter apprehended too. Peter was imprisoned until after Passover, guarded by four men and chained to two of them. Nevertheless he was sleeping when 'a light shone' and the angel appeared.

The vivid story of Peter's escape has all the marks of an eyewitness account, including the detail that Peter thinks he's dreaming! The angel is very practical, 'striking' Peter to wake him, telling him to get dressed, put on his sandals and wrap his cloak around him. The prison gate opens 'by itself' and the angel accompanies Peter the length of the street, then disappears. At that point Peter realises it isn't a dream and goes to Mary's house. Rhoda, overjoyed at hearing his voice, forgets to let him in! Angelic deliverance – but I believe the clue to that deliverance is in verse 5, 'the church was earnestly praying for him'. God sometimes limits Himself to the extent of our faith and prayers. When we pray, God acts, sometimes, as here, using angels as His agents.

I find this really challenging. When communism crumbled in Eastern Europe at the beginning of the 90s, I remember wondering, 'If I had prayed more or with greater faith would this have happened sooner?' Nothing is impossible with God – but He invites us to become partners with Him in the deployment of angels to 'impossible' situations!

Acts 12:1–17

'... Peter ... said, "Now I know without a doubt that the Lord sent his angel and rescued me ..."'
(v.11)

For prayer and reflection

'... pray in the Spirit on all occasions with all kinds of prayers and requests ... be alert and ... keep on praying for all the saints' (Eph. 6:18).

An avenging angel

Acts 12:11–24

'… an angel of
the Lord struck
him down …
But the word of
God continued
to increase …'
(vv.23–24)

Today's reading overlaps part of yesterday's, when we considered Herod's persecution of the young Church and Peter's angelic deliverance from prison.

Herod's anger at Peter's escape results in Peter's guards losing their lives (v.19). Herod travels to Caesarea where a deputation from the people of Tyre and Sidon (today's Lebanon) asks to meet him. These places relied on grain from Galilee, so any dispute with that area had serious economic consequences. The deputation recruits a mediator, Blastus, and on the appointed day Herod appears.

The Jewish historian Josephus records that the occasion was a festival in honour of the emperor Claudius and that Herod 'put on a robe made of silver throughout, of marvellous weaving'. Herod clearly intended to impress, both by his appearance and his 'public address'. The strategy worked and he was acclaimed as a god by his audience.

But Herod was a Jew. He knew only too well 'the first and greatest commandment': 'I am the LORD your God … have no other gods before me', yet he did nothing to stop the blasphemy of this heathen acclamation.

God acted in judgment, sending an angel 'immediately' to strike him. Five days later, according to Josephus, Herod died. *But the word of God continued … to spread* (v.24). Herod was dramatically removed by one of God's agents. The young Church which he had tried to suppress continued to grow.

Sometimes it seems as though godlessness will prevail, especially in places where Christians today are hounded and reviled for faith in Jesus. But 'our God reigns' and still vindicates His servants as He did in Acts. Angels haven't gone off duty!

For prayer and reflection

'I am the LORD; that is my name! I will not give my glory to another or my praise to idols' (Isa. 42:8).

Angels **at our side**

I n the previous chapter, Paul, on trial before Festus and Agrippa, exercised his right as a Roman citizen to appeal to Caesar – the emperor. Here he begins the sea-journey to Rome.

In ancient times ships never sailed during the winter months. It is now late autumn, but Paul's practical warnings (v.10) go unheeded; despite the late date, the ship's owner and pilot thought they could reach Phoenix, a bigger and better-protected port in which to spend the winter. They were wrong!

The ship, part of the fleet transporting grain from Egypt to Rome, is caught in typhoon-type winds and the ensuing storm rages for two weeks, during which time the ship is battered and the cargo and even the tackle thrown overboard. Paul can't resist saying, 'I told you so' (v.21) but at the same time he acknowledges that part of his earlier prediction won't be fulfilled – there will be no loss of life. The previous night an angel had spoken to Paul, reassuring him that he *would* get to Rome and that God had 'graciously given' him the lives of all his sailing companions. Paul encourages them to trust God with him, and, from this point on, takes charge.

Paul said the angel stood beside him. Some versions have 'stood by me'. Isn't that a wonderful picture of the angelic support available to us? There are angels at our side, God's agents 'on stand by' to encourage and assist those who trust God, especially when we are in difficult or dangerous situations!

When they jettisoned the cargo Paul must have thought that the ship and everyone on board would be lost, but God had other plans, using an angel to encourage Paul, Paul to encourage those aboard and the shipwreck to evangelise Malta – see chapter 28!

Acts 27:1–15, 20–25

'Last night, an angel of the God whose I am and whom I serve stood beside me …' (v.23)

For prayer and reflection

'As the heavens are higher than the earth, so are my ways higher than your ways and my thoughts than your thoughts' (Isa. 55:9).

WEEKEND

'Angels on assignment'

For reflection: Psalm 103

This psalm speaks of God's compassion for us in our human frailty. The final verses describe angels as 'mighty ones who do his bidding'. During severe disruption to UK rail services, a friend's teenage daughter had to travel alone at night to a remote part of Britain. We prayed for angelic protection for her; she got it – a woman with a WWJD wristband who accompanied her all the way!

In his book *Summer of Miracles*, in a chapter entitled *Angels on Assignment*, Jamie Buckingham, in theatre before surgery for cancer, describes seeing:

giant heavenly beings, shoulder to shoulder, between nine and ten feet tall … motionless, looking straight ahead. On the side of the room to my right there were at least twenty. I was aware of equal numbers standing around the other three walls. Huge celestial beings. Waiting. Watching. Guarding. On assignment.

He later comments to his wife that the angels 'weren't doing anything. Just standing there.' She responds, 'Oh they were doing something. That's why you're here.'

Angels on assignment; angels all around. Reflect and rejoice!

Angels – **sent to serve**

Those familiar with the book of Hebrews will know that its author aims to show that particular Old Testament prophecies pointed to Jesus, as did many other aspects of tabernacle and Temple worship and ritual. Jesus is the complete fulfilment of all God promised in the Old Testament.

That theme runs throughout Hebrews and in this first chapter the writer declares that Jesus was the final, full revelation of God's nature. If we want to know what God is like – look at Jesus! To emphasise Jesus' superiority over all created beings, the writer compares Him to angels, who are mentioned seven times in the chapter and we can gain further insights into angels from these references.

We see that angels worship God and Jesus in whose presence they dwell (v.6), whilst verse 7 stresses their role as God's agents, quoting from the Greek (Septuagint) version of Psalm 104. But the most telling comment, perhaps, comes in the final verse, where we are told that angels are 'sent to serve' those who are to 'inherit salvation' – that's us!

We have looked at angels in Scripture – in the past. But this verse reminds us that angels have a role today – they are 'ministering' (serving) spirits sent by God to help and support His children in times of need. There is undoubtedly a 'wow' factor here, but we must guard against giving angels undue emphasis. Tom Wright[1] sounds a timely warning here: 'Today ... many in the churches seem dissatisfied ... and are eager to expand their spiritual horizons ... to include angels, saints and other interesting distractions.' Angels are only servants; they are not to be worshipped. Jesus alone should be the focus of our adoration.

1. Tom Wright, *Hebrews for Everyone* (London, SPCK, 2003).

Hebrews 1:1–14

'He makes his angels winds, his servants flames of fire.' (v.7)

For prayer and reflection

'Let us fix our eyes on Jesus, the author and perfecter of our faith, who for the joy set before him endured the cross, scorning its shame ...' (Heb. 12:2).

Angels **in disguise**

**Hebrews
12:18–13:8**

'Do not forget
to entertain
strangers … by
so doing some
people have
entertained
angels …' (13:2)

**For prayer and
reflection**

'… I was hungry
and you gave
me something
to eat … thirsty
and you gave
me something
to drink, I was a
stranger and you
invited me in …'
(Matt. 25:35).

I n chapter 12 Hebrews begins drawing to a close, contrasting the terrifying atmosphere of the law-giving on Mount Sinai with our experience of 'Mount Zion', God's love and redemption in Jesus – notice the reference to 'angels in joyful assembly' (v.22). It ends with an exhortation to us to live thankful lives of worship, and chapter 13 gives examples of ways in which our gratitude to God can be worked out in daily living.

These include loving our fellow Christians (v.1), remembering those in prison (v.3), perhaps by praying for those imprisoned for their faith, and their dependants, and maybe helping those in our local prisons; we are similarly to remember the persecuted, identifying with them. We are to respect marriage and our lives should be characterised by contentment because God will meet our needs. All these sound fairly 'standard' Christian issues, but there's another very interesting one in verse 2.

Here we are encouraged to 'entertain' strangers, because – one day one of them might be an angel! What an intriguing thought! The obvious biblical examples are Abraham (Gen. 18) and Samson's parents (Judg. 13), but possibly the author of Hebrews had in mind Early Church examples of which we know nothing. Of course, hospitality was more part of the culture in New Testament times than, sadly, it is today in the modern West, but it can be such a blessing! I remember being welcomed as a student into Christian homes for Sunday lunch and we in turn have been greatly blessed by many visitors – from all over the world and of all ages – sharing meals in our home. It's something we can all do – even coffee and a chat counts!

What 'angels in disguise' might you entertain this week?

Deceiving angels

I n this section of his second letter to the Corinthians Paul appears very outspoken, even harsh. He was actually defending his reputation to the church in Corinth, which he had founded, and which was therefore close to his heart.

Reading between the lines, it seems that so-called 'super-apostles' had infiltrated the church, claiming superior revelation and a gospel 'better' than the message Paul had preached. Paul stoutly defends both his claim to be an apostle and the content of his gospel, and in condemning the 'false apostles' (v.13) he incidentally warns us of danger.

So far in studying angels we have considered only the 'genuine article', but there is a clear caution here about the possibility of being deceived by angels. Paul says Satan himself sometimes poses as an angel of light. It seems that Satan himself was once an angel, ejected from God's presence when he wanted to be like God – the sin of pride – taking thousands of other angels with him (Isaiah 14:12–14 and 2 Peter 2:4 may describe this, while Matthew 25:41 mentions eternal fire 'prepared for the devil and his angels'). These 'bad' angels do Satan's bidding, just as 'good' angels do God's.

If Satan can appear as something or someone good, how can we guard against being deceived? There is huge interest today in angels, but not all of it is helpful or right. Angels, as Tom Wright says, are neither to be worshipped nor are they to distract us from God – Father, Son and Holy Spirit. If we are unsure whether or not something apparently 'angelic' is from God, we can use two checks: Will this help me focus on God? And does it tie in with the truths I already know from the Bible? If the answer to either is 'no' – run a mile!

2 Corinthians 11:1–15

'… Satan himself masquerades as an angel of light.' (v.14)

For prayer and reflection

'Be on your guard; stand firm in the faith; be [women] of courage; be strong. Do everything in love' (1 Cor. 16:13–14).

Accompanying angels

**1 Thessalonians
4:13–18;
2 Thessalonians
1:6–12**

'This will happen
when the Lord
Jesus is revealed
… with his
powerful angels.'
(2 Thess. 1:7)

We have seen from Scripture different roles angels played in the past. We have thought a little about their role today, supporting and assisting believers. Now we learn that they will play their part too at the climax of history, when they appear with Christ at His return in glory, as Paul explains in these two passages from Thessalonians.

Obviously this is something beyond human comprehension and the pictures we have here and in the Gospels cannot fully describe what it will be like, but clearly it will be very dramatic – with the archangel's voice, the sound of a trumpet and Jesus attended by 'powerful angels'. Believers who have died will be raised and Christians still living will be caught up 'in the clouds' to meet Christ in the air. What a spectacle!

Matthew, Mark and Luke all record Jesus' words about this event, speaking of His return in glory accompanied by holy angels, who, according to His teaching in Mark 13, will be sent to bring believers from all over the earth – a great and triumphant ingathering of all God's children everywhere – brought home!

These passages indicate too that this second coming will precede the judgment, with angel-witnesses, for Luke 12:8–9 says that if we acknowledge Jesus here on earth, He will acknowledge us on that day 'before the angels'. These are awesome matters:

For prayer and reflection

'You also must be ready, because the Son of Man will come at an hour when you do not expect him' (Luke 12: 40).

Therefore with angels and archangels/and with all the company of heaven/we laud and magnify thy glorious name,/evermore praising thee and saying,/'Holy, holy, holy, Lord, God of hosts;/heaven and earth are full of thy glory./Glory be to thee O Lord most high.'
(Communion Service, Book of Common Prayer, 1662)

Yearning angels

I n this wonderful opening chapter of his letter, the apostle Peter reflects on the wonders of our salvation and all that God has freely granted us in Christ. The chapter 'pivots', however, on our theme verse for today: 'Even angels long to look into these things.' Before it, Peter describes the glories of our inheritance in Christ and the joy that brings. After it he says, 'Therefore ...' Because of this amazing salvation, ours both now and in the future, we should live lives of holiness and hope.

That brief sentence gives us a whole new perspective on our status as God's children. Angels, for all their privileged position, their ability to travel through space and time, to take different shapes, to do God's bidding, are limited in this respect: they have no knowledge of what it is to be human, no understanding of what it means to be made in God's image, no concept of what it feels like to have sinned – and to have been forgiven, brought home to our loving heavenly Father through Jesus' sacrifice on the cross.

As I was thinking about this, some lines of a hymn I sang as a little girl came into my mind: A song which even angels can never, never sing: 'They know not Christ as Saviour but worship Him as King.'

Another hymn says this: 'Praise, my soul, the King of heaven/To His feet thy tribute bring;/Ransomed, healed, restored, forgiven,/Who like thee His praise should sing?'

Who indeed? Certainly not the angels. We human beings may have been made 'a little lower than the angels' (Psa. 8:5) but we daily experience God's abundant grace – something the angels will never comprehend. Praise Him! Praise the everlasting King!

---

1 Peter 1:3–21

'Even angels long to look into these things.' (v.12)

For prayer and reflection

'You have been adopted into the very family circle of God and you can say ... "Father, my Father"' (Rom. 8:15–16, J.B. Phillips).

113

WEEKEND

Protected by an angel

For reflection: Psalm 34:1–20

In *Appointment in Jerusalem* Lydia Prince tells how her water supply failed, forcing her to cross the Jerusalem war-zone, carrying Tikva, an orphaned toddler, in order to reach the home of someone with her own water supply. Setting off, praying for protection, she recalled the final sentence of a friend's recent letter: 'We are claiming for you … Psalm 34:7: *The angel of the LORD encamps around those that fear him, and he delivers them.*'

Reaching a high barricade, Lydia realised she couldn't lift the toddler over it. Sensing she was not alone, she turned and saw a young man, who lifted Tikva over the barricade and then carried her, without hesitating over the route or speaking a word, right to the friend's home, where he put the infant down and walked away.

'However did you get here? … We phoned the police station … but they told us it was impossible for anyone to get through.'

I described the young man.

'El-hamd il-Allah!' cried Nijmeh … 'God has answered our prayers! We asked Him to send an angel to protect you and surely He did!'

Reflect on the story and the promise – and give thanks!

From fear
to faith

Rebecca Lowe

Rebecca Lowe is a writer, speaker and media consultant, based in Swansea, south Wales. She graduated from Oxford with a degree in Theology, then worked as a journalist becoming freelance following the birth of her daughter. She has written for a wide range of religious and secular organisations, including editing newsletters for the Christian charity, Care for the Family. She also acts as a volunteer media officer for the Christian relief and development agency, Tearfund. She is married to Rob and has a daughter, Stephanie. In her spare time, she enjoys reading, writing, playing the zither and walking in the Gower countryside.

From fear to faith

John 14:25–28

'Do not let your hearts be troubled and do not be afraid.' (v.27)

Fear has been described as one of the greatest scourges of 21st-century life. At a time when so many of us in the Western world have all we need in material terms, it seems ironic that we're increasingly weighed down by worries and anxieties.

A certain amount of fear, of course, is essential. Fear acts as an early-warning signal – a 'fight or flight' response, which stops us putting ourselves at unnecessary risk. Some fears can even be enjoyable – ask any roller-coaster enthusiast! But there are other fears, such as phobias or acute anxiety, which can hold us back and prevent us from getting on with everyday life. The Bible speaks of different types of fear. Fear, in the sense of reverence and awe, is often given as the only appropriate response to an awesome God. That is why Proverbs 9:10, tells us that: 'The fear of the LORD is the beginning of wisdom.'

Another sort of fear is that which relates to sin, guilt and conscience. When God asked Adam, after he had sinned, 'Why are you hiding?', he replied 'because I was afraid' (Gen. 3:10). His conscience and guilt provoked a fear response. This is often God's way of telling us we have done something wrong and need to repent.

Fear, then, can be useful, even helpful. But the problems come when our fears threaten to overwhelm us, growing out of all proportion to the thing we were originally afraid of. It is then that such fears become phobias.

The good news is that we don't have to put up with such fears – they have already been defeated by Christ! We don't have to do anything to earn this freedom; Jesus has already done it all for us. All we have to do is learn to put our trust in Him.

For prayer and reflection

Lord, I bring to You all the fears and anxieties which lie within my heart today. Please help me to have the faith to turn away from my own resources and put my trust in You.

'Excuses, **excuses!**'

Yesterday, we talked about the different types of fear. There are the 'useful' types of fear that protect us from danger, lead us to repentance, and can even bring us wisdom and blessing. Then there are the 'negative' fears – phobias of everyday things like spiders or flying, or more subtle fears, like a fear of failure or inadequacy – which threaten to paralyse us if we let them rule our lives. Today, we go on to examine the second type of fear in more detail, looking particularly at how it relates to responding to God's calling.

Have you ever felt that God was calling you to do something – perhaps outside your 'comfort zone' – but you let your fears of inadequacy persuade you that you weren't up to the job? If so, you're in good company. Here are some typical 'excuses' given by figures in the Bible:

- 'I'm a very poor public speaker', Moses (Exod. 4:10)
- 'I'm too sinful', Isaiah (Isa. 6:5)
- 'I don't know how to speak; I'm too young', Jeremiah (Jer. 1:6)
- 'I'm only from a humble background', Gideon (Judg. 6:15)
- 'Nobody will listen to me', Moses (Exod. 6:12)

It's reassuring to think that even some of God's most powerful leaders experienced the same emotions of fear, anxiety and personal inadequacy for the task.

When God calls us to do something difficult, it's easy to make our excuses, but consider this: God will never ask you to do something in your own power. With a genuine calling comes the promise of God's continued presence (see Jer. 1:8). If God is truly calling you to something, you can be assured He will not leave you in the lurch. Along with the call comes the blessing of His spiritual courage.

Jeremiah 1:4–11

"'Do not be afraid of them, for I am with you and will rescue you," declares the LORD.' (v.8)

Lord, forgive me for the times I've let my own fears of inadequacy get in the way of what You would have me do. Help me to do things in Your strength.

'Even if …'

1 Peter 3:13–22

'But even if you should suffer for what is right, you are blessed. Do not fear …' (v.14)

Fear of opposition is one of the key reasons often given for failing to answer God's call on our lives. It's hardly surprising, really. Nobody likes to stand out from the crowd. The thought of being rejected, opposed or possibly even physically abused is not exactly appealing.

Yet, according to this epistle of Peter, this is exactly what we can expect to endure if we are properly fulfilling our duty as a Christian. In 1 Peter 4:12–13, we are told: '… do not be surprised at the painful trial you are suffering, as though something strange were happening to you. But rejoice that you participate in the sufferings of Christ, so that you may be overjoyed when his glory is revealed.'

As Christians, we are called to 'stand up for the gospel' – even if that makes us unpopular. We are also called to live out the gospel in our actions 'to keep a clear conscience' even if that means standing up against what we know is wrong (v.16).

At the time this letter was written, the Early Church was experiencing very real persecution. Many Christians, including Peter, were eventually put to death for their beliefs. Most of us today will never have to face such direct opposition (though there are still, sadly, many countries where Christians are persecuted for their faith). But there will still be some areas of life where we are forced to take a stand – perhaps against some injustice we see in society, or to speak up for the things that matter to us.

At such times we can take courage from the fact that Christ is right there with us, every step of the way, sharing in our trials and promising to turn them into blessings.

For prayer and reflection

Have you made it your purpose to stand up for the gospel? Pray today for those Christians all over the world who are persecuted for their beliefs.

Stilling **the storm**

Whenever I re-read this well-known account of the 'stilling of the storm', I can't help feeling a certain amount of sympathy with the disciples. Here they were, in danger of drowning and Jesus was asleep on a cushion! How dare He ignore such a potentially life-threatening situation. How dare He not get caught up in all the panic!

I've never been a great one for sailing, but I was once caught up in a terrible storm. I was travelling home from France to England on a packed intercontinental ferry when, all of a sudden, the boat lurched violently to the left. Moments later, complete chaos ensued! People were running in all directions, children were screaming and adults were crying.

Eventually, the storm died down and we were escorted safely to dry land. Ever since, though, I've wondered whether our panic reaction created the situation. Perhaps if we'd all managed to remain calm, the boat would have continued sailing on serenely.

Jesus, of course, responds completely differently to the way we, in our lack of faith, would respond to fear. With a single word, He stills the storm and restores calm and normality. In doing so, He rebukes His disciples, not for their lack of sailing skills, nor their fear, rather, the fact that, in their panic, they had forgotten to place their trust in Him. Hadn't He promised to bring them safely to the other side? Did they really think a mere rainstorm was more powerful than His promise?

I don't know how good you are at dealing with stressful situations. I'm afraid I'm rather apt to run about like a headless chicken, complaining to anyone who will listen! If you're like me, perhaps it's time to listen to what God has to say.

Luke 8:22–25

'He got up and rebuked the wind and the raging waters; the storm subsided, and all was calm.' (v.24)

For prayer and reflection

Lord, often we are so busy running around in panic that we forget that You are with us. Help us to hear Your voice through the storm, calling to us, 'Peace, be still'.

'Don't fret the small stuff'

Luke 12:22–32

'Therefore I tell you, do not worry about your life …' (v.22)

Over the past four days, we've touched upon a wide range of fears – fear of answering God's call, fear of failure, and even the sort of life-changing fear that is felt in extreme situations.

But often, even more insidious than these 'extreme' fears, are the everyday worries and anxieties which creep up on us without warning, and threaten to paralyse us into inaction.

These are what I call the 'what ifs?' You know the sort of thing: What if I've left the gas cooker on by mistake? What if somebody breaks into the house while I'm away? What if I fail my job interview? What if my house sale falls through? What if nobody talks to me at the office party?

Sometimes, the exact cause of our worries isn't immediately apparent and manifests itself as a vague sense of impending doom – what the psychologists refer to as 'free-floating anxiety'.

The Bible makes it quite clear that we shouldn't allow our everyday worries and anxieties to overwhelm us. In Luke 10:41, Jesus gently reprimands Martha for 'fretting and fussing about so many things' rather than sitting and relaxing in His presence like her sister Mary.

In Luke 12:25, we are told that we can't add a single hour to our lives by worrying. The passage ends on a note of reassurance. Even though we can't see the final picture, God can, and He cares for our welfare, just as He does for all His creatures. The message is plain: if God is willing to put Himself out for a couple of ravens, how much more will He look after His children, who love and trust Him!

For prayer and reflection

Lord, help me to stop fussing about the little things which ultimately don't matter that much. Help me, instead, to sit at Your feet, like Mary, and listen to Your words.

WEEKEND

Water-walking takes practice!

For reflection: Matthew 14:22–34

Imagine how Peter must have felt when he first attempted to walk on water. Sure, the task was difficult, but he was more than up to the job. Hadn't Jesus told him that 'all things are possible to those who believe'? Unfortunately, it wasn't quite that easy. He started out confidently enough, but a few steps in, he lost his footing, started to panic and – just for a second – took his eyes off Jesus. Suddenly, he was plunged into a terrifying mass of deep, cold water. He was drowning!

Now imagine how he must have felt when the arm of Jesus reached out to pull him to safety. Imagine how relieved he must have been when he found himself safe and sound back on the boat with the other disciples, his clothes soaked, his dignity dented, but his lesson well learned.

Sometimes, the things we are asked to face seem far more than we can cope with, threatening to overwhelm us, to sink us. The solution is simple: Keep your eyes firmly fixed upon Jesus and He will offer you the strength you need to keep going. All you need to do is put your trust in Him. Unlike worldly sources of support, He will never fail you; He will never let you down. Why? Simple – because He loves you.

Are you ready to put your trust in Jesus?

The battle is the Lord's

1 Samuel
17:41–52

'… the battle is the
LORD's, and he
will give all of you
into our hands.'
(v.47)

L ast week we looked at some of the fears and anxieties which threaten to assail us in the course of our Christian lives. This week, we will go on to look at a supreme example of courageous living – that of King David. In 1 Samuel 17:41–52 we read the dramatic account of an encounter which was later to seal David's reputation as a courageous leader of men. On the eve of battle, the soldiers of Israel are gathered to pit their wits against their Philistine opponents. Into the midst of the throng comes a general called Goliath, a giant of a man with a fearsome and bloody reputation.

Up steps David – a mere shepherd boy, with no military experience, no armour and no weapon save five smooth stones and a sling (v.40). Everyone thought he was crazy even to think about taking on such an opponent (v.33). And yet David *knew* that he could defeat Goliath. What was the source of this extraordinary courage? I would suggest that there are two key factors:

He believed that God was in control. David knew that the battle was not his own to fight. The battle belonged to the Lord (v.47) and no amount of pre-battle boasting or posturing could change that.

For prayer and reflection

He knew that God could be trusted. As a shepherd lad, David had faced many dangers (v.36). Surely the God who had rescued him from lions and bears was more than capable of dealing with this new threat?

Lord, help me to remember the ways in which You have helped me in the past and to trust in Your promise to help me in the future.

Perhaps you're facing a stressful situation today, such as a job interview, a tricky meeting, or uncertainty about the future? If so, take a moment to reflect on God's past dealings with you. Surely the God who has helped you before will not desert you now, in your time of greatest need? Rest assured – the battle is the Lord's.

Take **courage**

The young David had good reason to be afraid. Yesterday we read how, as a youth, the shepherd boy David proved his worth by defeating the mighty Philistine general, Goliath. He went on to earn a reputation as a skilled military leader.

However, he was soon to face an even tougher opponent than Goliath, in the form of his previous ally, King Saul. To begin with, Saul was impressed by David's military prowess, but it wasn't long before jealousy set in (1 Sam. 18:8). When he couldn't dispose of his rival in battle, Saul pursued him on foot, intent on killing him. Finally, on the run and in fear for his life, David was forced to take refuge in a cave (1 Sam. 22:1).

A lesser man would surely have given up all hope at this point. But David stood fast, putting his trust in God. In Psalm 27:3, he writes: 'Though an army besiege me, my heart will not fear; though war break out against me, even then will I be confident.'

Despite his near-impossible situation, David never lost sight of the fact that God was in control. His faith was eventually rewarded and he became one of the greatest kings the world has ever known.

Are you feeling discouraged or fearful today? What objects or situations are you most afraid of in your life? Take courage from David's example. God is faithful and has great plans for you – but all in His perfect timing. 'Wait on the Lord; be strong and take heart and wait for the LORD' (v.14). Stick with it, for God is your stronghold.

Psalm 27

'The LORD is my light and my salvation … the stronghold of my life – of whom shall I be afraid?' (v.1)

For prayer and reflection

Spend some time reflecting on the following verse: 'The LORD is the stronghold of my life – of whom shall I be afraid?' (Psa. 27:1).

Facing up to your fears

'I will give your enemy into your hands for you to deal with as you wish.' (v.4)

As we saw yesterday, David and his followers had every reason to be terrified of King Saul. The king was violent, unpredictable and subject to furious mood swings. On one occasion, while David was playing his lyre, Saul threw his spear at him, intending to kill him (1 Sam. 19:9–10).

Eventually, David had to flee as the jealous king swore to hunt down and kill him, the man who had once been his favoured companion (1 Sam. 19:11). After months of running from Saul through wilderness, desert and mountainous terrain, David finally comes face to face with his would-be murderer, only to discover that the threat is not nearly so dire as might have been expected. Instead of being an immediate source of danger, Saul is vulnerable, separated from his men. Faced with an opportunity to kill his pursuer, David instead cuts off a part of his robe (1 Sam. 24:4) as a sign that he is prepared to be merciful, rather than seeking vengeance.

Most of us will, hopefully, never have to face such forms of danger, yet we can all learn something from David's response. Where other men might have continued to flee and to hide, David confronted the source of his fear head-on and, when he did, it was not nearly so threatening as he had at first supposed.

We can choose to spend our whole lives fleeing and hiding from the things we most fear but, by doing so, we risk denying what it means to be fully alive. The American preacher and peace activist Reverend William Sloane Coffin once said: 'We can choose to be scared to death, or scared to life.' We can let our fear paralyse us, or we can make it the motivating force to strive for something better. Which are you going to do?

For prayer and reflection

Lord, help me to stop running away or hiding from the things that scare or worry me. Help me to face my fears head on, secure in the knowledge that You are in control.

The darkest **valley**

I t has been said that death, and the fear of it, is the last great taboo. Even though we all know in our hearts that we must eventually die, it is something we prefer not to think or talk about.

As we've seen over the past week, the psalmist David was no stranger to death. He had seen it in the fields, where life was a daily battle for survival and rampaging lions would seize a newborn lamb given half a second's opportunity.

He had seen it on the battlefield, where bloody conflict between the Israelites and the Philistines had sent many of his closest allies into an early grave. And he had seen it in his own experience, when death threats from King Saul forced him to flee for his very life.

This beautiful psalm, which is often read at funerals, tells us that death is not the end of the story. Just as the shepherd David used to rescue his sheep from danger (1 Sam. 17:34), so we too have a shepherd who can be relied upon to save us from the jaws of death.

In John 10:11, Jesus describes Himself as the Good Shepherd, who 'lays down his life for the sheep' (John 10:11,17). Unlike others who might run for cover at the first sign of trouble, the Good Shepherd knows us, His sheep, by name, and will never leave us to fend for ourselves.

When we walk through the darkest valleys of death and despair, we can rest assured that Jesus will never leave us or abandon us. He loves us so much that He has already given His life for us, and nothing – not even death itself – can ever snatch us out of His hand. All we have to do is follow Him.

Psalm 23

'Even though I walk through the valley of the shadow of death, I will fear no evil …' (v.4)

For prayer and reflection

Lord, sometimes when everything about me seems dark, it's difficult to hear Your voice calling through the chaos. Will You help me to have the courage to follow You, even in the difficult times?

God is **our refuge**

'Therefore we will not fear, though … the mountains fall into the heart of the sea …' (v.2).

Over this past week, we've looked at how King David, a supreme example of 'courage under fire', dealt with potentially threatening situations. But now I want to ask you, how do *you* react when life doesn't turn out the way you expected, when your greatest fears are realised?

On Sunday 26 December 2004, suddenly and without warning, a terrible tsunami swept up from the north-west coast of Sumatra, drowning tens of thousands of people across South and Southeast Asia. Millions more were left homeless, their lives devastated. In the months that followed, the seaquake was followed by a soul-quake. People were asking themselves, 'Where was God in all this? How could such a thing be allowed to happen?'

Psalm 46 does not offer us easy answers to these questions. What it does do, however, is remind us of God's protection. No matter what happens, even if the world collapses, God is still with us (v.2). David, the psalmist, knew this all too well, having faced battle and conflict from all quarters. It is thought by many that Psalm 46 may have been written when the Assyrian army invaded and surrounded Jerusalem.

Even when disaster strikes and we think that God has abandoned us, says the psalmist, He is there with us, in the midst of our suffering, and He promises to see us through.

All of us face times of crisis in our lives – the loss of a loved one, the break-up of a marriage, forced redundancy, the diagnosis of a serious illness. At times such as this, it is reassuring to know that God is with us in the swirling current, even though it doesn't always feel like it at the time. All we have to do is trust Him.

For prayer and reflection

Lord, when I'm afraid and life doesn't seem to make any sense, it helps to remind myself that You are in control. Help me to make You my refuge.

WEEKEND

Take shelter

For reflection: Psalm 62:6
'He alone is my rock and my salvation; He is my fortress, I shall not be shaken.'

Most of our life, we battle on through our fears and frustrations. We put on a brave face for the outside world, trying to pretend that everything is OK, that we have it all under control. Normally, we can maintain the illusion only so long before the whole façade comes crashing down around our ears.

With God, though, things are different. He sees every moment of our lives and knows every thought. We cannot hide anything from Him.

We may not be able to hide *from* God, but, as this psalm shows, we can hide *in* Him.

In Psalm 62, God is described as a stronghold – a tower or fortress into which we can run for shelter or protection. In verse 8, He is described as being our 'refuge' (Hebrew: *Chacah*), someone in whom we can place our confidence, trust and hope.

When storms and battles are raging all around us, it is comforting to know that there is a place we can run to for cover, a place where God will protect us from all our fears, all our uncertainties.

Have you made Him your shelter?

When you are afraid, to whom do you run for cover?

Walking in the **fear of the Lord**

Acts 2:40–47

'Everyone was filled with awe, and many wonders and miraculous signs were done …' (v.43)

S o far, we've focused mostly on the negative types of fear. Not all fear is harmful, however. In fact, there are many times when fear is the only appropriate and useful response. For example:

- faced with imminent danger, fear enables us to take swift action (fight or flight)
- If we are delivering a speech, or acting in a play, fear, in the form of adrenaline, can add an element of excitement to the performance
- a certain amount of fear can be enjoyable, particularly when we accomplish new or challenging feats.

Without any fear, life would quickly become dull and predictable. Too much fear, however, can be debilitating and paralysing. If we're not careful, we can easily spiral into a cycle of being too scared to do anything. In Acts 2:41–47, we read that the disciples were accomplishing amazing things. The band of frightened and defeated men who had once hidden themselves away behind locked doors 'for fear of the Jews' (John 20:19) had been transformed into a real force to be reckoned with. On one day alone, 3,000 people were saved (Acts 2:41). How had they achieved such an incredible transformation? The answer is quite simple – they had gone from fearing other people to fearing God (see v.43).

Fear of the Lord, in its proper context, means letting go of our own needs, hopes, wants and desires and focusing instead on what God would have us do. If we try to accomplish everything under our own strength, the chances are, we'll never get very far. But once we start 'walking in the fear of the Lord and encouraged by the Holy Spirit' (Acts 9:31), miracles start to happen. Try it this week and see!

For prayer and reflection

Lord, forgive me when I try to do things in my own strength and then wonder why it all goes so horribly wrong. Help me to put You back in the driving seat.

With fear **and trembling**

Fear and trembling is not something we would normally associate with a relationship with a loving God. And yet, without the appropriate response of reverence and awe, we close ourselves to the treasures of God's wisdom and knowledge. In the Bible, we are told that fear of the Lord:

- is the beginning of wisdom (Psa. 111:10)
- prolongs life (Prov. 10:27)
- provides strong confidence and is a fountain of life (Prov. 14:26–27)
- prompts us to depart from evil (Prov. 16:6)
- leads to a satisfying life and spares us from much evil (Prov. 19:23)
- is the way to riches, honour and life (Prov. 22:4)

But isn't the concept of fear the very opposite to what it means to place our trust in a loving God? Not necessarily. In Psalm 103:13, we are told that 'as a father has compassion on his children, so the LORD has compassion on those who fear him ...' An example of what happens when we don't have the fear of God is given in Psalm 36:1–4: 'There is no fear of God before his eyes ... the words of his mouth are wicked and deceitful; he has ceased to be wise and to do good. Even on his bed, he plots evil ...' Who wants to live a life like that?

The fact is that, like a loving Father, God wants what is best for us. Such is the depth of His love that, later in the same psalm, the psalmist goes on to describe how the righteous will 'take refuge in the shadow of his wings' (v.7) and 'drink from the river of delights'.

If we meet Him with the appropriate attitude of reverence and awe, God can take our lives and transform them for the better – but He can only do so if we're prepared to let Him. Are you?

Psalm 36

'There is no fear of God ... he flatters himself too much to detect or hate his sin.' (vv.1–2)

For prayer and reflection

Lord, I'm slowly learning that to fear You is not to be in terror of Your judgment, but to have humility to accept Your guidance. Please help me.

'Do not fear what they fear'

'… do not fear what they fear … The LORD Almighty is the one … you are to fear …' (vv.12–13)

I n order to fully understand the concept of fear of the Lord, we need to go back to the Old Testament. In the Hebrew language in which the Old Testament was written, there are about 17 different words which are translated as 'fear'. The most common of these are *pachad* – often translated as 'terror' or 'dread', and *yir'ah* – which normally denotes an attitude of piety or awesome reverence.

At its simplest, *pachad* means fear of impending danger. Often the term is used in the context of coming judgment. So in Isaiah 2:10 and 2:19, for example, it is used to refer to those who have rejected God and set up their own idols to worship, who will flee from the terror of His wrath.

As Christians we no longer need to live in fear for our eternal destiny because we have been 'made new' in Christ. Thus, in Romans 8:1, Paul could confidently say, 'Therefore, there is now no condemnation for those who are in Christ Jesus …'

However, as those who have been set free, God's wonderful love and goodness should inspire awe and worship in our hearts. So we continue to live in an attitude of reverent awe (*yir'ah*) before God.

Where do you stand today in relation to these two forms of fear? Are you still clinging onto your old fears and insecurities, uncertain of the promise of eternal life that God has given you? Or are you at the opposite end of the spectrum – so comfortable in the assurance of God's goodness that you have forgotten to give Him the awe and reverence He deserves?

For prayer and reflection

Lord, forgive me for the times when I've let my old insecurities get in the way of trusting You. Help me to give You all the honour You deserve. Amen.

'An **awesome God**'

**Hebrews
12:22–29**

'... let us be
thankful, and
so worship God
acceptably with
reverence and
awe ...' (v:28)

Yesterday, we looked at two different forms of fear in the Old Testament – *pachad* (fear of judgment), and *yir'ah* (reverent awe). Today, I want to explore the concept of *yir'ah* in more detail.

The Hebraic word *yir'ah*, is often translated as 'respect', 'awe', 'piety' or 'reverence', but even these translations don't do it full justice. *Yi'rah* is perhaps best understood as living in a state of sensitivity to another. One Hebrew scholar describes it like this: '*Yir'ah* is the sense that you are being seen, being scrutinised. Every nook and cranny of your personality is open for inspection' (Rabbi Zalman Schachter-Shalomi).

When we open ourselves up to the reality of God's presence, the result is both reassuring and unsettling. On the one hand, we have the reassurance of knowing that He knows us completely and is with us always (Psa. 139:1–2). On the other, we become aware of His almighty and awesome presence, against which we are inevitably found to be wanting.

As today's Bible passage shows, awesome fear (*yir'ah*) is a proper and appropriate response when faced with the almighty power of God. He is the One whose voice shakes the very earth and will soon shatter the heavens, a 'consuming fire' (Heb. 12:29).

Yet all of this amazing power is balanced by a single word – love. God not only created the universe and put the planets in motion, He also made us and knows us intimately, '... the very hairs of your head are all numbered' (Matt. 10:30).

God deserves our reverent worship and yet He also inspires our love. If we truly 'fear' the Lord we will also be aware of His love for us – a love that covers over all our worldly fears.

For prayer and reflection

Lord, as I draw closer to You in prayer, help me to approach You with a renewed sense of reverence and awe.

A change of **perspective**

Luke 12:1–5

'... do not be afraid of those who kill ... But I will show you whom you should fear ...' (vv.4–5)

Once we begin to comprehend what it means to be walking in the fear of the Lord, we start to see life from a whole new perspective. Viewed from an entirely human perspective, a lot of what the disciples did in the Gospels and in Acts looks like madness. For instance:

- The apostles gave up perfectly good livelihoods and left family and friends to follow Jesus, a man they had only just met (Matt. 4:18–22).
- They associated with those society rejected – Samaritans and tax-gatherers and even adulterers – when it was quite clear such behaviour would get them into trouble (Matt. 9:11–12).
- They refused to follow the accepted religious practices of the day (Matt. 9:14–15).
- They even (in the case of Peter and the apostle Paul) faced persecution and certain death for the sake of the cause they believed in.

The reason the disciples could be so bold is that they had a new outlook on life. Where previously they had been terrified of other people's reactions, of persecution or injury or death, now they lived in the assurance of Jesus' enduring promise: 'And surely, I am with you always, to the very end of the age' (Matt. 28:20).

In Luke 12:4–5, we are told that there is only One whom we should ever need to fear – the One who has the power over our eternal destiny – God Himself. In other words, if we are in a right relationship with God, we need fear nothing and nobody else.

Placing such trust in something we can't properly explain or even fully understand might seem crazy from a worldly point of view, but that's not the point – viewed from an eternal perspective, it all makes sense.

For prayer and reflection

Ask the Lord to show you His will for your life today, and to give you the confidence to see it through.

WEEKEND

Perfect peace

For reflection: Isaiah 26:1–20

'You will keep in perfect peace him whose mind is steadfast, because he trusts in you.' (v.3)

Perfect peace – isn't that an incredible promise? The literal translation of this verse is 'peace, peace'. In Hebrew it reads 'shalom, shalom', a typical example of the Hebrew habit of repeating words for added emphasis. What the writer is saying is that this isn't just some momentary respite from the hustle and bustle of the world, like stepping into the bath at the end of a busy day, but a deep and lasting peace that nourishes and upholds us.

To be kept in this perfect peace, our mind must be steadfast. The Hebrew word for steadfast comes from the root 'to prop' and has the idea 'to lean upon or take hold of, bear up, establish, uphold, lay, rest upon or sustain'. In other words, perfect peace comes to the person who has learned to rest upon God, and is sustained by Him.

What is sustaining you today? Is your mind currently preoccupied with petty arguments, work niggles, disobedient children or worries about the future? If so, take some time out to let yourself rest upon the Lord, and enjoy the inflowing of His perfect peace.

Peace is not the absence of conflict but the courage to deal with it gracefully.

Fear-busting faith

'The Lord is my helper; I will not be afraid. What can man do to me?' (v.6)

Last week we looked at how maintaining a healthy fear (or awe) of the Lord can help us put our worldly fears and worries into perspective. This week, I want to go on further to examine some of the practical 'tools' that the Bible has given us for dealing with our worldly fears and anxieties, starting today with the tool of faith.

Faith is the opposite of fear. When faced with a fearful situation, we have two choices. We can either focus upon our negative fears, or we can focus on the positive promises that God has given us.

It's easy to say such things, but putting faith into practice does not always come easily. When I was in my early twenties I used to be absolutely terrified of going to the dentist. The situation got so bad that, at one point, I was even considering hypnotherapy to help me deal with my phobia.

Then one day a friend pointed me towards Hebrews 13:6 and it was like a revelation. I realised that I no longer had to be afraid of what others could do to me because Jesus was by my side, even in the dentist's chair. After that, I was not so afraid to put myself in others' hands because I knew that, ultimately, God was in control.

Jesus has promised that He will never leave us or forsake us (v.5). Not only that, but He will stand alongside us as our helper and protector in times of difficulty (13:6).

Such promises are not to be taken lightly – they are at the very heart of what it means to be a Christian. We might not always feel that God is with us, but He is, and that in itself is deeply reassuring.

For prayer and reflection

'Jesus Christ is the same yesterday, today and for ever' (13:8). Take a moment or two to meditate on these words.

Spiritual **dynamite!**

Our second 'spiritual tool' for dealing with worldly fear is the empowering gift of the Holy Spirit.

I don't know about you, but I've never been that brave when it comes to confronting others. I'm one of those people that, if their toes get trodden on, apologise to the person doing the treading.

The Early Church missionary Timothy was perhaps a bit like that, though (unlike me) he had every reason to be so. He was living in a time (c.AD 64) when Christians faced very real persecution. Paul, his spiritual mentor, was in prison with a death sentence hanging over his head. No wonder Timothy was afraid of speaking out.

Yet the apostle Paul saw things in a different light. Such timidity, he says, comes from man and not from God. Writing from his prison cell, Paul knew that shortly he was going to face death, yet still he could boast '... I have kept the faith' (2 Tim. 4:7). What gave him such extraordinary strength of conviction? The answer comes in the second half of 2 Timothy 1:7: the power of the Spirit.

When Jesus departed from His disciples, He left them with an incredible gift – the empowering of the Holy Spirit. Paul knew that he could do nothing in his own strength, but through the power of the Holy Spirit he was able to face prison and even death, secure in the knowledge of God's power and love.

When you are faced with difficult or fearful situations, it is worth reminding yourself of this incredible gift the Lord has given us. Through the power of the Holy Spirit, we can be inspired to love even our enemies or persecutors. We can conquer negative emotions such as anger or anxiety. Do you know the power of the Holy Spirit in your life?

2 Timothy 1:6–13

'For God did not give us a spirit of timidity, but a spirit of power, of love and of self-discipline.' (v.7)

For prayer and reflection

The Greek word for 'power' is *dunamos* – the same root which gives us the words 'dynamite' and 'dynamic'. Is there spiritual dynamite in your prayer life?

Welcome to **the family**

Romans 8:9–17

'… but you received the Spirit of sonship. And by him we cry, "*Abba*, Father."' (v.15)

For prayer and reflection

Lord, it seems incredible that You would even consider adopting someone like me as one of Your children. Thank You, Lord, for Your amazing grace and mercy. Help me to cling to this when times get tough.

We now move on to our third 'spiritual tool' for dealing with fear – the spirit of adoption.

Imagine you are working for a well-heeled firm of accountants. Your boss comes up to your desk one Monday morning, a strange look in his eyes. 'Stop working,' he says. 'You never need to work again.' 'What do you mean?' you reply, in horrified amazement. 'Are you firing me?' 'No,' says the big boss. 'It's better than that. I've decided to give you my salary instead. From now on, what is mine is yours.'

Of course, this is never going to happen (more's the pity!) but it does serve to illustrate something of what we're promised in today's reading. The word 'redeem' with which we are all so familiar goes back to the slave-buying terminology of Paul's day. At that time, the practice of slavery was commonplace. Slaves had no rights of their own. However, if a wealthy Roman citizen wished to release a slave from a harsh master, he could 'redeem' the slave by paying a price to secure his freedom.

Being set free would be incredible enough, but in Romans 8:17, Paul goes one further. Not only have we been freed from our bondage to sin and death, we have also been adopted as God's own children and '... if children, then we are heirs – heirs of God and co-heirs with Christ ...' (v.17).

This means that we need no longer be fearful for the future – our fears are placed firmly and squarely in the past because we are now part of God's family and, as such, inheritors of the promise of His kingdom. *You* have been individually adopted as a child of God. Take a moment to consider what that means.

Prayer power

Today we come on to our fourth 'spiritual tool' for dealing with fear – the amazing power of prayer. I am personally convinced that prayer is the most effective weapon we can have when dealing with situations which give rise to anxiety or fear. As evidence of this, we need look no further than the example of Jesus who, when faced with immeasurable mental anguish in the Garden of Gethsemane, prayed earnestly to God (Luke 22:44) until He received the courage to face even death on the cross.

Our English word for anxiety is derived from the Latin word *angere* which means, literally, to choke or to strangle. This is an apt description of what anxiety does to us. If we let our fears and worries grow unchecked, eventually they will rise up like weeds and choke the life out of us. Continuing with this analogy, prayer is like weedkiller. Once we start to focus on God's awesome power, our own fears seem less substantial and gradually wither and lose their grip.

Paul says that we should pray for everything – not just the things we think God wants to hear, but *everything*, (Phil. 4:6). We can pray thankfully, because we believe that God holds the answers to our prayers, even if they are not always the ones we would have chosen. We can also pray with confidence, because our God is an awesome God with the power to make things happen.

What is the result of praying such fear-busting prayers? The answer is given in verse 7, '... the peace of God, which transcends all understanding, will guard your hearts and your minds in Christ Jesus'. Do you want the peace that comes through prayer? I know I do.

Philippians 4:4–9

'Do not be anxious about anything, but in everything ... present your requests to God.' (v.6)

For prayer and reflection

Are you guilty of only praying the prayers you think God wants to hear? Spend some time opening up to the awesome power of God. Approach His throne with a renewed sense of wonder.

Amazing **love**

'There is no fear in love. But perfect love drives out fear …' (v.18)

We come now to our fifth and final spiritual tool – the incredible gift of love.

This passage in 1 John 4:18 has seen me through some tough times in my life, times which I call my 'fingertip' moments, when I feel as if I'm only clinging onto my faith by my fingernails. 'God is love' – that single phrase says it all. Who are we to worry, when we have the full force of divine love behind us?

When I was a child, I was constantly seeking approval from everyone. If I didn't get it from my parents, I tried to get it from my teachers or my peers. If it meant standing on a table singing three blind mice while balancing on one leg, I'd do it. I'd do anything, so long as I got the applause at the end.

Sometimes we can be the same way with God. Oh, we've read all the promises that He loves us and how He has sent His son Jesus Christ who died to free us from the bondage to sin and death, and how our sins have been forgiven, and yet … and yet. Somehow we can't quite accept that God, in all His glory, would want to bother with the likes of us.

For prayer and reflection

Lord, so often I'm seeking for others' approval without realising that I already have the approval of the One who matters most – You! Help me to live in the promise of Your abiding love.

The message of this passage is quite simple – God loves us, completely and unconditionally, just as we are. He loves us, not because we are perfect, but because He sees us through grace-coloured spectacles: 'If anyone acknowledges that Jesus is the Son of God, God lives in him and he in God' (v.15).

Thinking this way, we no longer need to fear illness, death, failure or loss because we know that, to paraphrase Romans 8:38, nothing, not even death, can separate us from God's love. '… perfect love drives out fear' – what an incredible promise!

WEEKEND

Stand firm

For reflection: Exodus 14:13

I t's easy to have faith in the good times, but how do you react when everything about you seems to be falling apart at the seams?

In the famous story of the crossing of the Red Sea, Moses and the Israelites were faced with a stark choice. They could either give up and return to Egypt, and a life of slavery or oppression, or they could keep on pressing on toward the goal of the promised land, even though they couldn't see it.

At one point, the frustrated Israelites beg to return to Egypt 'for it would have been better for us to serve the Egyptians than to die in the wilderness'. But Moses remains unmoveable, telling them 'Do not be afraid. Stand firm and you will see the deliverance the LORD will bring you today' (Exod. 14:13).

Perhaps you are facing a wilderness moment in your life at the moment? If so, take courage – stand firm and keep pressing forward in faith until you can sing with Moses:

'The LORD is my strength and my song;
    he has become my salvation.
He is my God and I will praise Him ...'

(Exod. 15:2)

A **faith-filled life**

Psalm 91

'You will not fear the terror of night, nor the arrow that flies by day …' (v.5)

The last few weeks we have focused on the subject of fear – looking in particular at how an attitude of faith or 'fear of the Lord' can be used to combat negative, worldly fears.

Today's reading brings us to a place where we can stand strong in our faith, confident in the Lord's provision to bring us through the very worst that life can throw at us.

No matter what we have to face, says the psalmist, be it the treachery of enemies, deadly illness, terrors by night, terrors by day, lions, warfare, evil, snakes or personal injury, the Lord will be with us. What an incredible promise!

One of my favourite images in Psalm 91 is that of the mother hen (v.4), who gathers up her chicks under her wings to protect them from danger. Walking through Swansea's Singleton Park earlier today I observed a similar phenomenon with a mother duck and her ducklings. No matter how busy the mother duck was with repairing her nest or searching for food, she always made sure her ducklings were within easy earshot of her call. If they moved too far away, she would quickly swim over and herd them back to safety.

For prayer and reflection

Lord, I thank You for Your amazing promise that You are there for me in times of danger or difficulty. Help me to listen for Your guidance in my life.

So long as we place our trust in God, we receive the promise of His ongoing protection. In verse 15, we are given the promise that God will protect those who acknowledge His name: 'He will call upon me, and I will answer him …'

Are you living within easy earshot of the Lord today, or have you moved too far away to heed His protective call? Take a moment or two to seek renewed closeness to the Lord.

Spiritual **encouragement**

One of the great secrets of living a life that is no longer governed by fear is the ability to actively seek out words of encouragement. The word 'encourage' means literally to live 'in' a state of courage. As Christians, we are all called upon to encourage others. In Romans 12:8, encouragement is listed as one of the gifts of the Holy Spirit, alongside such gifts as prophecy, serving and teaching. Ephesians 4:29 is a good guideline for the way we should conduct ourselves when speaking with others: 'Do not let any unwholesome talk come out of your mouths, but only what is helpful for building others up according to their needs, that it may benefit those who listen.'

The opposite of courage is discouragement. Place yourself for a moment in the shoes of Joshua, the Old Testament leader whom we read about in today's passage. His great friend and spiritual leader, Moses, had recently died, and now he was being called to take his place – not the easiest of boots to fill! For starters, it was well-known that the people he was leading were stubborn and apt to turn against their leaders in times of crisis. Then there was the small matter that the so-called promised land was already occupied by rather terrifying-looking warriors. No wonder Joshua was feeling 'discouraged'.

The words that God gave to Joshua, 'Be strong and courageous. Do not be terrified; do not be discouraged' are equally relevant to us today. But they are not given for us alone. We are also called to encourage others, and to build others up in the faith. Are you doing all you can to be a spiritual encourager today?

Joshua 1:1–11

'Be strong and courageous … for the LORD your God will be with you wherever you go.' (v.9)

For prayer and reflection

Lord, thank You for Your words of encouragement. Help me to resist focusing on the negative, particularly when dealing with others, and to share Your words of encouragement.

Contagious courage

Acts 27:27–44

'They were all encouraged …' (v.36)

As we come to the end of our series on fear, I want to invite you to a challenge: are you willing to lead a contagiously courageous life? Fear, as we've seen, is a powerful emotion, but just think how much stronger is an attitude of faith. As an example of this, think about the thing that scares you the most. Now imagine how much stronger is the ability to confidently say, 'I used to be afraid of___, but I'm not any more …'.

The apostle Paul knew all about contagious courage. As an Early Church missionary he had been regularly arrested, imprisoned, bitten by snakes, taunted and jeered at by the crowds and was shipwrecked on a number of occasions. In today's passage, we read how, having spent several days shipwrecked and been 'long without food', in the midst of their despair Paul encourages his crew, telling them not to lose heart or be afraid, because God has promised him that all of them will be saved (v.22).

Not only does Paul offer his crew words of encouragement, he also leads by example. Despite the fact that the ship is drifting far out from land, he instructs them to eat their remaining food supplies and throw the rest away – and proves his faith by doing so himself (v.35). Would we be so brave?

Just as Paul demonstrated his faith to his shipmates, so we too can become spiritual encouragers to those around us. There will always be storms in our lives – illness, financial worries, work pressures or family difficulties – but it is the way in which we handle them that marks us out. Remember, courage is contagious! If you can weather these storms of life, God might just end up using your experiences as the inspiration for others.

For prayer and reflection

'Courage is contagious. When a brave man takes a stand, the spines of others are stiffened' (Billy Graham). Are you a contagiously courageous Christian?

Spirit-inspired confidence

Wendy Bray

Wendy Bray's first book *In the Palm of God's Hand* (with BRF) won the biography prize at The Christian Book Awards in 2002. Since then she has authored or co-authored more than a dozen books, and written countless features and Bible reading notes. Curate at St. Pancras, Plymouth, Wendy has a special interest in exploring the way in which we understand and express our faith during times of illness and suffering. She is married with two adult children and lives in Devon.

Spirit-inspired confidence

Jeremiah 17:7–8

'But blessed is the man who trusts in the LORD, whose confidence is in him.' (v.7)

For prayer and reflection

Father, show me where I have placed my confidence, and as these weeks of reading and thought unfold, help me to transplant that confidence firmly in You.

The *Penguin English Dictionary* defines confidence as: '1. a consciousness of one's powers being sufficient ... 2. faith or trust in something or somebody'.

In essence, Christian confidence rejects the first for the guaranteed security of the second. Yet we have turned confidence into something more cosmetic: a characteristic dependent on style, talent, ability or success. True confidence, as we'll discover, doesn't depend on any of those fleeting things. True confidence is eternal.

True confidence is, essentially, trust. Not trust in a particular business suit that makes us feel as if we could own the company or win the case. Not confidence in our own ability, or even in that of a team member or strong and reliable friend or partner.

Interestingly, 'trust' and 'confidence' share the same Hebrew 'root' word.

In this passage from Jeremiah that root word extends to the source of a righteous man's (or woman's!) strength. Like the very roots of a tree itself, not planted, but *trans*planted in a safe and well-watered place.

When we ask God to take charge of the direction of our lives, He does literally transplant us, from a dry, arid, self-controlled (and often weedy!) plot to one that is well-watered with Him as a source of life. Of course, that doesn't mean that we will avoid times of drought or exposure to too much heat – they are still mentioned here. Rather, that we need not fear when that 'heat' comes, or worry when life appears to have 'dried up', because the faithfulness of God, the gift of His Son and the power of the Holy Spirit are our ever-flowing source. A source of life everlasting; that's something of which we can be really confident.

Confidence **for life**

For some of us, knowing God means embarking on what is a new, exciting relationship. For others, it has been a long-term, even life-long partnership. We are able to say that we have known God 'since my youth'. What we sometimes forget, amidst either experience, is that God has always longed for us and craved relationship with us. We were His hope, long before we knew He was ours.

That's hard to grasp, isn't it? Especially if our self-esteem has been battered by difficult relationships or we know a low sense of self-worth: that the God of the universe should seek relationship with us *first*, sometimes chasing us across the years until He catches us in an embrace and a whisper of 'I have always loved you'.

How could we not find confidence in such love?

I know a young couple whose lives were transformed by the confidence their love for each other gave. James was quiet, withdrawn and shy – nobody could reach him. Then he found himself working alongside Jayne: bubbly, warm and accepting, but scarred from a difficult childhood. She found in James the stability and thoughtful seriousness she needed. James found a bright personality who drew him from the shadows to show him that life – and love – were worth the risk. Jayne knew security for the first time – James came out of his hiding place and into the light. They both feel that they had been waiting for each other. They have grown into their marriage in confidence that was rooted in love, giving each other hope. Finding each other has transformed their lives.

God's love can transform us even more than that, because His is an everlasting love with an eternal hope. Will you let Him reach you and draw you from the shadows into His light?

Psalm 71:5–18

'For you have been my hope, O Sovereign LORD, my confidence since my youth.'
(v.5)

For prayer and reflection

Have I truly allowed You to catch and embrace me, Lord? What do I hold back? Draw me out of my own shadows and into Your light.

WEEKEND

The gift prophesied

For reflection: Acts 2:14–21
'God says, I will pour out my spirit on all people.' (v.17)

Accounts of life in the Early Church give us a glimpse of the power, joy and transforming delight of the promised and poured-out Holy Spirit – not to mention the confidence that resulted.

Over the next few weekends we will be focusing on just how life-transforming and confidence-giving the Holy Spirit is as He works in our lives – looking at the Early Church for something of His story.

Here Peter – the same bumbling, doubting, fear-filled Peter we so identify with – is transformed into a bold, articulate speaker. He speaks with clarity, power and incredible confidence, sharing a message that, as we read later, added 3,000 members to the Church: the result of the confidence and work of the Holy Spirit.

Can this really be Peter? The same fisherman who always seemed to get it wrong, put his foot in it and generally mess up? Yes it is! Such is the wonderful – and hilarious – grace of God.

I'm so encouraged by the fact that Peter's sincere, if often faltering, faith was so used and transformed by God's Holy Spirit. It means that He can use me too!

Read on, if you've time, and transport yourself to first-century Jerusalem to be caught up in the results of Spirit-given confidence!

Confidence in a **faithful God**

Have you ever heard someone say, 'I never know where I am with him' or 'She is always changing her mind'? An ever-changing, irresolute character is hard to deal with. We remain unsure, despite assurances. Experience teaches us to doubt and to never quite believe in the word given – however earnest the promise.

This beautiful psalm has the stability of God's character written between the lines for us to read. Speaking of righteousness, truth, faithfulness and security, it reminds us that God made the world we live in by His creative Word. That He has filled it with His love and that He holds firm to the plans He has for it, foiling the schemes of wayward nations and pushing forward His greater eternal purposes.

In simple terms, He made us, He holds us and He will keep us: period.

Whatever our TV screens and newspapers might tell us, God is in control, it is His world and He holds our future.

When my children were small my daughter – two years and nine months older than her brother – would often lend him her beloved wooden tricycle. She always made it clear that he might be driving it for a while now – but it belonged to her. Every so often, even as he sat on it, she would grasp the handlebar and steer it in the direction she wanted it to go. It's a crude and simple illustration, perhaps. But God has His eye on where He wants His people 'to go'. His plans remain unchanged. However often we appear to veer off His path, He will steer us – and our world – towards the fulfilment of His constant purposes. We always know where we are with God. Our names are ever before Him: engraved permanently on 'the palm of [His] hand' (Isa. 49:16).

Psalm 33:6–22

'But the plans of the LORD stand firm … the purposes of his heart through all generations.' (v.11)

For prayer and reflection

Where does your confidence for the future lie – in the decisions of men or the constancy of God? Lord, help me to trust the 'purposes of Your heart'.

Confidence **'whatever'**

2 Timothy 1:11–14

'… I am suffering … Yet … I know … he is able to guard what I have entrusted to him …' (v.12)

What an inspiration Paul's letter must have been to Timothy. Despite the probability that Paul was incarcerated in a cold, dark cell, he still held fast to his confidence, because it was confidence based on more than comfort or circumstances. He remained sharply and even joyously aware of the salvation he had been given and the promise that had been made by the Lord Jesus. His confidence was placed in the certain knowledge that the Saviour would 'deliver' what He had promised.

Paul encouraged Timothy to guard the gospel and keep the faith until 'that day', through the love of the Lord Jesus Christ and the power of the Spirit. His confidence was a 'whatever' confidence. 'Whatever' has been adopted by teenagers as a word implying indifference, a passive agreement or a 'don't care' attitude. So surely it is miles away from Paul's use here? I'm not so sure.

Paul was in some sense 'indifferent' to his suffering because it was taking him closer to his Lord. He was in agreement with what was happening to him because he knew that it was nothing compared to an eternity in His presence. He really did say, 'I don't care' about his circumstances. Because he knew they were only that: circumstances.

Paul's 'whatever' was a word of confidence. We so often let our faith drown in our circumstances. A little bit of discomfort and inconvenience, insecurity or uncertainty has us whining to God with a 'Why?' and a 'Not fair'. We lose sight of the bigger picture, allow our confidence to be shaken and forget that 'whatever' happens, God is in control.

Learn to say 'whatever' with a shrug of the shoulders. It might become your word of faith too!

For prayer and reflection

Pray thoughtfully and not lightly … Lord, give me the faith and boldness that will allow You to lead me along a path of trust that echoes with the word 'whatever'.

We are **inseparable**

W riter John Ortberg tells the story of a bear cub who becomes separated from his father in a snow storm. Lost in the blizzard the cub comes face to face with a wolf that has had his eye on the youngster for some time. Believing himself isolated and vulnerable, the cub can only do what he has seen his father do when faced with an enemy: rear up on his hind legs and growl. But when the little bear does so, his hind legs wobble and his growl is a mere squeak. He is not convinced – neither is his predator. The outlook is not good. Just as hope is almost lost the terrified cub watches in amazement as the wolf cowers, turns and runs away snarling. He then realises that behind his own weak attempts his father had appeared out of the storm. He had also risen to his more powerful height and growled like thunder to protect his son. The cub had thought he had been separated, but his father, keeping him in view, stepped in at the last to save him.[1]

We often feel as if we are separated from God by circumstances: fear, illness, redundancy, loneliness – all that Paul mentions and more. But our Father is Lord of all – even of what threatens us. Paul reminds us again that our circumstances will not separate us from God. He sees everything.

He will sometimes keep His distance or remind us of our dependence on Him as we wait, even until we believe He is lost. But His grace-filled love keeps us in sight, no matter how fierce the storm or the enemy. He will always rise up behind us at just the right moment. Nothing, absolutely nothing, separates us from the love of God.

1. John Ortberg, *Love Beyond Reason* (Zondervan, 1998)

Romans 8:35–39

'Who shall separate us from the love of Christ?'(v.35)

For prayer and reflection

We are inseparable. Remind me Father that, in faith, my sight often fails; my hearing is faint and my understanding dim – but that You are ever watchful. Nothing separates me from Your love.

No condemnation

Romans 8:1–4

'Therefore, there is now no condemnation for those who are in Christ Jesus …' (v.1)

As a child I would pass an almost derelict property on the way to school. An elderly woman lived there alone and, despite the fact that the house had been condemned and she had been offered alternative accommodation, she stubbornly refused to move. She died in the squalor that social services had tried to save her from, having chosen to live in a state of 'condemnation'.

Some of us choose to live in the self-condemned property that is our life; even when we are offered a brand-new one, free, purpose-built and secure. We prefer to live surrounded by the rubble of a life that we ourselves have condemned, with guilt. We allow our actions, our choices and circumstances to condemn us to low self-esteem, failing confidence, anger and depression.

We may struggle to build again, or blankly refuse because it takes too much effort. We prefer to live in our comfortably self-condemned life. But that's not the dwelling place God has chosen for us.

God's place is not one of condemnation but of grace. Grace in partnership with repentance and a desire to live His way. If we live God's way and 'according to the Spirit' there will be no condemnation for us – now or in eternity.

For prayer and reflection

If God doesn't condemn us, why do we condemn ourselves? It is His grace that justifies our very existence, His love that chose us and set us apart, so why allow circumstances, self-criticism or the painfully remembered words of others to condemn us?

Father God, show me a new dwelling place of grace free from guilt and condemnation – and help me move in.

A move may take effort, but it might be the only way to live in the confidence that comes from the assurance of God's love. 'There is no condemnation.' Where will you choose to live?

All 'yes' in Christ Jesus

W hen completing magazine quizzes we usually face A–D multiple choice questions or lines of boxes into which we must tick our 'yes' or 'no' – and even our 'maybe' answers. With choices A–D it is often easy to work out just which box we have to tick to come out on top. 'Yes' 'no' and 'maybe' need a bit more honesty on our part. It's not often that we are able to answer a complete set of questions in the affirmative – and even then 'yes' answers may indicate that we are as 'strategically challenged' at communication/confidence/casserole cooking as we always believed we were! The positives can end up making us feel negative!

But that's not the case here in Paul's' letter. These Corinthian Christians have found the message about Jesus to be entirely true: 'in him it has always been "yes"' (v.19) says Paul. He explains that Jesus is the fulfilment of all the promises that His Father has ever made. He claims us as His own and guarantees what is to come. There is no doubt. No wavering, no 'maybe' between the 'no' and 'yes' answers, just affirmation in the Person and love of Jesus.

It is through Him that our 'Amens' can be spoken with confidence. 'Amen' means 'It is true' or 'So be it'. It is a positive, God-confident statement at the end of our prayer or praise.

Yet so often we mumble it into our collars. We need to change our habits: say 'Amen' with assurance and to God's glory. Perhaps we should even adopt that exuberant action I so often watch my son exhibit. Think of Jesus, punch the air and shout 'Yes!' Jesus is the great affirmation of all God has done for us; let's not mumble the fact but proclaim it with confidence!

**2 Corinthians
1:18–22**

'For no matter how many promises God has made, they are "Yes" in Christ.' (v.20)

Answer 'Yes' or 'No':
- **Can you be confident in God?**
- **Has He promised His Holy Spirit to enable that confidence?**
- **Are you His precious child?**
Go on ... punch the air!

WEEKEND

The gift as promised

For reflection: Acts 1:1–7
*'Do not leave Jerusalem, but wait for the gift my
Father promised ...' (v.4)*

When my son was small he liked to know what the day might bring and needed some forewarning and security in the shape of promises and assurance. But he also had to learn that much would have to be taken on trust.

Jesus obviously sensed that the disciples, in their anticipation of losing Him, needed some assurance too. But they also needed to learn to trust Him in His absence. He gave specific directions as to what they should do and a broader picture of hope. He grounded those instructions and assurances both in the unshakeable promises of His Father and the everyday experience of remembered conversation. In effect, He told them 'this is what you must do'; 'this is what you can depend on' and 'this is what you already know'. The rest they had to trust Him for. Their confidence was built from three angles – knowledge, faith and action.

When we need confidence to do what God is asking us to do, we can do the same: know what we believe, have faith in His promises – and get on with the job in hand!

Read on to Acts 2:21 to discover just what happened when the disciples remembered their Master's promises.

Anointed by the Holy Spirit

Whether Jesus chose to read these beautiful words from Isaiah, or they happened to be those already selected for this particular day, we don't know. Either way, they were fulfilled before the very eyes of everyone in the synagogue, as the Son was anointed by the Father. Not the anointing of oil that those listening would have been accustomed to, but of the Holy Spirit.

Anointing with oil was both an everyday celebratory practice for bestowing honour, and a sacred one. Sacred anointing was a practice begun with Moses under God's direction (Exod. 30:22–31). It was first used for the anointing of Aaron and his sons as priests and for marking the Tent of Meeting and its contents. Even the fragrance and purity of the oil were given great attention by God.

The anointing of Jesus, however, was unique. It indicated both honour and fulfilment. This anointing with the Holy Spirit shows that He is the Messiah (which means 'anointed one') and that, as Old Testament prophecy indicates, He fulfils the roles of prophet, priest and king, each of whom were anointed by God.

It is true that God still 'anoints' us with honour today and often does so with His Holy Spirit, offering us guidance and strength to face special tasks or responsibility. This is often done in the context of prayer alongside others as we ask for God's help and wisdom. It is another way for God to equip us with boldness and confidence as we serve Him.

For Jesus this anointing with the Spirit marked the beginning of a teaching and healing ministry that was confident, bold and Spirit-filled.

If Jesus the Son needed the anointing of the Spirit for His work – how much more do we?

Luke 4:14–21

'The Spirit of the Lord is on me … he has anointed me to preach good news to the poor.'
(v.18)

For prayer and reflection

Father, fill me with Your Spirit, that, like Jesus, I may be confident in Your anointing, retain humility amongst Your people and carry grace and compassion to the lost.

Chosen by God the Father

Matthew 12:15–21

'Here is my servant whom I have chosen, the one I love, in whom I delight ...' (v.18)

Once again, the words of Isaiah are used to proclaim Jesus in fulfilment of Old Testament prophecy: this time as the chosen servant King. These words would have been familiar to onlookers who doubtless 'gossiped' them in speculation about who Jesus was and what His mission was all about. So much so that Jesus had to warn them not to tell others, in fulfilment of those words.

Jesus was – and is – that past hope fulfilled as well as our promised hope for the future.

His earthly life was spent offering that eternal hope to all who would listen and respond.

But of course, He didn't force His way into lives with an arrogant swagger, wielding a manifesto for the privileged or at the head of an accompanying army, as many of His contemporaries had hoped. God's way is not our way. No, He became His Father's servant – and also the servant of those He came to save.

If we look closer at these words and read around them we see that Jesus offered that hope with authority, gentleness, respect, dignity, grace and mercy – as well as a lot of very practical common sense!

The servant King offered His kingdom by serving others in order to bring them into the palace courtyards. No wonder this Man was unique!

We are 'chosen' by God to live our lives in just the same way – as servant children of the servant King, with the help, counsel and enabling power of the Holy Spirit. It's another source of true confidence.

Look once more at the ministry of Jesus that Isaiah prophesied. Look too at the practicalities of that ministry in the surrounding verses of Matthew. What are the hallmarks?

For prayer and reflection

How often does our daily personal 'servant ministry' carry those hallmarks of the 'chosen' servant King Jesus?

In the **joy of the Spirit**

I wonder what it was about Jesus that made Luke write that He was 'full of joy through the Holy Spirit'? What made that obvious? Something in His manner? In His beaming smile? It's certainly something I would love to have said about me! What better compliment? Certainly beats 'You look nice' or even 'I admire your confidence'. The irony is that it was Jesus' confidence in His Father that gave Him such joy. And it was a joy He shared not just with His Father in this amazing prayer, but with His followers.

The 'seventy-two' had just returned from their first preaching and healing mission 'with joy' (v.17) to tell Him excitedly of the wonderful things that had been done in His name. Jesus catches their excitement and praises His Father for the consequences and meaning of their experience. They had been engaged in the work of the kingdom of God, and they were buzzing!

Those followers – ambassadors of God's love – must have been somewhat sceptical when they set out on that first mission. Their instructions were clear but their apparent resources were few. Nevertheless God worked through them, resourcing them with the power and confidence that only the Holy Spirit gives, working through them and sending them back amazed.

God chose to reveal 'these things' to them (v.21); to involve them in His wider mission because of their willingness, cautious and sceptical or not, to go out in His name.

In the same way we can return 'with joy' when we go where He sends us, trusting in His resources rather than our own and living and working in the confidence of the Holy Spirit.

Luke 10:21–24

'... Jesus, full of joy through the Holy Spirit, said: "I praise you, Father ..."'
(v.21)

For prayer and reflection

Where does God want to send you to live and work in the power of His Holy Spirit? Your family, your community – or the wider world?

Empowered by the Spirit

'… God anointed Jesus of Nazareth with the Holy Spirit and power …' (v.38)

I n this great piece of oratory Peter gives us a template for what we would now call an 'evangelistic sermon' – sharing the gospel in a nutshell.

He begins by affirming his knowledge that God's message is for everyone who will hear it. Then he picks up on what His audience already knows: what they have seen and heard of the work and witness of Jesus. He explains that Jesus 'went around doing good' in the power of the Holy Spirit, anointed by God the Father, and reminds his audience of Jesus' resurrection and of his own commission to share the gospel. Then, after a clear invitation – that all those who believe in His name will know forgiveness – the Holy Spirit steps in, taking over where Peter had (almost) left off.

This is wonderful assurance for us. We may not be called to preach an evangelistic sermon. We may cringe at the thought of openly sharing our faith with others, no matter how much we long for them to know Jesus. But these verses give us confidence to do both. Not because we will necessarily come out with a message as eloquent and succinct as Peter's, but because God will always honour our attempts and will send the Holy Spirit to take over where we have left off.

Sharing our faith with a friend, work colleague or neighbour is never a conversation between just two people. When we ask the Holy Spirit to be present He will be: we can be confident of that.

Jesus 'went around doing good' in the power of the Holy Spirit. Peter testified to that in the same power by sharing his faith. Now – over to you. How can the Holy Spirit inspire and anoint you as you 'go around doing good' and as you share your faith?

For prayer and reflection

Next time you sit down for a coffee with a friend, simply ask the Holy Spirit to sit down with you. Who knows what He will bring to your conversation?

The promise of the Spirit

ometimes we have poignant conversations with those we love knowing that they will be our last together. That finality prompts us to make the most of those moments.

Jesus was also prompted to 'make the most' of these last conversations with His disciples. He has taught them all He can – yet they still have so much to learn. So He promises them that His Father will send Someone who will continue to teach them and remind them of all He has already shared with them – the Person of the Holy Spirit.

'... the Holy Spirit ... will teach you ... and will remind you of everything I have said to you.'
(v.26)

Too often, we think of the Holy Spirit as a nebulous 'thing'. We understand the concept of God's power displayed through the Spirit, but the Person of the Holy Spirit is more difficult. Yet the language used of the Holy Spirit is always personal language which includes personal pronouns, because He is a divine *Person*. It is He who gives new life, liberating us and enabling us to believe. He makes us God's children, equips us, inspires us, opens our eyes to God's Word, shows us more of the Father and helps us to pray. He will never overwhelm us in a way that we cannot cope with. Instead He will make us more and more what we were meant to be.

These verses clearly introduce His 'personhood'. He is described as Someone of truth and constancy who will live with us – and in us. We may find that idea puzzling. But as we get to know the Spirit more as a Person we realise that the loving Father and Son could not leave us to live in the world without the third Person of their Being so close to us that He actually lives within us and around us.

Shouldn't that unique closeness and security inspire a special confidence?

For prayer and reflection

Father, remind me that, as Jesus promised, a very special Person lives with me: the Person of Your Holy Spirit. Help me to make room for Him.

WEEKEND

The confident message

For reflection: Acts 2:22–36
'Brothers, I can tell you confidently ...' (v.29)

Peter's story is worth re-visiting for our weekend reflection because we recognise him as being a very normal flawed human being – just like us! He was an expert at putting his foot in it, impulsive, impatient, not terribly tactful, a bit of a coward and often slow on the uptake despite the fact that he loved Jesus – albeit weakly at times.

Yet in Acts we see Peter transformed and inspired by the power of the Holy Spirit into a bold, uncompromising witness for Jesus and for God's plan for all of us. 'Brothers, I can tell you confidently,' he says (v.29).

Peter's confident words were the result of three things: his knowledge and love of Jesus; his desire to share the message of salvation, and the power and witness of the Holy Spirit. The Holy Spirit was, in the real sense of the word, inspirational. I wonder how many conversations you and I will have this weekend with those same characteristics? Let's ask God to remind us of the way in which the Holy Spirit inspired practically the life and ministry of Jesus – and later, Peter, and ask Him to inspire our lives practically, too. Go and be inspired!

Lord, make me inspired, bold and confident in my faith and in Your story.

A **new lifestyle**

aving re-introduced ourselves to the Person of the Holy Spirit, we can begin to look at the way in which the special confidence He gives impacts and transforms our lives as we allow Him into what is essentially a partnership with us.

Paul's letter to the Romans is something of a Handbook of Christian Doctrine, covering a wide range of key theological themes. But don't let that put you off! It is also a practical faith-building foundation for the nitty-gritty of Christian living that is detailed elsewhere in Paul's letters. No less so in these verses, where Paul explains, in his typically uncompromising style, that our new lifestyle demands a new mindset: one controlled by the Holy Spirit.

We baulk rather at the idea of 'mind control'. It smacks of hypnotism, loss of freedom – even dictatorship. Yet if the Person of the Holy Spirit is really living within us and we are 'born of ... the Spirit' (John 3:5–6) who brought us into a relationship with the Father, we will want Him to dictate. He will not seize control, robbing us of choice and running off with our intellects, imagination and free will. No! He stands with us – even within us – to guide, help, inspire, empower, embolden, counsel, comfort, teach, love and sometimes rebuke. We just have to listen to Him as we learn more of His mindset.

No one is saying that's easy to do. We all have minds that wander; thoughts that shame us and imaginations that don't always entertain the dreams and desires they should. Thank goodness our minds aren't transparent! But of course they are to God. And for that reason we can be honest with Him and ask Him to strengthen that special 'mindset' partnership with the Spirit.

Romans 8:5–11

'The mind of sinful man is death, but the mind controlled by the Spirit is life and peace.' (v.6)

For prayer and reflection

What amazing possibilities, dreams, plans and desires might the Holy Spirit plant in my heart and mind if He is in 'mindset partnership' with me?

A **guaranteed deposit**

Ephesians 1:3–14

'Having believed, you were marked in him with a seal, the promised Holy Spirit …' (v.13)

'Guarantee' and 'deposit' sound rather businesslike don't they? We may even feel fazed by them: not altogether secure. Guarantees are rarely watertight in our cynical litigious world. Often they come with exemptions, opt-out clauses and small print, even when they are supposed to be safeguarding our position. Deposits should, technically, secure a purchase or place for us, but we can never be really certain of their value until whatever it is we had hoped for has been received and paid for in full. Our hope isn't secure.

But when God the Father gives the guarantee our hope is based on 'the word of truth' and marked by the Holy Spirit so we can be confident. It isn't even we who have to 'pay the bill.' Jesus paid the price in full. The presence of the Holy Spirit in our lives is a lifelong reminder of the completeness of that 'transaction'.

Too often we live our Christian lives unable to grasp that fact. We can't quite accept that everything is signed, sealed and later to be delivered. It might help to remember that we are already living in God's kingdom in this life. We've just got the best part of our inheritance to look forward to. Meanwhile, the Holy Spirit, our guarantee, can be the source of our confidence in that eventuality. He will remain with us until our hope is fulfilled.

It really is essential to read this whole passage to fully appreciate how Father, Son and Holy Spirit work together to give us this wonderful guarantee. As you slowly read it through again let the reality and wonder of its promise seep into your very being and warm your heart.

There is no hidden small print in this guarantee, the price is paid in full, our hope *is* secure.

For prayer and reflection

Father God, impress on me the magnitude and the grace of the price You have paid for me – simply because You love me.

The Holy Spirit **prays for us**

I am rarely lost for words in conversation(!) but am often lost for words in prayer. Sometimes words cannot express the depths of our pain – or our joy. At other times we know we can do nothing *but* pray – we just don't know *what* to pray. It's then that the Holy Spirit, living with us, will do the talking for us. When we turn to Him, expressing – even wordlessly – the depth of our emotions or the complexities of our situation He will catch them up in a prayer – audible or otherwise – which communicates in a way our inadequate words just can't.

I have often prayed through my tears alone. Overwhelmed with grief or pain, helplessness or frustration and unable to form any words, I have just wept my prayer to my Father God. Jesus knew this kind of sorrow (Matt. 26:38).

On one occasion, cancer treatment had weakened me until I could only whisper. Alone in my isolation room in hospital, unable to summon help, I felt at the very edge of my life. But I remembered that there is power even in the name of Jesus. As I whispered His name in the darkness I knew a sense of being lifted temporarily from my situation, as if in reprieve.

The Holy Spirit carried the name of Jesus as a plea and 'filled in the gaps' of my prayer. I knew amazing comfort, and then very necessary sleep. Even my dreams were filled with images of God's security and love. The Holy Spirit intervened for me from the depths of my weakness.

We don't have to find the words to pray – we just have to find the faith. Even faith that is weakened by sorrow or almost driven away by pain can be transformed by the Holy Spirit into the prayer we need to pray.

Romans 8:22–27

'… the Spirit helps us in our weakness … the Spirit himself intercedes for us …' (v.26)

For prayer and reflection

Ask the Holy Spirit to remind you next time you are 'lost for words' that He can find them – and carry them in prayer – for you.

The Holy Spirit **speaks for us**

Acts 6:8–15

'... but they could not stand up against his wisdom or the Spirit by whom he spoke.' (v.10)

As Christians living largely in a Christian community, we sometimes forget that our faith and our words are not always welcome in the wider world. Both may be severely tested as a result – by family, colleagues, even other Christians!

Yesterday we considered the way in which the Holy Spirit speaks for us in prayer. Stephen's story is an example of the way in which the Holy Spirit speaks through us in words.

We must always carefully assess any words we believe are Spirit-inspired, by lining them up against God's Word and/or by running them past the valued judgment of those older and wiser in their faith. But we must not be naïve enough to believe that having done so we will have an easy path ahead as a 'truth bringer'.

Stephen's ministry was powerful and effective: 'full of God's grace and power' (v.8). The wisdom and authenticity of his message was clear, but the opposition – even from those claiming to be faithful to God – was great.

Sometimes the truth hurts, and the truth bringer feels the heat of rejection and opposition as a result. Read on to the end of chapter 7 and you will see how Stephen remained faithful and uncompromising in his message. He was not afraid to challenge those who opposed that message (v.51). Right to the end he was aware of its truth and urgency. Filled with the Holy Spirit, he never wavered.

We may face opposition, even persecution, when we share words given by the Holy Spirit. But we must remember that no one can stand against their wisdom.

The twist in this tale, of course, is that Stephen lost his life at the feet of Saul, soon to be Paul, who approved his death. Such is the amazing grace of God and the power of His Holy Spirit.

For prayer and reflection

Holy Spirit, give me the wisdom to recognise Your words, the boldness to share them and the courage to face the opposition.

The Holy Spirit **enables us**

As a student I was involved in a challenge where six of us had to find the resources and skills to build a bridge or raft to cross a river – purely by improvisation and with severe restrictions on our resources. It was frustrating to scuttle off to find the means and have to pass punts, rowing boats, floating piers, kayaks and paddles as we made our search. We just weren't allowed to use them to cross that green and wet expanse. We had to find new initiative and method. Needless to say, there was much high-speed driving, bargaining, pleading and floundering around at the edge of the river. We got very wet in the process – but we made it eventually. We also learnt that paddling pools were not made to cross rivers.

So I am relieved that God does not leave us entirely to find our own resources – especially as a church 'team'. Instead He gives us, through the Holy Spirit, specific spiritual resources as 'he determines' (v.11).

We have to remember that these gifts are just that – gifts. We are not entitled to them and they are not to be boasted of, used inappropriately or kept to ourselves. They are, Paul says, 'for the common good'.

Everything that God the Father knows we will need to live lives of love, trust, obedience and service within and from our Christian communities is provided by these gifts: wisdom, knowledge, faith, healing, miracles, prophecy, discernment, tongues and interpretation.

God equips, enables and empowers us to do all He asks us to do for Him as we love and honour each other, by the power of His Holy Spirit. If we sincerely look to Him for our spiritual resources, we will not flounder around helplessly or sink. We need only ask.

---

1 Corinthians 12:1–11

'There are different kinds of gifts, but the same Spirit.' (v.4)

For prayer and reflection

Ask a wise Christian to pray with you regarding your own spiritual gifts. How might you confidently use the gifts of the Holy Spirit in the love and service of others?

WEEKEND

The 'how' of salvation

For reflection: Acts 2:36–41

'... they ... said to Peter and the other apostles, "Brothers, what shall we do?"' (v.37)

Having listened to Peter's amazing speech we now turn our attention to the results. Those who had been listening were moved by the Holy Spirit and the impact was amazing. They were 'cut to the heart' (v.37). How often can we say that of a sermon?!

The key thing is that the listeners asked what they should *do*. In recognising the truth of the gospel, the Holy Spirit had opened their eyes – they knew they must respond. Peter immediately tells them how: repent, be baptised and you will receive forgiveness and the gift of the Holy Spirit. In the best marketing terms he outlined the action – but he also explained the benefits!

It's also clear that the Holy Spirit was an essential part of their Christian lives from the very beginning. Their relationship with Him was fundamental. Peter wanted them to be equipped, inspired and confident in their faith. The Holy Spirit offered the way. When we try to live our Christian lives under our own steam we will always end up burning out, becoming discouraged or losing our focus. Our relationship with the Holy Spirit is as fundamental as it was to Peter's new converts.

Find a quiet place and open your heart and mind more fully to the Holy Spirit. Then *listen.*

Foundations of love

Ephesians 3:14–21

's a child I was enchanted by a much-loved chorus which told me that God's love is as wide as the ocean, as high as the heavens above and as deep as the deepest sea. It comes back to me often, and I find myself humming it as I picture a little pig-tailed, gap-toothed girl singing her heart out, believing absolutely every word with joy and wonder.

There are times when I could benefit from some aspects of that simple faith today.

These verses from Ephesians – and the chorus derived from them – are both simply profound and profoundly simple. Within their childlike simplicity and wonder we can find the key to our confidence as God's children.

Ask any childcare expert what a child needs to grow and thrive in confidence and they will say a foundation of unconditional love. Paul's beautiful prayer for the Ephesians, part of the Father's 'family' (v.15), illustrates just how similar God's heavenly parenting is.

Paul is praying that the Ephesian Christians will be rooted and established in Christ's love through faith (v.17), will know the 'fullness of God' (v.19) and will be strengthened by the power of the Holy Spirit (v.16). That prayer remains a valuable one for all of us.

Some of us will not have known such safe and loving security as children. So, Paul spells it out to us just in case we need some clarity and assurance (vv.18–19). Whatever our earthly experience we will not know just how wide, long, high and deep the love of Christ is, this side of eternity. Neither will we understand God's 'fullness'. But we can draw on that resource of boundless love and 'to the measure' (v.18) abundance to give us heartfelt confidence as His children.

'I pray that … he may strengthen you with power through his Spirit in your inner being ...' (v.16)

For prayer and reflection

Find a creative way to illustrate these verses for reflection, perhaps by displaying some stunning photographs of the ocean or sky, or planting some seeds and watching them take root.

An adopted **family**

Romans 8:12–17

'… you received the Spirit of sonship. And by him we cry, "*Abba*, Father."' (v.15)

I am privileged to know a family which includes two little girls adopted from Sri Lanka. They are much loved by their adoptive brothers and sister. Adoption means that they now share the same privileges as well as the same parents with all the security and love that go alongside.

In a similar way, we are adopted as co-heirs of Jesus. He is, of course, God's Son by nature. We are sons (and daughters!) because of the grace of God the Father, and we share what is rightfully the Son's because of that grace. This verse (v.17) does not mean that we must suffer in order to share that inheritance, but rather that despite the fact that we might suffer we can be assured of, and comforted by, a fulfilment of that inheritance – the glory of eternal life.

It's hard to get our heads around what this actually means. It seems fantastical, over the top, outrageous, that the King should share the Prince's inheritance with commoners! Imagine a monarch splitting up and sharing out the inheritance of his sons, giving to anyone who asked – there'd be a mutiny! Not least among the sons!

But that's exactly what God the Father does. We do nothing to earn these royal rights and privileges. His grace really is outrageous grace. That outrageous grace means that we will inherit the privileges and parenthood of Jesus – and the security and love that goes alongside them.

You are loved, chosen, empowered by the Holy Spirit, saved by the Son and destined for an eternity with the Father.

Just how much confidence should being the King's adopted daughter give you? Here's my advice – if you've got it – flaunt it! You are a true princess!

For prayer and reflection

Heavenly Father, help me to live in confidence, remembering that You have adopted me through grace because You love me greatly, and value me highly. In a phrase: 'I'm worth it!'

A way **to live**

Confidence before God is a wonderful concept. Where could confidence be more important? John writes that if we are obedient to God's way of living, Jesus will live in us by the Spirit He gave us. The result is confidence before God. We will stand before Him with honesty knowing that we have nothing to hide.

My daughter and I are very alike. That often pains me! Just recently I recognised my own teenage arrogance in her attitude. She had been lazy in preparing an important English presentation for a much-loved teacher who knows her well. Having been asked to prepare fully, she cut corners. She didn't follow his plan and bluffed her way through the presentation rather smugly. She had forgotten, however, that she would need to take questions afterwards and was floored by her inability to answer them because of her weak research.

Afterwards she was called to stand before her teacher and give account of herself but could not do so with confidence. He had seen through everything and she knew it. She had ignored his instructions, gone her own way, done less than required and blown it. The result was estrangement and wrath from the teacher who knows and loves her and her potential and, perhaps worse, great shame and sadness.

So often we live our Christian lives hoping to cut corners, ignoring the times when we have been disobedient and compromising on the right way to live. Not only do we disappoint our Teacher – but we live less joyously as a result and our confidence is weakened.

The Holy Spirit will not be able to impart confidence if we don't play our part fully. God sees our heart – let's make sure we can stand before Him with confidence.

1 John 3:21–24

'... And this is how we know that he lives in us: We know it by the Spirit he gave us.' (v.24)

For prayer and reflection

Father God, don't let me cut corners in following You and in so doing lose the confidence that Your Holy Spirit promises.

Freedom from fear

Isaiah 41:8–16

'So do not fear, for I am with you; do not be dismayed, for I am your God.' (v.10)

H aving hauled my way through eighteen months of lymphatic cancer treatment five years ago, I was just beginning to dare to live life to the full again when a completely new, unrelated breast cancer was diagnosed.

In the first few days after diagnosis I came across these verses – especially verse 10 – again and again. Two friends even sent them to me – quite separately. Their poignancy lies in the fact that last time around, God told me very clearly that I was held tightly in His hand. I even named my published diaries chronicling those days, *In the Palm of God's Hand* – so real was the image to me. This time around, in those early days, it was as if He were telling me that He would set me down on my own two feet, send me ahead and remain just behind me. That I could walk on my own and He would just uphold me with that righteous right hand.

Following surgery, and as I waited for further treatment, that was so. I did not know the moment-by-moment dialogue I knew the last time around but I knew a solid reassurance of His upholding me and being 'right there' should I need Him. That brought a new kind of freedom from fear.

God always offers us freedom from fear, but He doesn't always do so in the same way. It's important that we grow in the confidence that He is always with us through the power of His Holy Spirit – even if we don't 'feel' that is so.

The reason we often say 'Where are You?' and don't see God in the midst of our fear might be because He is standing behind us, upholding us gently with His hand, ready to catch us if we fall.

For prayer and reflection

Release yourself from the grip of fear with the words: 'When I am afraid, I will trust in you' (Psa. 56:3).

Eternal confidence

o, where does true confidence lie? Not in the
confidence we manufacture for ourselves
through accomplishment or training, celebrity
or status. That confidence evaporates with sudden
failure and falls victim to the ebb and flow of the tides of
popularity and success.

Our lasting confidence is in the Lord. In the love He
has demonstrated through His Son, in the power, peace
and purpose He offers us through the gift of His Holy
Spirit and in the hope of eternal life.

Faith means that our confidence in Him need never
run out on bad days, or desert us at crisis moments. It
does not have to grow less sure as we age, disappear
in the midst of pain or make poor company on a sunny,
laughter-filled day. It can transform all of those days
and moments with the joy and peace of the Holy Spirit.
Not just for today, this week and until the end of the
year, but for eternity. It is a hope that we can carry with
us until we stand before Him – in confidence.

The Holy Spirit is the source of that confidence and
He waits patiently for us to ask, ask again, and go on
asking, for His intervention in our lives. Yes, we will
mess up, we will get it wrong, and on more days than
we care to think about we will wobble in our faith and
even want to turn our back on it. But we will do so less
often if we can grasp the reality of the Holy Spirit as a
Person and a power who is relevant and real and who
longs to transform our day-to-day experience NOW –
and until eternity, until our hope is fulfilled – *if we will
only ask Him.*

'May the God of hope fill you with all joy and peace
as you trust in him, so that you may overflow with hope
by the power of the Holy Spirit' (Rom. 15:13).

Psalm 23

'… and I will dwell
in the house of the
LORD for ever.'
(v.6)

**For prayer and
reflection**

**Please – ask Him
now!**

The Lord's
Prayer

Alie Teale

Alie Teale has been a freelance writer and translator for over twenty years. She works in Higher Education professional services in London, shares her house with her four adult children, two pugs and a cat, and is a member of St Luke's Church, Cassiobury.

WEEKEND

The Lord's Prayer

For reflection: Matthew 6:9–15

When our children were smaller, we were sitting at the dinner table about to say our evening prayers together as a family, when our daughter asked, 'Are we going to say the tortoise prayer?' We looked at each other, wondering what she meant. Seeing our puzzled expressions, she quickly added, 'You know, the one Jesus *tortoise*.' Ever since then the Lord's Prayer has been known in our house as the 'tortoise prayer' and I have been unable to avoid a smile each Sunday when the minister pronounces, 'Let us join together in the prayer Jesus taught us.'

The idea of a tortoise usually brings to mind a slow animal with deliberate movements – and that is what we are going to do with the Lord's Prayer in the course of the coming month – go through it slowly with time to ponder each of its seven petitions.

You could read through it meditatively over the weekend. The form of the prayer we will be using is one in Matthew 6:9–15, which is the version most of us are familiar with from our prayer books. I do pray that this slow amble will give us time to see something fresh in what can become over-familiar words.

Hallowed be Your name

I have been reciting the Lord's Prayer all my life; as a result, the way I understand it has been influenced by the way I learnt it as a child. We learnt each phrase as a unit; and the whole prayer committed to memory one unit after another until it made a whole. As a result, until I thought about the prayer more carefully, I always assumed the phrase 'hallowed be your name' stood alone. This was rather confusing – because, even a child can figure out that God's name is already hallowed, holy or sanctified, just because of who God is. It never occurred to me that 'hallowed be your name' or 'may your name be honoured' was part of a longer request which essentially reads 'Our Father, hallowed be your name ... *on earth as it is in heaven.*'

Read this way it is easy to see that, yes, God's name is holy or hallowed in itself, but that our prayer should be that God's name is honoured and kept as holy down here on earth as it is in heaven where He is worshipped and glorified by holy beings.

Thinking about it carefully, this is precisely the direction we have from God in the second of the Ten Commandments: that we do not misuse the name of the Lord our God (Exod. 20:7). In other words, we are to use God's name properly so that God is honoured and His name not brought into disrepute. Thus praying 'hallowed be your name' is quite a dangerous prayer if we take it seriously; it implies we are asking that God's name be honoured on earth, and the first place that this is going to start is right here in each one of us. How? By being holy as He is holy.

1 Samuel 2:1–10

'There is no-one holy like the LORD; there is no-one besides you; there is no Rock like our God.' (v.2)

For prayer and reflection

If the honour of God's name on earth depended on the way other people perceived you and the way you live your life, where do you think it would stand?

173

... Hallowed **by my words**

Psalm 19:1–14

'May the words of my mouth and the meditation of my heart be pleasing in your sight, O LORD ...' (v.14)

Apart from seeing the glory of God in the natural world around them and the Holy Spirit revealing God to people as they read His Word, the Bible, the only other way people on earth can see what God is like is by the difference He makes in the lives of those of us who say we are His children. God calls us to be holy as He is holy (Lev. 11:44; 1 Pet. 1:16), and the only way that other people can see we are set apart for God (that is what 'holy' means) is by what we *say* and by what we *do*.

Of these two things, our words are the most crucial as they reveal what is hidden in our hearts (Matt. 12:34). If our hearts are full of bitterness, anger and unforgiveness (Eph. 4:31), then this will be reflected not only in what we say, but in the way we say it. No matter how hard we try to cover it up, it only takes one slip of the mask and our true nature is revealed.

All of us need major heart surgery and regular check-ups if the thoughts of our hearts and the words of our mouths are going to bring honour to God's name on a daily basis. The heart is deceitful above all things (Jer. 17:9), and often we think God cannot see into its dark corners or that we can keep their secrets hidden from those around us. Remember, although we look on our outward appearance, God looks right into the heart (1 Sam. 16:7). He sees into every dark corner we think is hidden.

If God's name is to be honoured as a result of our words, then the dark corners of our hearts need to be brought into the Lord's light.

For prayer and reflection

'Create in me a pure heart, O God, and renew a steadfast spirit within me. Do not cast me from your presence or take your Holy Spirit from me' (Psa. 51:10–11).

... Hallowed **by my deeds**

They say actions speak louder than words, so if the Lord's name is not to come into disrepute, then our actions are as important as our words. Very often we say one thing and do another, or we behave one way with a certain set of people and another way with others. Our fallen human nature makes this behaviour understandable – but not excusable. In the first instance our spirit may be willing, but our body, ie our physical desires, may be weak – leave a packet of chocolate biscuits lying around and I will prove it with no problem. There is nothing wrong with chocolate biscuits if you are blessed to have them, but excess, greed and selfishness are not part of God's ideal for His children. We all have physical desires that we need to discipline if God's name is not to fall into dishonour.

The tendency to behave in one way with certain people and another with others stems from our innate desire to want to be accepted – no one likes to be left out or laughed at. I only have to look at the dynamics among the children around our family meal table to see that demonstrated. But some of us show greater inconsistency in behaviour; the person we appear to be at church on Sunday is not the person who turns up at work on Monday morning.

The important thing to remember is that it is far more important to be accepted by God than the 'in crowd' of the moment, even if that means there are times when we are not included because of what we stand for – but that is what holy means – 'set apart'. People recognise the difference God makes in our lives and often do the 'setting apart' for us.

2 Peter 3:11–14

'You ought to live holy and godly lives as you look forward to the day of God ...' (vv.11–12)

For prayer and reflection

'Search me, O God, and know my heart ... See if there is any offensive way in me, and lead me in the way everlasting' (Psa. 139:23–24).

May **Your kingdom come**

'… God placed all
things under his
feet and appointed
him to be head
over everything …'
(v.22)

The second petition of the Lord's Prayer is 'your kingdom come'. As I thought about the idea of God's kingdom, I realised my understanding of it was actually quite naïve, because I had not exchanged my childish perceptions for mature ones.

My understanding was coloured by the fairytales I had read as a girl where the prince wins the hand of the princess and is given half the 'kingdom'. This conjures up notions of blue birds and cherry blossom, but is devoid of any notion of the authority that belongs to 'kingdom'. Perhaps this is because, in England, we have no immediate experience of the absolute power that monarchs had in Europe in the past. In other parts of the world, people have no problem understanding absolute authority, and often suffer at its hands; thus it is no surprise that in these countries there is a greater understanding of the kingdom of God, ie God's rule over and against any human or supernatural power.

God's kingdom stems from the fact that Jesus came into the world, died for us on the cross and was raised again to life by the Father. In doing this, Satan's rule over mankind was broken and those who receive Christ move from being under the rule and authority of darkness to living under the rule and authority of the Light of the World. In today's reading Paul prays that believers would have the eyes of their hearts opened so that they might truly understand the shift that has occurred in their lives as a result of their becoming part of God's kingdom – His incomparably great power for us who believe. The challenge is to wake up from the deception we have allowed ourselves to be drawn into and live as daughters of the King.

**For prayer and
reflection**

**Almighty Father,
open the eyes
of my heart,
that I might
understand the
length, breadth,
height and depth
of the meaning
of the kingdom
of God – and live
accordingly.**

Your kingdom come **on earth**

**Matthew
28:16–20**

'… make disciples
of all nations …
teaching them to
obey everything
I have
commanded …'
(vv.19–20)

After I had written yesterday's notes, I went downstairs to find the family watching the movie *The Return of the King*. I walked in right in the middle of the battle between the forces of evil and the forces of good. I was struck by the thought that once we have a clearer understanding of the meaning of 'kingdom', it is impossible to avoid the image that Christians are in the middle of a vicious battle between Christ and the powers of darkness. The devil's subtlest ploy is to convince us that he doesn't exist and to deny there is any spiritual struggle at all. Wrong – he does and there is.

Waking up to the reality of our struggle against powers and principalities (Eph. 6:12) can be frightening, but we have no need to fear. Jesus assures us that all power and authority in heaven and on earth has been given to Him (Matt. 28:18). The second petition of the Lord's Prayer commands us to pray that the authority Jesus has in heaven – His kingdom – will also prevail in all its fullness on earth. One of the ways God's kingdom will come on earth is by more and more people hearing and understanding the good news of salvation and asking Jesus to be their Lord. We need to pray earnestly for that. We must also be prepared to be part of the answer to our own prayers – people will not hear unless someone tells them (Rom. 10:14), and we must be willing to be that spokesperson. Just as the first petition of the Lord's Prayer challenges our everyday words and actions to be a letter from Christ (2 Cor. 3:2), the second challenges us to speak openly about Him. You don't need to cross the world to do that – perhaps just your street.

For prayer and reflection

Father, give us Your Word so the gospel may be preached throughout the world, be received in faith, work and live in us, and prevail over sin, death and hell.

WEEKEND

Our Father in heaven

For reflection: Matthew 7:7–11

When Jesus taught His disciples to pray, He began with the words 'Our Father in heaven' to demonstrate that the kind of relationship He had with God was one His followers could know. This relationship was very different to that modelled by a servant and a master, or a criminal and a judge, which is the way many people relate to God.

Jesus' idea was that people would understand they could ask God for what they needed and expect to receive it with the same confidence children have when asking their parents for something, knowing they will receive it.

Today we hear a lot about people's lack of a father, or the negative mental image they have of the idea 'father' because their own father has treated them badly. That is why Jesus calls God 'our Father *in heaven*' – because a heavenly Father is the perfect father, the father we all wish our own could live up to. I am convinced that even someone with a bad father must have the capabilities to imagine what a good father is like – God is that Father, and He is there for you.

The day of the Lord

Whenwe pray that God's kingdom will come to exist on earth the same way as it exists in heaven, what we are in effect praying for, besides people coming to know Jesus as their Lord and Saviour, is the return of Jesus Christ and God's establishment of the new heaven and the new earth. Whatever form that will actually take, it will mean that God will at last dwell with mankind, and people will experience the kind of relationship they were designed to have with Him before sin entered the world.

In the past, the idea of the imminent return of Christ fuelled a passion to reach as many people as possible with the good news of salvation before Judgment Day when the lost would be cast into the lake of fire.

These days, due to ideas that arose in the nineteenth century, talk about hell can be a taboo subject – in fact many Christians think hell doesn't exist. This means the motivation for praying in God's kingdom on earth is reduced. While these ideas were growing, changes in the way the second coming was understood made Christians think this was an event a long way off; that it was something that wouldn't happen until people had created a perfect society on earth themselves.

Although this idea generated much social action in the late nineteenth century, it led people to think Jesus' return was not so imminent. The end result of such thinking was that the urgency to share the gospel waned. Big changes in thinking take many decades, but these changes are probably why some Christians do not have the evangelistic urgency of earlier generations. It is so easy to imbibe the spirit of the age without even realising it. Does your ideology need a wake up?

Revelation 21:1–8

'Now the dwelling of God is with men, and he will live with them.' (v.3)

For prayer and reflection

Lord, may my mind not be conformed to current ideas without even questioning them. May I know for myself what Your Word says and what it means for my life.

What is **God's will?**

Ephesians 1:3–14

'And he made known to us the mystery of his will … which he purposed in Christ.' (v.9)

The third petition of the Lord's Prayer reads: 'Your will be done on earth as it is in heaven' (Matt. 5:10b). But what is God's will? We ought to know, because God the Father 'has made known to us the mystery of his will' (Eph. 1:9), which is 'to bring all things in heaven and on earth together under one head, even Christ' (Eph. 1:10). This is God's ultimate intention, His ultimate desire – most of us don't think that big – the cosmic scale is beyond our immediate concern and imagination. We would probably say God's will is that we serve Him and bring glory to His name. Yes, but that is not the big picture, just our small part.

Think about it for a moment, the first three petitions of the Lord's Prayer are asking that three big things are accomplished on earth just as they are in heaven: that God's name is honoured by and in all creation, that His authority is acknowledged by and in all creation and that His will is done by and in all creation. The last petition actually encompasses the first two; if the first two are fulfilled, the third is fulfilled automatically. So when we pray these first few lines of the Lord's Prayer we are supporting the fulfilment of God's ultimate purpose in creation – to bring everything in earth and heaven together under Christ.

Unifying all things in heaven and earth could only be achieved by Christ's death on the cross, His resurrection and ascension; this was the way God planned to put things right in fallen creation. This is why Paul talks about 'God's will being *purposed* in Christ'; he means God planned it that way, even if our minds can't fathom the mystery of how it works.

For prayer and reflection

Lord, Your purposes are mind-stretchingly too big for me to grasp; I abandon myself to You and marvel that my prayer matters – and I pray 'Your will be done'.

Not as I will, **but as You will**

The perfect instance in history where God's will has been done on earth as in heaven was in the Garden of Gethsemane when Jesus struggled with the thought of what lay ahead of Him if God's purpose for history was to be fulfilled. We have three records of what Jesus prayed. The first time He prayed He asked His Father that 'this cup be taken' from Him if it was *possible* that there was another way for fallen creation and a perfect God to be reunited – but He also prayed that God's will would be done. The second time His words had changed; He prayed, 'If it is *not possible* for this cup to be taken away unless I drink it, may your will be done.'

Between the two prayers, when Jesus had stopped to chide the disciples for sleeping, He had realised there was no other way – this was God the Father's perfect plan. The second prayer was thus a cry for strength and resolution under the most difficult of circumstances. I'm sure Jesus knew this before the first prayer, but this reflection of His humanity encourages us when we have the seemingly impossible and incomprehensible to face because we are following our understanding of God's will for our lives.

The third time Jesus prays He prays the same words as the second prayer. I think this third prayer is a reflection of complete submission and surrender to the perfect will of God that is accompanied by an experience of peace that only those in such difficult circumstances can know. When the soldiers arrived, this depth of surrender and trust in God had produced a depth of resolution in Jesus that allowed Him to say confidently, and proactively, 'Rise! Let us go!'

Matthew 26:36–46

'Are you still sleeping and resting? Look, the hour is near ...'
(v.45)

For prayer and reflection

O God, grant me a willing spirit to sustain me when the road ahead is dark and difficult and I can't understand why I have been poured a bitter cup.

Living to **please God**

**1 Thessalonians
4:1–12**

'… we instructed
you how to live …
to please God …
and urge you … to
do this more and
more.' (v.1)

We've thought a little about God's ultimate will – that all things in heaven and earth be united in Christ – and how Jesus surrendered Himself to allow that to happen. While it is important to be aware of the cosmic picture, it is also important that we are aware of God's will for us at the human level. The link between God's cosmic will and His will for our individual lives is the example of Jesus that we looked at yesterday. Jesus' surrender to God's will made the final unification of all things in God finally possible, although we will not see the total fulfilment of that until Jesus' return. Our individual surrender to God every day and in every way edges in the coming of God's kingdom on earth.

Surrendering to God's will is not only a decision we make in our heads by faith that moves us from the kingdom of darkness to the kingdom of light, but it is also a heart thing – surrendering our desires so that we can become more and more like Jesus by learning to think, say and do only the things that bring honour to His name. This process is called sanctification. This basically means becoming more and more holy as we live for Jesus every day.

Some people think it is enough to believe that Jesus has saved us and that we don't need to do any more about it, but if we have become new creations in Christ, that newness should shine through in our behaviour, or it is not worth very much. This doesn't mean that doing God's will is enough to save us, but it does mean our salvation is cheap if we are not willing to take up our cross and follow Christ in all we say and do.

For prayer and reflection

**Arm yourself with the same attitude as Christ … and live the rest of your life not for evil desires, but rather for the will of God …
(1 Pet. 4:1–6).**

Give us today **our daily bread**

The fourth petition of the Lord's Prayer reads, 'Give us today our daily bread'. I am very conscious that these notes are read by women in countries where prayer for something as basic as bread is a very real necessity. In Britain, due to the trend for carbohydrate-free weight-loss diets, the last thing many women would want to eat is bread. So when we pray this prayer for our daily bread, it is so important to step outside the mindset of our over-privileged culture and be grateful for what we so often despise, reminding ourselves we are praying to be provided with the basic necessities of life not its luxuries.

Not only does this petition prompt us to pray for the provision of life's basics but for everything that allows us to enjoy them – think what it takes to put that loaf of bread on your table. In Britain few of us know anything about hoeing, sowing, watering, reaping, winnowing, grinding and baking – a loaf that takes all day to make can be received with much more thanks than one grabbed off a supermarket shelf. Few of us even think to pray that no drought, locusts, deluge or warfare might destroy the crop we have worked so hard to produce – it is beyond our experience.

Perhaps those of us who have much, need to stop, realise how much we actually lack because of the lifestyle our culture imposes on us, and pray for those who lack basic necessities – and for ourselves who have lost much of our basic humanity in the face of excess.

Matthew 7:7–12

'For everyone who asks receives … who seeks finds; and … the door will be opened.'
(v.8)

For prayer and reflection

'We all have enough that we lack, but the great want is that we do not feel nor see it. Therefore God also requires that you lament and plead such necessities and wants, not because He does not know them, but that you may kindle your heart to stronger and greater desires, and make wide and open your cloak to receive much.'

Martin Luther

WEEKEND

The gratitude attitude

For reflection: Psalm 103:1–5

I read in a newspaper that people who count their blessings live longer than those who don't. Apparently the regular listing in a journal of three good things, however small, that have happened to you during the day is a major contribution to a positive attitude – and that is good for your health. I suppose the discipline of list-making is the resort of the person who has no one to thank. Those who know God as Father know all good gifts come from Him, and this prompts a thankful response in prayer in the evening – as well as a constant grateful attitude in the heart through the day.

It's quite easy to remember to thank the Lord for special things – like a free ticket to the final day of the cricket test against Australia at the Oval – but what about the everyday things? It takes a burst water main for us to remember to thank the Lord for clean water, or a fuel blockade before we thank the Lord for ease of transport, or an illness before we thank God for our health.

Let's not forget to thank God for the things we take for granted.

The secret of **contentment**

The Lord's Prayer encourages us to ask God to provide the things we need every day to get by, and we read in Matthew 7:7 that everyone who asks receives. In that light, today's verse provides something of a conundrum – being content whether we are well fed or hungry.

This confused me until my husband reminded me that Paul's watchwords were something Paul tried to live by in his capacity as a travelling evangelist and teacher. When you are 'on the road for Jesus' you can find yourself sleeping on the floor and eating beans on toast, or you can find yourself in a penthouse suite with room service. What Paul is talking about is that workers for Christ shouldn't stipulate the penthouse with room service, but be content with what they are offered. There is a real danger that the 'minimum' a speaker expects can increase as time goes by, just as there is a danger that those who invite a speaker might think they can treat the person shoddily because the speaker should put up with anything for the sake of the gospel (1 Thess. 5:12–13)!

Paul's watchword is often applied to those who don't travel and preach. The danger here is that it leads to the thought that we have to be content with the way things are, that there is no point trying to make things better for ourselves and our families. In this way Paul's watchword can sometimes become a tool for social oppression – there is nothing wrong with wanting to make things better for your family, although there will be times when we need to be content with little, and times when we can rejoice in blessing. What is wrong is to allow self-advancement and the desire to accumulate to push Jesus off the throne of our hearts.

Philippians 4:10–20

'I have learned the secret of being content in … every situation, whether well fed or hungry …' (v.12)

For prayer and reflection

Lord, do not give me too much that I forget You, nor too little that I steal and bring dishonour to Your name.

Seek first the kingdom of God

....

Matthew 6:25–34

....

'… do not worry about … what you will eat or drink; or about your body, what you will wear.' (v.25)

....

For prayer and reflection

....

'You do not have, because you do not ask God. When you ask, you do not receive, because you ask with wrong motives, that you may spend what you get on your pleasures' (James 4:2–3).

After Jesus taught His disciples the Lord's Prayer He told them not to worry about food and clothes, but to look at the birds and the flowers that God feeds and clothes without them asking. Jesus wanted the disciples to understand that God knows we need these things, and that He provides them as a matter of course.

This doesn't mean that Jesus was telling us at the beginning of Matthew 6 to ask for what we need and then contradicting Himself at the end of the chapter; it means that Jesus wanted His disciples to get their priorities right. It's rather like when one son came to me and said he needed a new pair of jeans. I already knew he needed some because I'd seen the tears in the knees when I'd folded the laundry. I'd also already planned time to go and buy some for him, but I was so pleased he'd asked – and he was pleased and surprised that I was already on the case. So we went and bought jeans and a couple of other things too. It would have been rather different if he had come to me and asked for a completely outlandish, expensive piece of clothing. Firstly I wouldn't be able to afford it and secondly I would have said 'no' on principle. It's the same sort of thing with God – He's already on the case when it's something we need, but we aren't likely to get the unnecessary thing we want from wrong motives.

The way to deal with wrong motives is to put seeking God's kingdom first above everything; holding our desires up to the Light shows them for what they really are. Then we know which ones are worth bothering God with and which we need to pray forgiveness for!

Forgive us our debts

The fifth petition of the Lord's Prayer reads 'forgive us our debts, as we also have forgiven our debtors'. The debt that we owe God is our sinfulness. Today's reading shows us that not a single one of us can claim to be free of that debt, we have all sinned, and do so every day. A thorough examination of the motives behind our prayers is enough to show this is true – we easily fool ourselves because the human heart is deceitful above all things (Jer. 17:9). Our good deeds are not much better. If we thoroughly examine the reasons why we do some of the so-called good things we do we find that 'our righteous acts are like filthy rags' (Isa. 64:6).

Martin Luther summed up this human situation as follows: 'The flesh in which we daily live is of such a nature that it neither trusts nor believes God, and is ever active in evil lusts and devices, so that we sin daily in word and deed, by commission and omission, by which the conscience is thrown into unrest, so that it is afraid of the wrath and displeasure of God, and thus loses the comfort and confidence derived from the Gospel.'

Thinking about the inescapable situation we find ourselves in as a result of our fallen nature can lead us to despair – this is a debt we can't repay however hard or long we try. Paul wrestled with this problem when he wrote 'What a wretched man I am! Who will rescue me from this body of death?' To which he added 'Thanks be to God – through the Lord Jesus Christ' (Rom 7:24–25).

Today's reading highlights God's rescue plan in a nutshell: If we confess our sins *Jesus* is righteous and just and He will forgive us our sins and cleanse us from all unrighteousness. Taking time to keep short accounts with God is very important if His kingdom is to come in our lives.

---

1 John 1:5–2:2

'If we claim to be without sin, we deceive ourselves and the truth is not in us.' (1:8)

For prayer and reflection

'... my sin is always before me ... cleanse me ... and I shall be clean ...'
(Psa. 51:3,7).

As we **forgive** our debtors

Matthew 18:21–35

'Shouldn't you have had mercy on your fellow-servant just as I had on you?' (v.33)

When we come to a realisation of the length and depth and breadth of our sinfulness – as I tried to depict yesterday, hopefully without depressing you too much – we come to a much better understanding of how much God has forgiven us in Jesus Christ. This is partly what Paul meant when he prayed that the Ephesians would know the length, depth and height of God's love – love that had to be that big in order to cover the enormity of our sins.

When we understand how much we are loved by God, and how much we have been forgiven and are forgiven on a continual basis, then our hearts are overwhelmed with love for God in return (Luke 7:36–50). This kind of love generates compassion in the heart; suddenly it becomes clear to us how fallible our fellow human beings are, that they can no more help the things they do than we can, and there is nothing better we can do in response to God's love for us than forgive those people we perceive are in debt to us due to their intentional or unintentional thoughts, words and deeds.

When I say 'those people we *perceive* are in debt to us', what I mean is that our own deceitful hearts can never see a situation for what it truly is, we have a tendency to colour things in our favour. The times I have experienced most forgiveness from God have always resulted in a change in perception. Suddenly my own fault becomes blazingly clear and more repentance is required. This is a very humbling experience, and very necessary, as it stops us becoming bitter and critical and prevents us cultivating all those horrible attitudes that grieve God's Holy Spirit.

Forgiveness helps us build others up rather than tear them down (Eph. 4:29–32).

For prayer and reflection

'Bear with each other and forgive whatever grievances you may have against one another. Forgive as the Lord forgave you' (Col. 3:13).

Forgiving **ourselves**

I was at a conference last week where the speaker was talking about forgiveness. After mentioning how we need to receive God's forgiveness and forgive others, he mentioned the importance of forgiving ourselves, but he didn't explain the biblical background for the last statement.

As I have recently become aware of how much modern pop psychology has been surreptitiously attached to the gospel, I began to think about the biblical basis for 'forgiving ourselves'. I know from my own experience how important it is if we are to live effectively for the Lord once we have confessed our sins to Him and received His forgiveness, but I wasn't sure where I could find anything about this in the Bible.

As I lay thinking about this in bed, the nearest thing I could think of relating to this subject were Jesus' words, 'Love your neighbour as yourself' (Matt. 19:19). This isn't exactly 'forgive others as you forgive yourself', yet if we love others with the love of Christ then we will forgive them as He forgave us. By implication this means that love incorporates forgiveness and if we are loving others with a love with which we love ourselves, then this 'self-love' must include 'self-forgiveness'. I hope you see what I mean! Besides, if God can forgive us our sins when we confess them, isn't it rather presumptuous for us not to forgive ourselves and move on? If we don't, then in a way we are saying we know better than God – which of course we don't.

So next time you ask God to forgive you, forgive yourself. If the thought of your sin keeps bothering you, remind yourself you are forgiven and use it as an opportunity to resolve in Christ's strength not to commit sin again.

Jeremiah 31:31–34

'... they will all know me ... For I will forgive their wickedness and will remember their sins no more.' (v.34b)

For prayer and reflection

Is anything you have asked God to forgive still bothering you? Bring it to the cross and ask the Lord to help you forgive yourself and to know His loving embrace.

WEEKEND

Does God tempt us?

For reflection: 2 Peter 1:5–7

D oes God tempt us? The short answer to this question is 'No'. In James 1:13–14 we read:

When tempted, no-one should say 'God is tempting me.' For God cannot be tempted by evil, nor does he tempt anyone; but each one is tempted when, by his own evil desire, he is dragged away and enticed.

God may not tempt us, but He does test us. In 1 Peter 1 we read that these times of testing usually come in the form of various hardships. The intention is to refine our faith. In 2 Peter 1:5–7 we see the kind of progression that faith can make in difficult circumstances: self-control leads to perseverance which in turn leads to godliness. Times of testing may be from God but the devil then sneaks in with the temptation to sin – like Job, we can be tempted to curse God for our misfortune. It is a constant challenge to be able to face up to the reality of a bad situation and not sin by charging God with wrongdoing.

I am constantly challenged by Job's words: 'The LORD gave and the LORD has taken away; may the name of the LORD be praised' (Job 1:21).

Three kinds of **temptation**

W e now come to the sixth petition of the Lord's Prayer: 'lead us not into temptation'. Although we are a new creation in Christ (2 Cor. 5:17) and our sinful nature has been crucified with Him (Gal. 5:24), we still live in a fallen world in which we are subject to trials and temptations every day. If we are to watch out for temptations so that we do not fall into them (Matt. 26:41), then we need to know in what form they come.

Throughout Christian history temptation has usually been categorised into three types traditionally called 'the world', 'the flesh' and 'the devil'. If you look right back to the Garden of Eden where the Serpent tempted Eve, these three types of temptation are seen at work all at once. The fruit was 'pleasing to the eye': this represents the kind of temptations thrown at us by the world – things we see and hear that tempt us to covetousness and the desire to accumulate material things. The fruit was also 'good for food': this represents the kind of temptations that test our 'flesh', ie our bodies – the desire to overeat, to drink too much, or indulge in sexual licence. And, finally, the fruit was seen as 'desirable for attaining wisdom': this represents the kind of temptations that come from the devil. These include any matters of the conscience, seeking to control others for our own prowess, and spiritual compromise.

All these things are related to seeking power for oneself rather than submitting to God and are well illustrated by Satan tempting Jesus to throw Himself off the roof of the Temple and be saved by angels so that everyone would worship Him (Luke 4:9–12).

Genesis 3:1–19

'… the fruit … was good for food and pleasing … and also desirable for gaining wisdom …' (v.6)

For prayer and reflection

Where is your weak point – the world, the flesh or the devil? What tactics could you use to be alert to the particular temptations that the enemy lays in your path?

Looking for the **emergency exit**

**1 Corinthians
10:1–13**

'… when you are
tempted, he will
also provide a way
out so that you can
stand up under it.'
(v.13)

After yesterday's reading, perhaps you managed to identify particular temptations that you are subject to. There is nothing to be ashamed of if you have temptations – we all do. The good news is that 'no temptation has seized you except what is common to man' (1 Cor. 10:13) – nothing you have experienced is anything new. Unfortunately, the other thing that is not new is being so self-assured you are standing firm that you take your eyes off Jesus and fall into the temptation. Having the temptation is not a sin, but entertaining that temptation for longer than it takes to cast it out in the name of Jesus – well that definitely leads to sin.

Martin Luther wrote that if you let the head of a serpent through even a very small gap, then the rest of the body slips through very easily with no stopping it – and those of us who have lived in hot countries know how long and deadly a thin snake can be. So it is wise not to give the devil a foothold in your life, it can be very difficult to shake him off.

The key then is to plug the gaps before the snake can get its head through. That is why I encouraged you to identify your weaknesses – these are the areas where there are most gaps to plug. God promises to provide a way out when we are tempted – but although the door may be labelled 'emergency exit', it is no use in an emergency unless we have identified its position beforehand. For example, if your temptation is to gluttony then don't walk to work past the bakery!

Whatever your weakness or situation there are emergency exits that God provides, but we are the ones who carry the choice to use them.

**For prayer and
reflection**

**'How gracious
he will be when
you cry for help …
your ears will hear
a voice behind
you, saying, "This
is the way; walk
in it"'
(Isa. 30:19–21).**

Being **prepared**

When I was a child I lived in Africa and never saw a lion although I was always on the lookout. Now I live outside London where you wouldn't expect any animal action. But recently things changed; I woke up one night to a horrendous sound. Outside our window I witnessed a fox mauling a cat. Thankfully that cat escaped, but a few nights later another cat didn't. As you can imagine, now I do not let my cats out of the house once it begins to get dark and I guard the door when anyone comes in or goes out. The cats nag me, but I have to be self-controlled and not give in – I know what the consequences could be. Every night, although I am asleep, part of me is alert to the sounds outside the house in case I have to try and rescue someone else's pet. Three years ago someone told me they had witnessed something similar, and I was sceptical – things like that don't happen in 'nice' places like this, but now I know they do.

The same kind of things can happen to us in a variety of ways – everything appears to be safe and cosy, we hear of dreadful things that other people have had to face, but we find it hard to believe because our own experience leads us to think that what we are hearing is make-believe or at least exaggeration. And then the unthinkable happens – we witness a poor innocent falling prey to a temptation that has come from a direction that we, and they, never anticipated.

The watch words we need to remember are 'self-control' and 'alertness', then we will be ready to resist and stand firm in our faith when a temptation comes from an unexpected quarter.

1 Peter 5:6–11

'Be self-controlled and alert. Your enemy the devil prowls around like a roaring lion …'
(v.8)

For prayer and reflection

'This is what the LORD says to me, "Go, post a lookout … When he sees chariots … let him be alert, fully alert"'
(Isa. 21:6–7).

Deliver us from the evil one

Romans 8:28–39

'… neither angels nor demons … will be able to separate us from the love of God …' (vv.38–39)

In the final petition of the Lord's Prayer Jesus teaches us to pray to be delivered from the evil one. By this He means that we should pray to be saved from the schemes of the devil. Traditionally these have been described as attacks on the body, attacks on our soul, attacks on our material possessions, and attacks on our good reputation. These days we don't often think about being delivered from evil in a physical or material sense – we have tended to spiritualise the idea. But if you look at Romans 8, Paul talks about the kinds of evil Christians were undergoing: trouble, hardship, persecution, famine, nakedness, danger and 'the sword'. All these things are actual evils, not spiritual ones.

We read in John 8:44 that the devil was a murderer from the beginning, so he is set on the destruction of the children of God and will use any means. It therefore follows that when we pray to be delivered from evil, we have as much cause to pray for a trouble-free life, ease, liberty and justice, food, clothing, bodily protection and freedom from any form of assault on anything that pertains to us in this life – spouse, children, home, business etc – as we have cause to pray for the protection of our faith against the lies that the devil throws against us and the temptations he shoots across our path. I can't explain in this short space why sometimes we aren't delivered from physical or material suffering, but we can take comfort in Paul's teaching that in all our afflictions we are more than conquerors through Him who loved us – ie through Christ our *Lord* – because the Father has put all things under Jesus' feet by giving Him kingdom authority.

For prayer and reflection

The devil's biggest victory is to convince us he doesn't exist. If you don't think he does, imagine he might. How would that change your prayer life?

Deliver us **from the time of trial**

A s well as being a prayer to deliver us from moral and/or spiritual evil, the last petition of the Lord's Prayer is sometimes translated 'deliver us from the time of trial'. The reason for this is to stress the part of Jesus' teaching that emphasises the imminence of the end of the age and His return.

As we saw at the beginning of this month of notes, Jesus' return will usher in the fullness of God's kingdom that we are praying 'will come on earth as it is in heaven'. However, the Bible teaches us that before this happens, there will be a time of trial on the earth during which true believers will be persecuted for their faith. This is mentioned twice in Revelation. The first instance occurs in the letter to the church in Philadelphia (Rev. 3:7–13). Some Christians believe the letters to the seven churches in Revelation represent seven periods of history between the birth of Christ and His return, and thus that the letter to the church in Philadelphia represents Christ's words to believers in the days before His return.

Here Jesus promises that those who have kept His commands and endured patiently will be saved from the time of trial that will come to test those who live on the earth. This time of trial (v.10) is frequently linked to Revelation 20:2–3 and 8, where we read that, having been bound for a thousand years, Satan is released 'for a short time' to deceive the nations and to gather them for battle. It is understood that during this time of trial many Christians will be martyred (John 16:2), but the hope of glory is promised to those who have been faithful and have 'come out of the great tribulation' (Rev. 7:13–14).

Revelation 3:7–13

'I will also keep you from the hour of trial that is going to come upon the whole world …' (v.10)

For prayer and reflection

It is impossible to avoid the fact that the Christian faith carries an eschatological hope, and in praying the last petition we are acknowledging that hope, whatever form it may actually take.

WEEKEND

The power and the glory forever

For reflection: Revelation 19:1–10

The Lord's Prayer that I learnt as a child ends with the words: *'Yours is the kingdom, the power, and the glory forever. Amen.'* These words are not part of the main text, but a footnote in the translation of the Bible that I use. However, I don't think they should be a footnote in our thinking when we pray the Lord's Prayer.

After dwelling on temptation and being delivered from evil it is very uplifting to shift one's focus away from the difficult things that we have to face as children of God and look up into the face of Jesus and remember that kingdom authority has been given to Him. It is significant that the footnote also mentions power. Think about it – power and authority don't automatically go hand in hand, you can have one without the other. Those who wield power without proper authority are usually oppressors; those who have authority but no power achieve nothing.

Our God has an authority and a power that perfectly complement each other – besides providing us with salvation, they bring Him the glory He deserves. Salvation, glory and power belong to our God.

'Hallelujah! Salvation and glory and power belong to our God … Hallelujah! For our Lord God Almighty reigns.
Let us rejoice and be glad and give him glory!'(vv.1,7)

Make it so

When we pray the Lord's Prayer we usually end by saying 'Amen'. This is not a way of signalling our prayer is over, like a full stop ends a sentence; there is more to it than that. 'Amen' means 'I agree', so when we say this word we are in essence signing our name at the bottom of a petition that is going to be presented to heaven's highest court of appeal by the best advocate we could ask for – Jesus (Matt. 10:32; Rom. 8:34). Not only does 'Amen' mean 'I agree' but it is also a very special use of language called 'performative' – language that can make things happen, but only if the person uttering it has the authority to do so.

When we say 'Amen', we are thus also saying 'Make it so' – but do we have the authority? The amazing thing is, that although the things in the Lord's Prayer that we are decreeing be 'made so' are of unimaginable scope, we do have the authority to make such decrees because Jesus has delegated some of His authority to us: 'And I confer on you a kingdom, just as my Father conferred one on me' (Luke 22:29).

Think also about the words Jesus spoke to Peter: 'I will give you the keys of the kingdom of heaven; whatever you bind on earth will be bound in heaven, and whatever you loose on earth will be loosed in heaven' (Matt. 16:19). So think – when we pray 'your kingdom come on earth as it is in heaven', our words are 'loosing' God's kingdom on earth even if its fulfilment is still in the future.

I will leave you to chew over this bit of linguistic philosophy and conclude our series on the Lord's Prayer with a wonderful quote from Martin Luther:

2 Corinthians 1:18–22

'And so through him the "Amen" is spoken by us to the glory of God.' (v.20)

For prayer and reflection

'There is no nobler prayer to be found upon earth than the Lord's Prayer which we daily pray, because it has this excellent testimony, that God loves to hear it, which we ought not surrender for all the riches in the world.'

Encounters

Chris Ledger

Chris Ledger worked as a counsellor, supervisor and trainer in the NHS, and now has a private practice. She enjoys speaking at Christian meetings and is a regular tutor on Waverley Abbey Resources *Insight* days, also co-authoring several books in the *Insight* series. At Greyfriars Church, Reading, she is a Licensed Lay Minister, and in her spare time enjoys having fun with her five grandchildren.

Encounters

'Greetings, you who are highly favoured! The Lord is with you.' (v.28)

T his month we will be meeting ordinary people like you and me, whose encounter with Jesus has much to teach us.

No one could get more ordinary than Mary. As an unwed, teenage 'nobody' from provincial Galilee, she was plucked incognito to become one of the most favoured of all women – the mother of Jesus; she was to carry God's own flesh. Our tabloid papers would have made sensational reading, '*Pregnant teenager swears she has never had sex*'. Mary makes two responses to the angel's news: the incredulous question, 'How will this be ...?' (v.34) and then the response of complete surrender, 'I am the Lord's servant ... May it be to me as you have said' (v.38). As a Jewish woman, Mary would have learnt about God through the book of Moses, the Psalms and the prophets. Knowing something of God's graciousness and the fact that the Messiah would come, probably made it easier for her to say humbly, 'Yes, I am willing to carry this baby.' Mary was truly thrilled to have Jesus living and growing within her womb, and on sharing her news with her cousin Elizabeth she burst out in praise (vv.39–56).

Today God is asking us the same sort of question He asked Mary, 'Are you willing to let me into your life?' Have you completely surrendered your life to God, as Mary did? Are you holding anything back? Some of us may experience difficulty in surrendering our career, family, or hopes and dreams, and we find ourselves echoing Mary's question, 'How will it be?'

What is your personal struggle? Let's learn to trust God and let Him be the living centre of our lives. Then we may find ourselves like Mary, worshipping Him: 'My soul magnifies the Lord' (v.46).

For prayer and reflection

In favouring Mary, God raised womanhood to a dignity it had never known. 'Lord, I choose to be Your servant ... have Your way in my heart and life. Amen.'

A **righteous** man

I wonder what God was trying to demonstrate in choosing an ordinary, humble carpenter to be the foster father of Jesus – perhaps that ordinariness doesn't stop us from being people of spiritual stature that God can use.

Joseph, a Nazarene, would have been devastated to discover that his fiancée, Mary, was pregnant. Having never touched her in a dishonourable way, he knew he wasn't the father and, as 'a righteous man' (v.19), his immediate thought wasn't for himself, but for Mary. He wanted to protect her honour and public image, so decided to quietly divorce her. Anyone who has suffered a broken engagement will know something of the deep sorrow of an aching heart. But God had a rescue plan! Suddenly an angel appeared and told Joseph not to be afraid to take Mary as his wife, for the Holy Spirit had enabled her to conceive a special son. Again we catch a glimpse of a selfless man. Once married, Joseph put aside his own physical desires and waited to consummate the marriage until after the baby was born. Then came that joyous moment, when Joseph held his foster child in his arms, and whispered, 'Jesus.'

Joseph challenges me, as I see in him a man of deep devotion to God. He's been through a roller-coaster ride of emotions; happily engaged, then dramatically contemplating breaking off the relationship, to be quickly followed by marriage, but holding back on sex. But never once do we see him complaining. He is more concerned to be obedient to God and care for his beloved Mary, than he is for himself. How do we respond when Jesus comes into our lives and turns our plans upside down? Do we shout and scream, or quietly think of others more than ourselves and get on with what God requires of us.

Matthew 1:18–25

'... he gave him the name Jesus.' (v.25)

For prayer and reflection

How would people describe you? Righteous and selfless? 'The fruit of the righteous is a tree of life ...' (Prov. 11:30).

An **anxious** couple

Luke 2:41–52

'Your father and I have been anxiously searching for you.' (v.48)

Whilst caring for a child have you ever discovered he or she has gone missing? We once lost our toddler whilst out shopping and my thought, 'What if someone's hurt her?' gave rise to an awful sickening anxiety. Fortunately she was found safe and sound two miles away. What an anxious time Mary and Joseph must have had as they searched for three days before they found their lost son.

Jesus (aged 12) and His parents had been in Jerusalem for the Feast of the Passover. As the large number of families returned home there would have been a lot of chatting amongst the adults, and playful teasing amongst the children – it would have been easy for the absence of a child to have gone unnoticed. Immediately Jesus' parents found He was missing, they returned to Jerusalem, eventually finding their son in the Temple. Much relieved, Mary gently scolded Him and Jesus replied, 'What's the fuss about? It's important for Me to be in My Father's house.' For Jesus the Temple symbolised His Father's presence and He was saying that His relationship with His Father was of the utmost importance to Him.

In our Christian journey we may experience anxiety because we don't feel Jesus' presence. Sometimes, like Jesus' parents, we may at first not even notice He is missing in our busy lives. Note how they *sought* after Jesus, and how important it is for us when we are anxious, to *seek* after Him – 'He who seeks finds' (Matt. 7:8). Anxiety is a state of mind in which the 'What ifs,' can pervade our attitudes, causing emotional, physical and spiritual distress. I cope with anxiety by trying to distract my thoughts away from the worries – by meditating on a particular Scripture verse, or by singing a worshipful song. Sometimes that's easier said than done!

For prayer and reflection

'Cast all your anxiety on him because he cares for you' (1 Pet. 5:7).

A **suffering** woman

A crowd gathered – shouting and gesticulating. A crowd bent on killing her son. As Mary nervously inched herself forward to the foot of Jesus' cross, her mind flashed back 33 years. She was in the Temple, hearing Simeon's words, 'A sword will pierce your own soul too' (Luke 2:35). Now she knew the meaning. She felt the sharpness of the blade penetrate her innermost being. Feeling indescribable pain, her emotions were denied any expression … she felt numb. Nausea swept over her as she saw her son, wracked in pain, hanging on a cross like a common criminal. Mary suffered with Him – this was part of motherhood. Then in the midst of this heart-rending scene, Jesus saw the suffering in His mother's face. Immediately He comforted her, 'Dear woman, here is your son', and said to John, the disciple, 'Here is your mother' (vv.26–27). Jesus reassured Mary that in her suffering He cared for her.

Like Mary, when we see our loved ones in pain, we invariably suffer as well. Perhaps you have a family member dying with cancer; or your teenager has gone 'off the rails'. Whatever the cause, suffering can bring feelings of helplessness, loneliness, anxiety, and such a depth of sorrow that a dull ache pervades all.

How do you cope with suffering? Pain can make some women bitter, but for others it refines. Are we willing to admit that we are suffering and let God enter our pain, or do we pretend it isn't there? Larry Crabb says, 'We Christians are often practising Buddhists. We kill desire in an effort to escape pain, then wonder why we don't enjoy God.' Mary challenges us to allow God to draw near to us in our pain. We next read of her praying in the Upper Room (Acts 1:14).

John 19:16–27

'Near the cross of Jesus stood his mother …' (v.25)

For prayer and reflection

Jesus, help me to learn how to place my suffering in Your hands. Just as You transformed the pain on the cross to triumph, transform my pain into something beautiful.

WEEKEND

Love one another

For reflection: John 13:34–35; Ephesians 4:2; John 4:7–12

I n the weekend readings this month we will be looking at our responsibilities towards 'one another' and begin with the command to 'Love one another'. I don't know about you, but I find it much easier to love those people I like and I have to work really hard at loving those I don't! One aspect to loving others is being really patient with them even when they drive you round the bend. We learn from 1 Corinthians 13:4 that 'Love is patient'. Patience is the ability to endure irksome people long-sufferingly and to tolerate their most annoying ways.

Think of the people you'll come into contact with over the next week, and make a list of all those you find aggravating, who try your patience or who you may ignore. Use the following categories – family, friends, colleagues and neighbours. Now think of how you can go out of your way to bless them.

Consider:

- speaking to someone you would normally ignore
- reacting differently when someone annoys you – see him or her through Jesus' eyes;
- responding with love in a new way starting this weekend.

Remember – to love is constructively to seek the welfare of others.

A **desperate** woman

Mark 5:24b–34

'Daughter, your faith has healed you … be freed from your suffering.' (v.34)

nly another woman can even begin to think what is was like for this woman to suffer with a menstrual bleed for 12 years. Imagine how drained and uncomfortable she felt, with no mod cons such as running water or disposable feminine aids (with the latest absorbency and scent!). Enough to drive any of us to despair! As if physical misery were not enough … a menstruating woman was ostracised from community life as she was deemed to be ritually 'unclean' (Lev. 15:25–28), as was anyone she touched. Alongside this woman's emotional rejection came poverty, as she had spent all her money seeking out doctors for a cure.

With all hope of living a normal life faded, she didn't sit in a pool of self-pity crying 'Poor old me', but having heard about Jesus and His miraculous healings she went in search of Him … but so had everyone else!

'I don't want to miss Him, I need to push through the crowd … now … reach out and touch His hem.' Her last few steps were a public nightmare as she was trembling with fear, but Jesus looked straight into her face. In that brief second she knew she was not only healed, but accepted. 'Daughter, your faith has healed you. Go in peace and be freed from your suffering.' All the pain, hurt and rejection melted away. Her encounter with Jesus changed her life.

In what areas of your life are you suffering? Physical, emotional or perhaps relational? Rather than despairing in the situation let's be like this woman of faith and turn to Jesus. With determination let's push through our fears and cynicism and reach out to touch His hem … then receive His healing love.

For prayer and reflection

Jesus said, 'Have faith in God' (Mark 11:22–24). How can we increase our faith? By strengthening our hearts as we meditate on the promises of God. Today, declare aloud one of God's promises.

A **thankful** man

Luke 17:11–19

'He threw himself at Jesus' feet and thanked him …' (v.16)

I n today's encounter we meet others rejected by society because they too were unclean – the ten lepers. This story challenges our attitudes.

Jesus was on His way to Jerusalem when He met the lepers. Leprosy was perceived by the Jews to be a mark of God's displeasure. Because the disease was thought to be contagious, lepers were considered unclean (Lev. 13) so they had to wear bells around their ankles, warning people to keep away. Consequently they were isolated from loved ones, rejected by society and cut off from the worship of God. What sort of people do we reject in our society today?

Interestingly, the lepers didn't directly ask to be healed. 'Jesus, Master, have pity on us.' Jesus replied, 'Go show yourselves to the priests.' Why did He say this? Because only a priest had authority to pronounce they were healed and give permission for them to return into society (Lev. 14). 'As they went, they were cleansed.' Obedience to Jesus brought healing. Imagine how they felt as they saw new skin grow over diseased areas, and deformed joints restored. How joyful they must have been. Yet only one of them returned. Praising God with a loud voice, he 'threw himself at Jesus' feet and thanked him'. He was a Samaritan. What a bombshell! Jews didn't have anything to do with Samaritans … but Jesus did, for He crossed the barriers of culture. Do we easily cross cultural barriers?

When Jesus answers prayers or gives unexpected blessings, how do we respond? What is our attitude? Are we like the nine lepers forgetting to show any appreciation, or are we like the one leper, full of thankfulness and praise?

For prayer and reflection

'On your feet now – applaud GOD! … sing yourselves into his presence … Enter with the password; "Thank you!" Make yourselves at home, talking praise. Thank him. Worship him' (Psa. 100, *The Message*).

A **crippled** woman

For 18 long years this woman was crippled in her body with a 'spirit of infirmity' (AV); bent double (possibly with arthritis), causing her range of vision to be restricted, and mobility affected. Unable to look anyone in the eye, she was mercifully spared the embarrassment of her fellow worshippers' contemptuous glances in the synagogue.

But Jesus saw her, tucked away amongst the women – He notices everyone – and He called her over. She shuffled forward. As Jesus' sandalled feet came into sight she heard Him say, 'Woman, you are set free from your infirmity.' Gentle hands helped her to unbend. Jesus did not despise her, but treated her with respect. After 18 years she found herself looking into someone's face – His eyes were full of love for her. Immediately she burst into praise, knowing that this healing was a gift from Him.

Just as Jesus initiated an encounter with this ordinary crippled woman, releasing her from her infirmity, so He can touch our lives. Perhaps we feel emotionally crippled, recognising that deep within us we are so hurting that we have never broken free from childish attitudes and behaviours. Although we are adults we may find ourselves crippled with childish desires which insist on their own way, sulking when we don't get it. Or perhaps we feel timid like a child, unable to speak up for ourselves and so crippled that we hide away, never reaching our potential.

All of us are crippled to some degree from experiences in the past – are you able to pinpoint what is giving you a distorted view of life and how this may affect the way you behave? Let's allow the gentle touch of Jesus to free us to become mature adults.

Luke 13:10–17

'Woman, you are set free from your infirmity.' (v.12)

For prayer and reflection

Jesus, healer and restorer, please set me free from childish and immature attitudes. Show me if I have a distorted image of You and help me to see You as You truly are.

207

A **blind** man

Mark 10:46–52

' "What do you want me to do for you?" Jesus asked him.' (v.51)

Jesus and His disciples are journeying through Jericho on their way to Jerusalem, when they pass a blind man begging at the roadside. Hearing the commotion, this man, Bartimaeus, calls out, 'Jesus, Son of David.' But the crowd rebuke him – after all what use is such a man to anyone? But Bartimaeus isn't to be silenced; he knows what he wants, so shouts even louder. Stopping His journey, Jesus asks, 'What do you want me to do for you?' The man didn't have to think twice … 'I want to see.'

Jesus replied, '… your faith has healed you,' and Bartimaeus immediately received his sight. What a joy to see shapes, colours, movement and smiling faces for the first time. His life took on a different dimension.

This encounter teaches us much. Bartimaeus wasn't discouraged when the crowd shouted abuse at him, for he was determined to meet Jesus. His request for healing was specific and he firmly placed his faith in Jesus, (nothing else). His healing ended years of darkness – physical and spiritual – for we see Bartimaeus begin a spiritual journey by following Jesus.

Are we in spiritual darkness? Perhaps we're blind to our own faults; or blind to where Jesus wants to lead us and can't see what He wants to do in our lives.

These verses also challenge us to be more like Jesus … to be ready to stop what we are doing, set aside our own agendas and be there for needy, vulnerable people. I don't know about you, but I sometimes find it difficult to know when to stop and help others, and when to look after my own needs.

Jesus got the balance right, he was able to do both.

For prayer and reflection

Jesus asks you personally today, 'What do you want Me to do for you?' How will you answer? 'I want … '

A **curious** man

W e spend another day in Jericho, with the crowds elbowing one another in an attempt to catch a glimpse of this amazing man, Jesus. He had just healed Bartimaeus, what was He going to do next? There was one man who was curious to know – Zacchaeus. Physically small in stature, he was a chief tax collector, who had probably gained his wealth by underhand methods. Determined to satisfy his curiosity, Zacchaeus threw aside his dignity, ran ahead of the crowd and climbed a tree.

Here is an ordinary healthy man, with no perceived need, apart from a desire to satisfy his curiosity to see Jesus. Curiosity often draws us to acquire knowledge, to seek out the secrets of nature, and attracts us to discover love in others. How curious are we to learn more about Jesus and His ways? Let's see where Zacchaeus' curiosity led him. Re-read the verse for today. Jesus invited Himself! 'I *must* be your guest.' He didn't ask if it was convenient! Jesus displayed the sovereignty of His grace in choosing such a sinner, just as He graciously chooses us and comes into our lives. What was the result of Zacchaeus' curiosity? A new man was born ... a man of compassion, 'I will give half of my possessions to the poor;' a man of honesty, 'For all those I have cheated I will pay back four times the amount.'

Curiosity about Jesus can be dangerous! It can change us. Zacchaeus welcomed Jesus into his house – is Jesus welcome in yours? There are some houses where He wouldn't stay long because the talk, the atmosphere and the whole surroundings would be offensive to Him. What about our inner house? Is that fit for Jesus to enter? Or does it need cleaning and disinfecting?

Luke 19:1–9

'Zacchaeus, come down immediately. I must stay at your house today.' (v.5)

For prayer and reflection

Jesus, birth in me a greater curiosity to see 'what You are up to'. As I welcome You into my heart please do something new and transform my life.

WEEKEND

Accept one another

For reflection: Romans 14:13; 15:7; 1 Peter 3:8

Following Christ calls us to embrace love as a way of life, and accept others for who they are. Let's be honest with ourselves – are we prejudiced against others?

Just because people are individuals and may choose to do things differently from us, doesn't mean they're wrong and we're right. No doubt many of us subtly carry preconceived opinions of others and are biased in how we perceive them to be, and expect them to act. 'Who are you to judge your neighbour?' (James 4:12). Judging others hardens the heart and it is not long before criticism is given a free rein. Our little tongues spew out words, like sewage spilling over, contaminating others. But an accepting heart gives us such a different picture, one of life and growth as love is poured out.

Think of one person who plays a part in your life whose differences you find hard to accept.

Ask God to help you learn from these differences – perhaps you will gain a new perspective, or see new ways of doing things. Rejoice that we're all different and not everyone is like you!

Remember – accepting others holds no judgment or prejudice.

A **despondent** man

Today we meet a paralysed man lying by the pool of Bethesda, hoping to benefit from its healing waters. The dialogue between the man and Jesus is filled with implications for us.

Jesus asked the man, 'Do you want to get well?' 'Of course,' is the reply we'd expect. But let's think about it. What would be the implications if this man became well after 38 years of paralysis? He was a beggar and could lose a lucrative income if he was cured, and his condition meant he might never have learned a trade.

It's a question we would do well to ask ourselves. Many Christians hold on tightly to the things that paralyse them spiritually. Jesus can heal us of these things. But if He does, there will inevitably be change, and this can be scary – for with change comes fear, insecurity, stress and sorrow. Some of us may feel so comfortable living in the landscape of our inner lives that we want things to remain the same. I knew a disabled lady who didn't want to get better because losing her disability living allowance would bring frightening changes.

The paralysed man didn't answer Jesus' question. Instead he offered an excuse. 'I'm all alone. I have no one to help me.' While what the man said was true, perhaps despondency had clouded his ability to see how things could change and he had lost the will to be cured. His words implied, 'I can't help myself and God isn't here to help either.'

Paying no attention to his excuse, Jesus said, 'Get up and walk.' Only as the man obeyed did he experience healing.

Jesus doesn't come to us today accepting our excuses and saying 'Poor you' in harmony with us. His message is 'Get up and walk'.

John 5:1–15

'I have no-one to help me into the pool ...' (v.7)

For prayer and reflection

What areas of your life do you want Jesus to heal? Are you despondent? Pray that Jesus' healing love will penetrate deeper than your fears, and give you hope.

An **adulterous** woman

John 8:2–11

'Then neither do
I condemn you …
Go now and leave
your life of sin.'
(v.11)

Have you ever been caught red-handed in an activity that caused guilt and shame? That is bad enough, but then to be dragged into a public place and have your sin exposed – what humiliation. Little wonder this woman trembled as she stood before the crowd, knowing that adultery was subject to death by stoning. Sounds unbelievably cruel, doesn't it?

The atmosphere was electric. The woman was a pawn in a game as the Pharisees tried to trap Jesus. They were desperate to accuse Him, so they questioned Him. 'In the Law Moses commanded us to stone such women. Now what do you say?' (v.5). Nothing happened – silence fell. Jesus was writing something in the dust with His finger. Eventually He straightened up, saying, 'If any one of you is without sin, let him be the first to throw a stone at her' (v.7). One by one the men peeled away, until eventually the woman found herself standing alone with Jesus. He didn't condemn her, nor did He condone what she had done, but told her to sin no more. Still trembling, she marvelled, 'I can't believe it. This man Jesus has saved me from certain death.'

For prayer and reflection

What areas of our lives are ungodly? Let's repent and remind ourselves, 'there is no condemnation for those who are in Christ Jesus' (Rom. 8.1).

We may not be like this promiscuous woman giving ourselves to another man, but it is all too easy to give ourselves to other things that are not godly. Perhaps there have been times when we have experienced the heaviness of guilt and the overwhelming darkness of spirit following sin's enticement … ending up feeling exposed and ashamed of ourselves. Yes, we deserve to be punished, for 'the wages of sin is death' (Rom. 6:23). But Jesus has paid the penalty for our sin by dying on the cross; thus like this woman we are saved from death to enjoy a gift of life.

A **paralysed** man

I n our society there seems to be a strong dislike for the little word 'sin'. Those using it are accused of imposing their morality on others. This word also aroused intense feelings in today's story.

When the paralytic man was lowered through the roof and Jesus pronounced forgiveness for his sins the religious teachers retorted that this was blasphemous – the Old Testament Law taught that only God could forgive sins. Jesus then healed the paralytic, demonstrating that God was working through Him, confirming His authority to forgive sins. We aren't told if there's any connection between this man's sin and his paralysis, but perhaps a past sin had given rise to a guilty conscience and this emotion had then become expressed in his body as paralysis. Whatever the reason, this man allowed God's forgiveness to penetrate the core of his being, and he was healed.

Have you a guilty conscience for past sins? Perhaps you have had an abortion, hurt or deceived someone, or had a secret affair. Receiving forgiveness can be difficult for some women because they have such low self-esteem they feel they don't deserve such a gift; whereas others may think they can work hard and clear the debt themselves. Then there are those who have a clear intellectual understanding of forgiveness, but whose hearts have never been touched. They're still trapped.

Allowing Jesus' forgiveness to penetrate our whole being breaks the bonds that paralyse our ability to be the women God has purposed us to be. I have had the privilege of seeing women freed from migraines, chest palpitations and depression as they have received the fullness of Jesus' forgiveness for past sins.

Mark 2:1–12

'Son, your sins are forgiven.' (v.5)

For prayer and reflection

There are no sins too big for God to forgive. 'Daughter, your sins are forgiven.' Father, help me to receive Your forgiveness into the centre of my being. I'm forgiven! Alleluia!

An **impetuous** woman

John 20:10–18

'Then the disciples went back to their homes, but Mary stood outside the tomb crying.' (vv.10–11)

hat comes into your mind when you think of Mary Magdalene? A seductress with flirtatious eyes? A prostitute? Passionate? She had been trapped by what others called 'demons'. Her behaviour was bizarre and she longed to be 'normal'. Then she met Jesus – an encounter that changed her life (Luke 8:2). He drove out the 'demons' that had ruined her life and then welcomed her into His group of friends – there was no hesitation. The natives of the small town of Magdala were shocked. It was one thing for men to become His disciples – but a woman? Her place was to stay at home!

But Mary didn't stay at home; she stayed close to Jesus. At the cross – Mary was there. When Jesus' body was taken to the tomb – Mary was there. Looking into the tomb she saw two angels who spoke to her. Then Jesus revealed Himself to her, but she didn't recognise Him at first. (How typically characteristic of an impetuous nature!) But when He called her name her spiritual eyes were opened. She was the first person to see Him, and was given the responsibility to go and tell the other disciples. How wonderful that Jesus had entrusted Himself and the news of His resurrection to a woman with such a history. No doubt she ran laughing and crying to tell the disciples, but how sad that they didn't at first believe her, they thought she had 'lost it' (Luke 24:11)!

This story of Mary brings hope to us all, as whatever our past, it is a reminder that Jesus values us and entrusts us with His truth. As women, He doesn't perceive us as second-rate people. Jesus needs fervent women in His Church today and has a place for you – a role uniquely yours.

For prayer and reflection

Stay close to Jesus and whatever He has called you to do, remember it is ' "Not by might nor by power, but by my Spirit," says the LORD Almighty' (Zech. 4:6).

A **compelled** man

Simon, an unknown man, was innocently getting on with his life. He was travelling from Cyrene (about 800 miles from Jerusalem) and 'was passing by on his way in from the country' (Mark 15:21). He had long wanted to come to Jerusalem, particularly to the Passover and probably knew little or nothing about the turmoil going on in the city. Was it mere chance that he was there in the street just as Jesus stumbled by with His cross, on the way to Golgotha? Simon 'passed by' neither too soon nor too late. Just think of how many divine interventions had worked together to bring him to encounter Jesus at this specific time – but so the Lord would have it, and so it came about.

Quietly mingling with the crowd, Simon was greatly surprised when a rough hand gripped his arm. 'Shoulder that cross,' bellowed a stern voice. Simon felt forced to comply – there was no resisting a Roman centurion. Being compelled to carry Jesus' cross brought Simon closer to Jesus. As the crossbeam was lifted onto Simon's shoulders he caught a glimpse of Jesus' face – what anguish he saw, love mingled with sorrow. Walking behind Jesus and following in His footsteps, perhaps Simon thought, 'I am so privileged to carry His cross.' Jesus had often said, 'If anyone would come after me, he must deny himself and take up his cross daily and follow me' (Luke 9:23), and now this principle is illustrated in a real situation.

C.H. Spurgeon said, 'They see Jesus best who carry his cross most.' Today, Jesus' love compels us to be cross-bearers. This may mean quietly submitting to God's providence, speaking out against rampant sin, or resisting self-promotion. What does it mean for you?

Luke 23:26–31

'... they seized Simon ... and put the cross on him and made him carry it behind Jesus.' (v.26)

For prayer and reflection

When we take up our cross, it will cost us, change us and challenge us. My prayer is, 'Help me Jesus'.

WEEKEND

Encourage one another

For reflection: Hebrews 3:12–13; 10:24–25; 1 Thessalonians 5:11

Sharing our lives with others in our fellowship builds a relationship from which the giving and receiving of encouragement can flow. Regardless of gifting we are all called to encourage one another. The Hebrews readings remind us that our resolve to follow Christ may weaken under difficulties and thus we are to encourage one another to keep pressing on with our walk with the Lord, despite obstacles and fatigue. The Hebrew word 'encourage' literally means, 'to stir up, to provoke, to incite people in a given direction'.

When going through a particularly difficult time I can recall a friend leaving a candle and card on my doorstep. The card, with a beautiful picture of a sunrise, simply said, 'After every night there's a morning'. Lighting the candle and meditating on the words and picture renewed my confidence in God's faithfulness. What an encouragement.

Think of a friend facing difficulties. Consider:

- Giving a card, flowers or chocolates;
- Giving time to listen and encourage;
- Exploring new creative ways to encourage.

Remember – 'Encouragement is the kind of expression that helps someone want to be a better Christian, even when life is rough' (Larry Crabb).

A **wealthy** man

W e know this man had great wealth (v.22); was a ruler (Luke 18:18); and was young (Matt. 19:22); hence he is invariably referred to as 'the rich young ruler'. Note how keen he is to encounter Jesus. He runs to Him, asking, 'What must I do to inherit eternal life?' He assures Jesus that he has kept all the commandments required of him. Then Jesus looks him in the eye and lovingly says, 'Go, sell everything you have and give to the poor ... Then come, follow me' (v.21).

The story takes an unexpected turn. The man's face falls; this is the last thing he wants to hear. He was not about to relinquish his riches. So, with a heavy heart he walks away and, interestingly, Jesus makes no attempt to dissuade him. The conditions have been set. It was a straight choice, wealth or eternal life. Security with money, or a quality of life with love. 'Now this is eternal life: that they may know you, the only true God, and Jesus Christ ...' (John 17:3).

In spite of the Jews favouring the rich, Jesus says, 'It is hard for a rich man to enter the kingdom of God'. Indeed, 'It is easier for a camel to go through the eye of a needle' (v.25). Why? Because money tends to make us selfish, materialistic and can pull us away from depending on God. Money brings freedom to go anywhere, at any time, to do anything, and can distract us from being disciplined Christians, searching for God's will day by day. There is nothing wrong with wealth, or in having many other good things, but unless they are surrendered to God they can be stumbling blocks to a deeper relationship with Him.

What is your stumbling block?

Mark 10:17–29

'How hard it is for the rich to enter the kingdom of God!' (v.23)

For prayer and reflection

**Reflect on:
'... all things are possible with God' (v.27). Then pray, 'Almighty God, I surrender to You my money and ... (list the things that cause you to stumble).'**

217

A **poor** woman

Mark 12:41–44

'… she, out of
her poverty, put
in everything …'
(v.44)

Yesterday we learnt about a rich man. In contrast, today we find out about a poor woman. The wealthy ruler gave nothing, but the poor widow gave all.

Financially reliant on her family and struggling to make ends meet, this widow carefully budgeted. She only had 'two very small copper coins' but she knew exactly what she wanted to do with them. Unashamed of her threadbare clothes, she walked barefoot into the Temple. The rich men jostled her as they arrogantly strode up to the treasury box, ostentatiously throwing in large amounts of money. Money from their abundance. In contrast the woman kept her head down and inconspicuously dropped her coins into the box, whispering, 'God, this is Yours.' Unbeknown to her, Jesus was watching and saw her extravagance. Drawing His disciples' attention to this woman's generosity, He said, 'The rich gave what they'll never miss, but she gave what she couldn't afford – she gave everything.'

What are we to make of Jesus' words? Giving money itself has no value to God, but giving has everything to do with the heart. How generous are our hearts? 'Each man should give what he has decided in his heart to give, not reluctantly or under compulsion, for God loves a cheerful giver' (2 Cor. 9:7).

Today's story disturbs my comfort zone. Am I prepared to give everything to God? When God asks me to give sacrificially I am tempted to think about what I could do with the money, so I have to remind myself that *everything* belongs to God – we just share in what He has! What is it 'that demands my soul, my life, my all'?

As Isaac Watts says, 'Love so amazing, so divine'. A love that Jesus demonstrated on the cross.

For prayer and reflection

Jesus take my heart … where there is self-indulgence, may there be generosity; where there is fear to give and let go, may there be trust and peace.

A **humble** man

Mark 1:1–8

'… I am not worthy …' (v.7)

ulfilling prophecy, God sent John the Baptist to prepare the way for His Son. At birth John was filled with the Holy Spirit and anointed, 'he will be great in the sight of the Lord' (Luke 1:15). Being born about six months before his cousin, Jesus, they probably spent their childhood years together, going their own ways when John went into the desert. Here he lived a hermit's life, eating locusts and wild honey. Then, when Jesus was about 30, John appeared preaching on the banks of the Jordan.

John was fearless in his denunciation of wrongdoing, calling his listeners to confess their sins, repent and prepare themselves spiritually for Jesus, the true Messiah. When asked by the Jewish authorities to give an account of himself, John describes himself merely as a 'voice'. His early years with Jesus had so impacted his life that he said in effect, 'My task is to call your attention to one who is more powerful than I, the thongs of whose sandals I am not worthy to stoop down and untie'. John's one desire dominating his heart and mind was to let Jesus take centre stage while he retired to the wings. 'He must become greater; I must become less' (John 3:30). Oh that we might have the same desire and become humble!

Growing in humility is a lifetime's work and the quality that stunts this growth is pride. Pride has to be bigger and better than anyone else; it knows it all, is not teachable, it wants to impress, it cannot receive, and seeks the glory of man. If we cannot lay aside pride, we'll run out of humility and God cannot increase in us. So let's despise the pride in ourselves and refuse to yield to it anymore. May we be like John and humbly point people to Jesus.

For prayer and reflection

Lord Jesus, help me to put a sign on my heart that says, 'Jesus is centre stage', and may I grow in humility.

An **ambitious** woman

Matthew 20:20–28

'Grant that one of these two sons of mine may sit … in your kingdom.' (v.21)

Ambition! No doubt you have met workmates ambitious for promotion, status and financial reward; or friends ambitious for an upfront ministry; or parents ambitious for their children – pushing them to achieve the things they themselves missed out on. How ambitious are we? Ambition is not wrong. It's what we do with our inner drive to succeed.

Salome, a mother who was ambitious for her sons, John and James, was married to Zebedee (a fisherman), came from a humble background and unexpectedly found herself exalted to a privileged position. She became the proud mother of two of the three disciples closest to Jesus (Peter being the other). Salome had heard Jesus speak many times of His new kingdom and she desperately wanted her sons to achieve what she couldn't – a position of honour when the new kingdom of Israel was established. So much so, that she became a 'pushy' mother.

Along with James and John, she came to Jesus requesting a favour. Her maternal pride and jealousy drove her to ask for the wrong things. 'Please award my two sons the highest places of honour in Your kingdom, one on Your right and one on Your left.' How 'pushy' can you get! No wonder the other disciples were furious. How arrogant to think that her sons were more special than they were. What was Jesus' answer? 'You don't know what you are asking.' High rank in the kingdom of God calls for drinking His cup, and that cup for Jesus, meant death.

Let's ask some personal questions – in what areas of life am I 'pushy'? Am I ambitious to achieve and to gain status, in order to feel good about myself or am I driven by God's love, and ambitious to be found doing His will?

For prayer and reflection

Heavenly Father, forgive me when I harbour self-seeking desires in my heart. Help me to remember these words, 'Do nothing out of selfish ambition' (Phil. 2:3).

A **religious** man

I feel annoyed when people label me 'religious'.
I explain that my faith is not about legalistically
keeping to a set of rules, but about having a
relationship with Jesus, and I would rather they call me
'Christian'.

Nicodemus was a religious man, a Pharisee, who
kept religious laws to the 'nth' degree. Many Pharisees
opposed Jesus, and those who didn't practise what they
preached He called 'hypocrites' (Matt. 23:13,15,23,25).
It would appear that Nicodemus broke this mould for he
was courteous throughout his conversation with Jesus.
Why he came to Jesus at night is speculative, but the
physical darkness mirrored his inner spiritual darkness.
As a dev-out orthodox Jew, Nicodemus assumed his
credentials automatically assured him a place in the
kingdom. So what a shock when Jesus said that only a
spiritual birth would bring him into God's kingdom and
enable him to have a spiritual life, just as physical birth
brings physical life. Becoming a Christian has nothing to
do with religion, but everything to do with experiencing
a spiritual rebirth; knowing that light has penetrated the
inner darkness of a sin-hardened heart that now belongs
to Jesus. Nicodemus became a transformed man and one
of Jesus' followers (John 7:50; 19:38–42).

I believe that religious symbols and rituals have their
place and can be very helpful in drawing us closer to
Jesus, providing we don't feel so legally bound to them
that they become more important than Jesus. Pippa
believed that to be a good Christian she should go to
church twice every Sunday, and she felt riddled with
guilt when she couldn't. Are you legalistically bound by
'shoulds and oughts' in your walk with Jesus?

John 3:1–21

'... no-one can see
the kingdom of
God unless he is
born again.' (v.3)

**For prayer and
reflection**

**Forgive me,
Jesus, when I put
more importance
on religious
rules than my
relationship with
You. May I do
things out of love
for You, rather
than because I
'ought' to.**

WEEKEND

Serve one another

For reflection: Galatians 5:13–15; 1 Peter 4:9; Ephesians 5:21

If we love one another then we will serve one another, and if we serve one another we shall not destroy others by 'biting and devouring' them. Love is constructive because it serves. Jesus said, 'I am among you as one who serves' (Luke 22:27). He demonstrated a servant heart by pouring His life out to the last drop for others, and it didn't matter to Him whether He received praise or blame.

To be a servant to others is to meet their needs, to be useful and to carry out duties. In serving one another it's important that we don't use others as 'objects' to serve us, in order to meet our own needs; but rather to respect one another and give ourselves freely to serve them genuinely and wholeheartedly.

Over this weekend consider ways you can serve others.
- Make a cake, go shopping or mow a lawn for a needy person;
- Offer hospitality;
- Visit someone who is downhearted or housebound;
- Commit yourself to a practical need in the church.

Remember – 'Truly to love somebody is not to possess him for myself but to serve him for himself' (John Stott).

An **uptight** woman

W hen Jesus travelled up to Jerusalem, He often stayed in Bethany, a little village a couple of miles out of the city. Here He enjoyed the welcome hospitality of His friends, Mary, Martha and Lazarus.

On this occasion Martha was stressed because her well-known guests, all 13 of them, had dropped in unexpectedly. She was an energetic, practical person with a servant heart and possibly felt over-responsible for her guests thinking everything had to be 'just right'. Making them feel at home was her pride and joy, but she battled with herself. She was irritable because her sister wasn't doing what she expected her to do, ie help. Martha became furious. Flouncing into the dining area, she caught sight of Mary still sitting, listening to Jesus. She exploded, 'It's just not fair!' Martha didn't seem to care that she was accusing her sister in the presence of her guests and, embarrassingly, demanded that Jesus should tell Mary to help her.

How do we handle tension in our lives? No doubt many of us find ourselves getting uptight like Martha and perhaps become irritable with our nearest and dearest. But how much of our rushing around is really necessary? Are we trying to make a good impression? Who are we trying to please? A servant heart is important, as Jesus obviously felt at home with the ever-practical Martha, so what was the problem? It wasn't the unprepared vegetables and messy kitchen – it was her attitude towards Mary.

Today there is often tension in church between the Marthas and the Marys. Do others irritate us? Yet we need both these characteristics – practicality and devotion – if we are to serve God's humanity, and worship His divinity.

Luke 10:38–42

'Martha, Martha … you are worried and upset about many things …' (v.41)

For prayer and reflection

Jesus values spiritual fellowship more than physical nourishment (v.42). Do we become 'uptight' and irritable because we love doing God's work more than we love God?

Two **grieving** women

'Lord, if you had been here, my brother would not have died.' (v.32)

For prayer and reflection

Thank You, Jesus, that You loved these sisters with their totally different personalities and that You understand the way I grieve. Help me to trust You with the big picture.

The next meeting between Jesus and this family was under extremely sad circumstances. Lazarus was seriously ill. Having sent this news to Jesus, the sisters had absolute confidence that He would respond immediately and come. But Jesus delayed His coming and Lazarus died.

When Jesus finally arrived in Bethany, He received two different responses from the grieving sisters – there is no right or wrong way to grieve. Martha had possibly grown impatient with the four days of weeping and wailing at the funeral wake, and rushed out to meet Jesus. Whereas Mary, paralysed with grief, chose to stay at home. Perhaps she felt the pain too deeply, or was too disappointed in Jesus' delay to go out and greet Him. When she eventually went to Him, in true 'Mary' devotional style, she fell at His feet. 'If you had been here, my brother would not have died.' Words also echoed by her sister (v.21). These words express faith and perhaps reproach. 'You should have been here. You could have changed things!' What was Jesus' reaction to their grief? To weep with them.

When we pray for some important and desperate need, eg a child suffering or unemployment looming, we launch our desperate prayers heavenward, confident in Jesus. But if our child dies, or we have to move house because of unemployment, we're torn by doubt and disappointment. When praying in difficult circumstances I've often felt like throwing rocks at the silent sky! Why doesn't God respond? But Jesus had a purpose that people weren't able to grasp until Lazarus was raised (v.42). Don't let God's apparent failure to answer prayer rob you of His love, for He is working behind the scenes.

A **worshipping** woman

It was Passover in six days' time, and on His way to Jerusalem Jesus again stopped off in Bethany. He was the honoured guest at a special dinner. Martha was busying herself in the kitchen (no irritability with Mary this time!); and Lazarus, who had just come back from the dead, was reclining next to the Master. What was Mary up to?

She was a woman of profound inner thoughts. Reminding herself of the times Jesus had spoken about His coming suffering, she sensed His days on earth were numbered. Was this His farewell meal? With a deepening desire to thank her Lord, she took a little jar and poured sweet-smelling drops of perfume upon Jesus' feet. The perfume, a funeral embalming oil, was very costly – perhaps it represented her life savings. But for Mary the cost didn't matter; this act of worship expressed her devotion to a Lord she loved with all her heart and soul. Humbly she knelt before Him, lovingly drying His feet with her hair. What a picture of true worship. Her loving act 'filled the house' with fragrance. There is always something beautiful about doing things out of love, rather than out of a mere sense of duty, or obligation. It is like fragrance filling the air.

But one person found this sweet smell offensive. Judas angrily questions the wisdom of her action, calling it an act of extravagance. Jesus defends Mary, 'Leave her alone. It was intended that she save this perfume for the day of my burial.' Although Mary probably never knew the significance of her actions, she represents a model for the worship of Jesus. Her humble spirit and desire to bless Him challenges us.

True service for Jesus starts with kneeling at His feet.

John 12:1–11

'Then Mary … poured [expensive perfume] on Jesus' feet and wiped his feet with her hair.' (v.3)

For prayer and reflection

'Come, let us bow down in worship, let us kneel before the LORD our Maker' (Psa. 95:6); 'worship at his footstool' (Psa. 99:5). I love You, Jesus.

A **weak** man

**Matthew
27:11–26**

'I am innocent
… It is your
responsibility!'
(v.24)

Over the past few weeks we've met many
people, with their different personalities
and characters and have seen the impact
Jesus had upon them. The last person we meet is Pilate,
the Roman Governor of Judea – a cruel, weak man with
a reputation for being corrupt and inhumane. He hated
the Jews. This story reveals him as an absolute coward.

The Jews despised Jesus because they viewed His
claim to be the Son of God as blasphemous, so they
brought this charge against Him at the Sanhedrin.
However, because they had no power to carry out
capital punishment, they handed Jesus over to
Pilate for execution. It's clear that Pilate found Jesus
innocent. 'I find no basis for a charge against him'
(John 18:38; 19:4,6) and he became frightened as
he tried to withstand the Jews' pressure on him to
have Jesus crucified (John 19:8). His fear caused him
to take a cowardly way out. He chose to avoid any
responsibility by offering the crowd either Jesus, the
teacher and healer, or Barabbas, an insurrectionist who
had committed murder. 'It's your responsibility. You're
judge and jury.' When the crowd chose Barabbas, Pilate
was shocked. He had made his choice and was hating
the outcome. He had put reputation above integrity and
tried to wash his hands of the whole affair.

How often does our desire to please the crowd, thus
saving our reputation, win over our desire to please
God? Are we courageous enough to speak out for truth,
committing ourselves to do what is right, whatever
the cost – or do we cowardly run away? I recognise I
sometimes have a tendency to please man rather than
God. But as with Pilate, Jesus stands before us, and we
must decide who we will choose to please.

**For prayer and
reflection**

**'The fear of the
Lord leads to life'
(Prov. 19:23).
When I am
tempted to fear
man more than
You, Lord, please
give me a gift of
courage to choose
Your ways.**

Ephesians –

seeing the full picture

Anne Le Tissier

Anne writes books, magazine articles, and Bible reading notes, impassioned to disciple women and encourage them to fulfil their potential in and for God. She also hopes to expand her boundaries and reach out through fiction.

Anne is a wife, mum and granny, enjoys hill walking, playing and listening to music, a good film, a good read, growing her own veg, and relaxing over a meal with close friends and family. She dislikes offal, and soggy dishcloths.

Seeing the full picture

Ephesians 1:3–10

'… to bring all things in heaven and on earth together under one head, even Christ.' (v.10)

A skilled artist sees the overall picture in his mind's eye before he sets even a brush stroke on the canvas. Some artists can create pictures in such manner as to obscure the intended image for as long as possible. A dab here, a few lines there, they invite avid viewers to guess what the picture will be, as they skilfully bring together its random components into one intended whole.

Reading Paul's letter to the Church in and around the vicinity of Ephesus, circa AD 60, it might well be compared to a work of art. Scattered throughout six chapters, various topics appear ad hoc, or so it would seem – salvation, grace, church, lifestyle, unity, relationships, prayer and even armour, for example. But on further reflection they all blend together into one glorious whole, one eternal purpose, one intended theme of life both now and for the future; an exquisite picture in which we all have a special part to play.

Rather than leave us guessing until the end of the letter, however, let's take a sneak preview at that overall image to help us engage with its detail. It is God's plan to reconcile all people to Himself through the Lordship of His Son Jesus Christ, thereby enabling believers to share in His risen life. Indeed, we were chosen to share in the power, wisdom and riches of God both now and for eternity. Through each of our lives that make up His Body, the Church, Christ continues to fulfil God's purpose that He began with His earthly ministry; and therein we find all manner of implications for your life and mine today.

For prayer and reflection

Thank You, Jesus, that Your blood bought my life not only for my sake, but that I too may take up my role in fulfilling God's glorious will.

WEEKEND

Life from God's perspective

For reflection: Ephesians 1:22–23; 3:10–11; 4:14–15

It's not just Paul's letter to Ephesus which may compare to art, for our lives too may sometimes appear like a painting in the making. A splash of colour here, a scrawl of squiggles there, that leave us guessing haphazardly what picture God had in mind when He designed its random parts – a conglomerate of diversified activities, beliefs, opinions, relationships, responsibilities, obligations, ministries, hobbies, memories, dreams, regrets, aspirations and so on. Surveying them all from our limited perspective may sometimes be disheartening as we struggle to juggle their separate parts, tugged this way and that to maintain momentum.

Does this describe you? Then pause this weekend, and pray for fresh perspective. For God appointed Jesus to be head over all and to fill everything with His fullness, to bring order and purpose to our work, relationships, faith and ministry. Our loving Father planned our lives from design stage to completion – lives filled with His ongoing potential and purpose to fulfil His will and satisfy our needs: physically, mentally, emotionally and spiritually.

Jesus said, '… I have come that they may have life, and have it to the full' (John 10:10).

A canvas **in a picture-frame**

Ephesians 1:1–2

'… the faithful in Christ Jesus.' (v.1)

Paul's letter, written from prison, travelled with Tychicus to the west coast of Asia Minor (modern-day Turkey), to the wealthy port of Ephesus. As the capital of a Roman province, it remained beneath the watchful eye of Rome's ruling governor, but its Greek and Jewish inhabitants were permitted sufficient liberties to live, work and worship in accord with their cultural dictates. And so, with warmth, Paul greeted the believers 'in Christ Jesus', a term used frequently throughout this letter concerning faith, salvation, spiritual blessings, purpose, love, power, tasks, unity and the Church. And just as the themes of Paul's letter all fit within this framework, so also the picture of our lives sits securely in Christ.

Everything that encompasses who we are – our faith, salvation, purpose, talents, responsibilities, relationships and role in the Church – find meaning for life 'in Christ Jesus'. When we fully appreciate who we are 'in Christ', our sense of self-worth and our need for a purpose no longer arise from the things we do, the people we know or our perception of success, ability, knowledge, spirituality and so on. Jesus is the frame in which our living canvas sits. In Him we find comfort, hope, strength, inspiration, guidance and purpose for life – and so He brings meaning into every detailed facet of the picture of our lives.

But a canvas without a supporting frame turns at the corners, folds in on itself then crumples to the floor. Is your life sitting 'in Christ' – and if not, who or what is propping you up? Choose today to discard those temporary crutches that will inevitably fail, and find all the support you need by engaging with life 'in Christ'.

For prayer and reflection

Lord Jesus, as You are the One who encompasses my entire life, help me to distinguish then discard anything in which I seek the support that only You can provide.

Living with **heavenly power**

I
f Paul sent us a letter in which he praised God for giving us a millionaire's inheritance from long-lost Aunty Flo, the cancellation of our mortgage debt or the new-found cure for our loved-one's fatal illness, I feel sure we'd be hugging the postman, jumping for joy and joining Paul with shouts of praise to God. But do we get as excited to hear that God has 'blessed us in the heavenly realms with every spiritual blessing in Christ'? Somehow, it doesn't hit the spot with quite the same impact! But Paul, who had died to the flesh-life, saw and lived his new life in Christ from God's eternal perspective (Gal. 2:19–20), and it's on these heavenly realms that we also need to focus.

This place is the spiritual environment where the forces of good and evil battle to win control over men's hearts (Eph. 6:12). Without the protection of Christ's perfect blood it's a dangerous place to go, but we who believe and are therefore in Christ, may receive its spiritual blessings. These priceless, heavenly gifts include an intimate relationship with God as Father, the infilling of the Holy Spirit, an awesome heavenly inheritance, the enabling of God's immense power, the comfort of His unconditional love and purpose in life, just to name a few of those mentioned (1:17,13–14,18–20; 2:8–10). Furthermore, Paul confirms that not one believer is excluded from these blessings (2:11–18).

Absolutely nothing can ever hope to compare with such amazing promises, but it's only as we live in Christ and as we set our minds and hearts on this heavenly realm, that we then begin to appreciate their value and potential.

Are you hugging the postman yet – I rather think you should!

Ephesians 1:3

'… blessed us in the heavenly realms with every spiritual blessing in Christ.' (v.3)

For prayer and reflection

Lord, please help me to set my mind and heart on You in the heavenly realms, that these blessings may excite me far more than anything or anyone on earth.

Using the **eyes of your heart**

**Ephesians
1:15–21**

'… that God …
may give you the
Spirit of wisdom
and revelation, so
that you may know
him better.' (v.17)

As much as we might believe in the powerful potential of yesterday's promised blessings, some of us may not feel we've experienced them to the extent that Paul describes, while others may be too overwhelmed with the physical needs of life to get all that excited. When a loved one is suffering with an incurable disease or our business is threatened with bankruptcy, 'heavenly realms' and 'spiritual blessings' may not feel like pressing priorities.

Simply knowing about God's immense power and purpose is one thing, but we need to know Christ and how to engage with His power for ourselves if we want it to have any impact. Paul was able to face extreme physical hardship (irregular income, ill-health, torture, imprisonment and so on) because he learnt to live his physical life in the heavenly realms of spiritual blessings. His feet remained firmly on the ground but the reverend submission of his heart, mind, hands, feet, mouth and body became a fitting channel through which God could empower his life and impact the lives of countless others.

Paul wasn't disregarding the hardships of life with irrelevant spirituality; moreover he was and is offering invaluable guidance to help us live the victorious life in Christ that we often hear preached from the pulpit.

**For prayer and
reflection**

**Lord, I do want to
know You better,
please enlighten
the eyes of my
heart.**

We cannot see Jesus with our physical eyes but as we learn to live life in the heavenly realms we can seek to know Him with the enlightened eyes of our heart. Why? '… in order that' we may begin to live in the power of those glorious spiritual blessings, no matter what difficult circumstances harass our earthly lives. But as Paul's prayer infers, we cannot do it alone, we need God's Spirit to teach and reveal to us how to live such a life.

Sealed **or filled?**

I f an artist were depicting this letter with paint, he might lavish a wonderful colour across the expanse of the canvas, one that would ultimately touch every part of the picture – that which is the Holy Spirit, longing to fill every part of our lives. For as we saw yesterday, how can we live an empowered life unless the Spirit fills us, and how can we know Jesus with the eyes of our heart unless the Spirit reveals Him to us? But to receive His ever-increasing wisdom and revelation we need to move on from our initial conversion experience.

God deposits His Spirit into our hearts upon our first confession of faith, guaranteeing our future heavenly inheritance and the salvation of our souls. But perhaps some of us remain at the point of being sealed with the Spirit without seeking the further infilling that Paul's letter describes (3:19). This may simply be through ignorance of the Scriptures or may result from a worldly life that grieves the Spirit's holiness (4:30).

Either way, it leads me to wonder how often we try to make sense of our lives using limited human thinking; how many of us continue to live in our own strength and abilities, giving the appearance that we're living the life of faith, perhaps even assuming an air of perceived 'spirituality', when in reality we're nigh on empty of God's wisdom and power.

The seal of God's Holy Spirit is a mere foretaste of our glorious inheritance awaiting us in eternity but, likewise, a tempting taster of what we may enjoy with ever-increasing measure during our life on earth. Indeed, Paul encourages us to attain to 'the whole measure of the fulness of Christ', not merely a part (4:13).

Ephesians 1:13–14

'... marked in him with a seal, the promised Holy Spirit.' (v.13)

For prayer and reflection

Thank You, Lord, that I am sealed in You for eternity, but I pray for an ever-increasing measure of Your Spirit to empower my life for the present.

Filled **to the measure**

**Ephesians
3:12–21**

'… that you may
be filled to the
measure of all the
fulness of God.'
(v.19)

S tuttering tongues and fearful hearts burst into confident praise and proclamation (Acts 2). It was Pentecost, and the effect of the Holy Spirit poured out onto the cowering disciples was life-changing. But Paul wrote to the Ephesians long after Pentecost, for it was not intended as a one-off experience. Being filled with the Spirit is an ongoing lifetime goal, a journey of inward transformation as we keep trusting by faith, submitting to Christ as Lord and conforming to His nature and will, that we may be His fitting representatives in this godless, sin-weary world.

So where should we begin in our quest to be filled to increasing measure with His Spirit, the One who will teach us the life of the heavenly realms? Should we sign up for Bible college, stop mixing with non-believers or learn some special liturgy? No, Paul prays that first of all we might grasp the enormity of God's love. This is our starting point – grasping, knowing and engaging with God's outstanding love, and Scripture explains the reason why: 'We love because he first loved us' (1 John 4:19). So we can only truly love others as we first appreciate and receive God's love for us. And unless we love, the potential impact from being filled with the Spirit is nullified (1 Cor. 13:1–3).

That, therefore, is why we must first grasp the width, length, height and depth of God's love in order to be filled to the measure. So let's take time to open our hearts afresh to the spiritual blessings of the Father's awesome love. For without its living impact upon our hearts, the struggles of our earthly lives can sap its potential nourishment while any aspirations we have for His anointing are meaningless.

**For prayer and
reflection**

**'I have loved
you with an
everlasting love;
I have drawn
you with loving-
kindness' …
'Never will I
leave you; never
will I forsake
you' (Jer. 31:3;
Heb. 13:5).**

WEEKEND

Life in God's love

For reflection: Ephesians 2:1–9

Imagine yourself in a safe and secret place with God. He is sitting in the middle of the room, waiting for you patiently in the warmth of this candle-lit haven. He owns all the time in the world to embrace you, talk with you, care for you and listen to you – to love you as only He knows how. Perhaps you've known Him as Lord for some time, but are you still trying to earn His favour?

Have you taken on too much at church to impress Him with active service?

Have you set yourself rules and expectations to try and prove that you're good enough for Him?

Or are you constantly steeped in condemnation because you think you're too great a failure to deserve such grace and love?

Nothing and no one can satisfy you more and nothing you can do or say can make Him love you more. So,

Keep yourselves in God's love as you wait for the mercy of our Lord Jesus Christ to bring you to eternal life.

(Jude 21)

For a lack of self-worth and the enemy's lies may otherwise convince you that God does not or cannot really love you as much as Scripture says.

Living as **children of light**

Ephesians 5:1–9

'Be imitators of God, therefore, as dearly loved children.' (v.1)

Very young children are quick to imitate others – picking up words they overhear that would not normally be part of their vocabulary, for example; and you have probably heard a parent say, 'Don't do that or Johnny will copy you'. Furthermore, loving parents teach and encourage their children to live according to their own preferred behaviour code and moral standards, hoping that as they grow up they will reflect that upbringing in their adult relationships, work and so on.

I trust that we've emerged from the weekend basking in the radiance of God's love, for we are His dearly loved children and as such, Paul instructs us to imitate Him – to live a life of love (vv.1–2), bearing the fruit of goodness, righteousness and truth (v.9). In fact, God Himself throws down the gauntlet, '... be holy, because I am holy' (Lev. 11:45) and Jesus reaffirms it, 'Be perfect, therefore, as your heavenly Father is perfect' (Matt. 5:48).

We may well respond that it's impossible to be perfect while living in this imperfect world, but we've a divine challenge that we should not be seeking or settling for anything less.

So how can we hope to live a life without 'even a hint ... of any kind of impurity' (Eph. 5:3), for the strongest of will-powers and the best of intentions will never be sufficient to imitate God's ways? Well we certainly can't do it alone, but as we submit to the Spirit living within, allowing Him to transform our lives with ever-increasing measure, then the greater a reflection of God we shall become.

It's no wonder, therefore, that God longs to fill us with more of His Holy Spirit, and tomorrow we shall consider the part we can play to provide Him with greater capacity.

For prayer and reflection

Lord, You know that although I feel willing, in reality I'm weak (Matt. 26:41). Please overrule, infill and transform my life with Your goodness, righteousness and truth.

Getting **rid of the old**

magine you have a bowl filled with stones, and a jug of water – the bowl is your life, the stones represent aspects of your old self and the water is God's Holy Spirit. Even with stones inside, the bowl can be filled with water, just as God sealed you with His Holy Spirit on your first confession of faith. But if you were to remove some stones, it would create extra capacity to top up the bowl with more water.

Similarly, if we're going to create more capacity within our lives for God to fill us increasingly with His Spirit, something that is currently blocking us up will simply have to go. And so, Paul says, we must 'put off our old self ... be made new in our attitudes ... and put on the new self created to be like God'; or as John the Baptist once said, 'He must become greater; I must become less' (John 3:30).

To decrease and get rid of this old self, therefore, we have to make daily choices that will empty our lives of the worldly trash, increasing the capacity for the Spirit to reproduce God's righteousness and holiness in and through our lives. Consequently, the Spirit can renew the attitude of our mind and clothe us in the new self created to be like God (Eph. 4:23–24). And how long do we have to keep making these choices that remove our old self? – 'until we all reach unity in the faith and in the knowledge of the Son of God and become mature, attaining to the whole measure of the fulness of Christ' (4:13).

It's a life-long commitment to a life-long transformation, but one which will strengthen the Spirit's power within us with ever-increasing measure.

Ephesians 4:17–24

'... put off your old self ...' (v.22)

For prayer and reflection

Take time to allow the Spirit to highlight which 'stones' are getting in His way, then remain willing and obedient as He shows you how to remove them.

Victory in battle

**Ephesians
4:25–29**

'… and do not
give the devil a
foothold.' (v.27)

When we talk or hear about spiritual warfare we may back off, leaving it to those whom we perceive to have that specific prayer ministry. But there's a word here for all of us concerning the spiritual warfare we engage with daily in the heavenly realms as we live out our normal routines.

Paul begins to list just some of the numerous sinful traits that characterise our selfish and proud fallen nature, accompanying each prohibition with a positive command: put off deceitful pretences … live out the truth; stop stealing … work with your hands; prevent unwholesome talking … speak to encourage. And in all of this, Paul says, 'do not give the devil a foothold'.

As we seek to 'put off' and 'get rid of' our sinful self, we cannot actually take it off physically like a piece of clothing or get rid of it like the stones from yesterday's bowl, but we do so by acting in the opposite spirit to that which self would want. And this, therefore, necessitates obedience to the Holy Spirit's guidance. For example, when self tempts us to deceive we must choose to speak the truth; when tempted to criticise we choose to encourage; when tempted to be rude we choose to be kind; when tempted to hate we choose to love; when tempted to resent, we choose to forgive; when tempted to be greedy, we choose moderation.

When we indulge self we give the devil 'a foothold'; an opportunity to use our sinful nature to permeate his ungodly ways in and through our lives. But when we choose to put off that old self and live according to the Spirit of God – the Spirit of goodness, righteousness and truth – our lives will be filled to ever-increasing measure with His holy characteristics.

For prayer and reflection

What aspects of your sinful nature are still fighting for a place in your life? Live in the ways of God's Spirit and accomplish the victory you've longed for.

Our **Father's sorrow**

Ephesians 4:30–32

'And do not grieve the Holy Spirit ...' (v.30)

When our children rebel against the love we've showered upon them, the guidance and disciplines we've given to protect and support their health and welfare with their best intentions at heart, it's most upsetting. But how much more do we grieve the Holy Spirit with a lifestyle that ignores the guidance and discipline of our heavenly Father?

As parents, guardians or youth leaders, our reactions may vary with frustration, annoyance, anger, sadness, hurt and so on, but the deep distress and sorrow intimated by the word 'grieve' reminds us that selfish behaviour cuts to the heart of the One who loves us perfectly and wants His chosen best for our lives. The more we appreciate God's love for us, the greater our awareness of just how much we hurt Him when we live in open rebellion to His holy, righteous ways. And as our appreciation and love deepens in response, we'll experience an ever-increasing desire to please Him rather than grieve Him with our behaviour.

'This is love for God: to obey his commands ...' (1 John 5:3) – to obey the Spirit's guidance as to how to live out lives in all righteousness and truth, that we may imitate our Father and clothe ourselves with Christ (Rom. 13:14). Some of us may find it tempting to skim-read passages like Ephesians 4, assuming that such traits as stealing or rage have never been personal pitfalls. But let's first provide sufficient time for the Spirit to highlight aspects of our lives that sadden Him, the unintentional sins that we may not even be aware of.

Remember, we cannot earn His love, but because we love Him, we're aiming to please Him rather than to grieve Him.

For prayer and reflection

'Search me, O God, and know my heart ... See if there is any offensive way in me, and lead me in the way everlasting' (Psa. 139:23–24).

Our **Father's joy**

Ephesians 5:10–16

'… and find out what pleases the Lord.' (v.10)

When you genuinely love someone, you not only behave in such a way so as not to offend or hurt them, but you make an effort to do things that you know will give them pleasure.

Paul writes, 'find out … be very careful … make the most of …' Pleasing the Lord is not a passive pursuit but an active determination to touch His heart with love. Jesus always did what pleased His Father (John 8:29) and His Spirit living within can show us how to do likewise. We can also study Scripture which gives plenty of helpful advice as to what will please God; for example: consecrated bodies (Rom. 12:1), an active faith (Heb. 11:6), praise (Heb. 13:15–16), a befitting lifestyle (Col. 1:10), prayers and intercessions (1 Tim. 2:1–4).

Furthermore, the original Greek translation of Revelation 4:11 suggests that we were made for His pleasure. As we were each created uniquely, we can seek our own special way to touch our Father's heart. But, primarily, simply spending time alone with Him will delight Him far more than we can imagine – more so than the joy we bring when we spend time with human loved ones. He loves you – just as you are. And as you share your time, listening, talking and singing love songs of worship, it's a guaranteed path towards an even more wonderful relationship.

For prayer and reflection

Doing something special to touch our Father's heart won't make Him love us more, but it will express how much we love and appreciate Him. What might you do today?

Finally, remember that 'Those controlled by the sinful nature cannot please God' (Rom. 8:8). If we're merely giving Him lip-service while continuing to live the life of the flesh, we will grieve His Spirit intensely. A lukewarm Christian life is enough to make Him sick – He would rather that you were hot or cold than tepid in between (Rev. 3:15–16). 'Be very careful, then, how you live' (Eph. 5:15).

WEEKEND

Live life with love

For reflection: 1 Corinthians 13:4–7

Jesus said that the greatest commandment is to love God with all that we are, and the second is to love others as we love ourselves (Matt. 22:37–39). Indeed, Paul wrote to the Ephesians that we should live a life of love (Eph. 5:2).

But, as today's passage clearly spells out, loving others isn't merely a superficial façade, and if we take the time to meditate upon its words, I guarantee they will be extremely challenging!

God loves you in all the ways this passage describes, but is this how you love your family, your friends, your church fellowship, your colleagues at work, your acquaintances, the people who really wind you up, the person who has hurt you deeply – your 'neighbours', no matter the colour of their skin, their religious beliefs or the attitudes of their heart?

Meditate on this passage, one word or phrase at a time, asking the Spirit to bring to mind people or situations where you have not loved in this manner. You may even need to take just one word (or phrase) per day for a while, and ask Him to remind you of it during your usual routines.

Choice rather than chance

Ephesians 1:4,11

'For he chose us in him before the creation of the world ...' (v.4)

A s an artist approaches his easel, before one stroke of his paintbrush even gets close to the canvas, he already had in mind the picture that he will paint.

But God had the unique design of our lives in mind before He'd even begun to create the world! Even as His Spirit hovered over the waters of the deep (Gen. 1:2), God chose our lives for the purpose He would assign to us.

Think about that for a moment – thousands of years ago, God knew us, loved us and had already planned our unique purpose that would dovetail into His kingdom work. And so, when the time came for Him to create us in our mother's womb, He knit into our being all the seeds of potential that would some day be used to fulfil His plan.

We were certainly not an accidental result of an unplanned pregnancy or the repercussion of a forced conception, nor were we merely the product of chance. Our earthly parents may not have chosen to have us in the way or the time that they did and we may not have chosen the circumstances into which we were born – but God chose us and will even use the sad and difficult situations of this fallen world that have been part of our lives, for a very special purpose.

As God continues to fill us with His Spirit, it is not only for our own comfort or peace of mind or to transform us into His likeness, but also to empower us for the tasks He has chosen for us to do.

'For we are God's workmanship, created in Christ Jesus to do good works, which God prepared in advance for us to do' (Eph. 2:10).

For prayer and reflection

'Before I formed you in the womb I knew you, before you were born I set you apart' ... 'See, I have engraved you on the palms of my hands ...' (Jer. 1:5; Isa. 49:16).

Equipped **for service**

Ephesians 4:7–12

'But to each one of
us grace has been
given as Christ
apportioned it.'
(v.7)

G race' is a theme that paints its hue into various parts of our picture. Just as we receive God's love and forgiveness by grace – that is, freely and undeservedly (Eph. 2:8–9) – so Paul continues to use the word 'grace' with regard to receiving spiritual gifts.

We do not deserve God's gifts any more than we merit His love, but as we were chosen for His divine purpose, we must rely on His Spirit's equipping to fulfil our specific role. And so we each 'have different gifts, according to the grace given us' (Rom. 12:6), in order that God's purpose be fulfilled in its entirety.

It's a privilege and the greatest fulfilment that life can offer to serve God in this way. Perhaps, however, some of us feel phased and frustrated as we struggle through an endless and stressful list of things to do. Or maybe there are times when we hanker for the gifts given to others which we perceive as more important than our own. And so Paul writes, '... do not be foolish, but understand what the Lord's will is' (Eph. 5:17), for it's His work that we aspire to.

Christ, who descended, had to ascend in order that we could receive the outpouring of His Spirit into our hearts and consequently the empowering to continue His earthly ministry (John 7:39; 14:12–14). Thus we need to spend time discerning His will and as we do so, we'll then be encouraged to nurture any gifts lying dormant, or cease certain activities that distract us from God's path.

God isn't going to empower us to try and copy someone else's work, but the more we align our daily routines to the purpose He ordained for us, the more His Spirit can bring to fruition the gifts that we shall require to do His will.

For prayer and reflection

Lord, I acknowledge that it's not by my ability, nor by my strength, but by Your Spirit that Your purpose is fulfilled (Zech. 4:6). Teach me to serve You accordingly.

Which part are you?

**Ephesians
2:11–22**

'… built together
to become a
dwelling in which
God lives by his
Spirit.' (v.22)

When you hear the word 'church', what image comes to mind – a building, a help-centre, a nationwide religious organisation? Yesterday's reading concluded that God distributes His spiritual gifts among us '… so that the body of Christ may be built up' (Eph. 4:12). As we are all 'in Christ' and are all filled with one and the same Spirit, we are intrinsically linked. Indeed, we are all held together by Christ, the chief cornerstone, and called the Church, 'which is his body' (1:22–23) – a temple in the making in which God's Spirit lives.

Jesus, who no longer owns a human body, relies on each part of His Church Body to fulfil its role and complete His work, for '… God has arranged the parts in the body, every one of them, just as he wanted them to be. If they were all one part, where would the body be? As it is, there are many parts, but one body' (1 Cor. 12:18–20).

The gifts that the Spirit enables within our lives are not given to develop our own reputation but to serve God and in so doing, administer His grace in its various forms as we also serve one another (1 Pet. 4:10); a further reminder of our need for the constant infilling of His Spirit to nurture and empower those gifts.

What part have you been chosen to play in Christ's Body, the Church? The human body encounters pain or disability when part of it stops functioning properly and so, too, Jesus feels the pain when we stop fulfilling the purpose God chose for us. He needs and esteems equally each and every part of His Church, but are we trying to duplicate someone else's role or have we removed ourselves, gone AWOL?

**For prayer and
reflection**

**'From him the
whole body,
joined and held
together by
every supporting
ligament, grows
and builds itself
up in love, as each
part does its work'
(Eph. 4:16).**

The tie **that binds**

Looking through Ephesians, we've been reminded of our high calling – one that requires us to live holy lives and imitate God's character; one that equips us for a divine purpose. Today we learn it's one that requires us to live up to that call throughout all relationships with other believers.

If we could sit next to God in heaven and survey every Christian around the world, we'd observe a diversity of race, culture and social background. Diversity, however, does not imply disunity, for we all share in common one body, Spirit, hope, Lord, faith, baptism and God (vv.4–6). This bond of peace that will unite us can only be found in Jesus, for He Himself is our peace (2:14). Nevertheless, we do have a responsibility to 'make every effort' to maintain unity and must therefore choose to align ourselves to the ways of His Spirit who will teach us how to dovetail with the lives of countless others.

Are we united with everyone in our local church fellowship or do we allow our petty grievances, opinions and personal preferences to break Christ's bond of peace? And what of the bigger picture, the worldwide body of Christ? Are we at one with other denominations who confess the same faith or are we refusing to interconnect owing to alternative styles of music, liturgy and so on?

Christ's peace lives in you and in me, but it's only as we allow His Spirit to overrule our fallen human instincts that His bond will unite one to another; as we make every effort to live in complete humility with gentleness and patience, relating to one another in love (v.2). Unity does not merely request but commands God's blessing (Psa. 133) – surely this is ample motivation.

Ephesians 4:1–6

'Make every effort to keep the unity of the Spirit through the bond of peace.'
(v.3)

For prayer and reflection

If we're struggling to dovetail harmoniously it is as much our responsibility as anyone else's to resolve conflict and let go of personal grievances that hinder the Spirit's work.

Relating to **and serving Jesus**

**Ephesians
5:21–6:9**

'Serve
wholeheartedly, as
if you were serving
the Lord, not men.'
(6:7)

I've often thought I'd be such a 'good' Christian if it weren't for other people! It's far easier to be gentle, patient, kind and so on when there's no one else to relate to, but not so easy when engaging with other imperfect people like me! Paul, however, summarises some key pointers to maintaining both the Spirit's unity among believers and His witness to unbelievers, through various examples of relationships: submit, love, obey, honour, and don't exasperate or threaten.

Wives do you submit to your husbands or is there an element of rebellion – an argumentative or critical spirit, for example? Husbands, (if you happen to be reading your wife's Bible notes!), Paul proffers a most challenging goal, but if you love your wives as Christ loves the Church, your wife's response will be all the more natural and loving. Children (under 18), are you obeying your parents or constantly pushing the boundaries they've set? Children (of any age), do you respect your parents in thought, speech and action? Parents (of any age), are you being so pernickety that your wound-up kids have become distanced from you? Employees, are you conscientious concerning your contractual obligations, whether or not the boss is around? Employers, Christ is our overall Master, do you treat your employees as He treats you?

Whether spouse, parent or child; whether worker, employer or job-seeker; whether friend or acquaintance; whoever you are and whatever you do, no matter the variety of people that interact with you, love and serve them equally to the best of your ability – just as though you were looking into the face of, or working for the business of, the Almighty King of kings.

**For prayer and
reflection**

**Lord, by Your
Spirit, remind
me that it's You
I'm relating to in
the lives of other
believers, and it's
You I am serving
no matter who
I'm with.**

WEEKEND

Live life with purpose

For reflection: Ephesians 3:1–9

Paul was chosen as an apostle to the Gentiles, to reveal and clarify the mystery that reconciled Jew and Gentile to God through Jesus. He recognised that it was only by God's grace and empowering that he could fulfil this role; certainly not through any merit of his own. Consequently, engaging with life from God's perspective, he simply got on with the job in hand – despite opposition, difficult people, hardships, imprisonment, a human sense of inadequacy and so on. While men thought they could control or hinder him, Paul lived in the reality that Christ was Master of his time and circumstances.

What about you?

Are you seeking fulfilment through personal aspirations, or serving the purpose that you were specially created for?

Are you constrained by other people's expectations, or freed to live life from God's perspective?

Are you imprisoned by a lack of self-worth, or empowered by the Spirit as you live your life for God?

Think carefully about these things, 'for it is God who works in you to will and to act according to his good purpose' (Phil. 2:13) – but you and I have to choose to give Him full control.

Signposts to heaven

**Ephesians
1:11–12**

'… in order that
we … might be for
the praise of his
glory.' (v.12)

J esus came to earth and provided men with an
image of their invisible God (Col. 1:15). Jesus
revealed God's glory to the disciples
(Matt. 17:1–5), God's grace and mercy to the sinner
(John 8:3–11), God's love to the unlovely (Luke 5:12–15),
God's holiness to the unholy (John 2:14–17), God's
compassion to the needy (Mark 6:34–44), God's wisdom
to those with worldly wisdom (Mark 11:18), God's power
to those with worldly power (Matt. 27:54) and so on.
In fact, Jesus never fell short of revealing His Father's
character, fulfilling His Father's purpose and pleasing
His Father's heart, and so countless numbers turned
their lives away from the things of this world in praise of
Almighty God.

Paul's letter encourages us to be filled with God's
Spirit (5:18) and to live a life of love (5:2); a life befitting
God's holiness (4:24), worthy of God's call (4:1), united
with other believers (4:3), fulfilling God's work (2:10) and
so on. Why else, but 'for the praise of his glory' (1:12).

As Christ's ambassadors, God continues to make His
appeal to men through your life and mine (2 Cor. 5:20),
and so our lives must attract rather than repel, woo
rather than hinder, draw rather than put off their hearts
to the glorious love of God. But as soon as we start
promoting ourselves or criticising and falling out with
others, we focus their minds upon our frail humanity
which cannot save a soul. Rather, as our lives are
empowered by God's Spirit within, they are the means
by which we guide others to Him.

We are to be signposts in the world that point
mankind towards God in heaven – but are we?

**For prayer and
reflection**

**'Live such good
lives … that,
though they
accuse you of
doing wrong, they
may see your
good deeds and
glorify God on the
day he visits us'
(1 Pet. 2:12).**

Standing strong

There were unimaginable celebrations in heaven the day we committed our lives to Jesus, but there was equal wrath in hell! Another soul lost from Satan's evil kingdom and handed back to God for eternity.

In fact, the more we seek God, the angrier Satan becomes; after all, we're living as traitors in his territory, serving another Master. He knows full well that an increasing measure of God within us will have an increasing effect on God's kingdom and a decreasing effect upon his. He'll therefore do anything to thwart our progress and minimise further damage dealt by Christ's light on his darkness.

Remaining in unity with those who've hurt us, living a life of love when we're angry and imitating God's holiness when we're tempted to satisfy self, are by no means easy standards to attain, let alone maintain – and impossible if we try to do it alone. It may feel like we're constantly battling the flesh-life, pride, repercussions of sin, physical hardships and so on, but our struggle is against rulers, authorities and powers of this dark world, and spiritual forces of evil in the heavenly realms (6:12). If Satan catches us off guard, previous mechanisms may kick in instantaneously tempting us to seek strength and comfort through alternative means than God. That, of course, is exactly what he would want us to do, and so Paul writes, 'be strong in the Lord' – a daily dependence upon His strength and protection to fulfil His holy purposes.

So next time someone hurts us, who or what will we reach for to ease the festering pain – the biscuit tin, the shops, a sympathetic but ungodly ear ...? Rather, let us reach out for God, resist the deception of worldly satisfaction and find our strength in the Lord.

Ephesians 6:10–12

'... be strong in the Lord and in his mighty power.' (v.10)

For prayer and reflection

Lord, I'm a walking target, but grant me greater discernment to detect Satan's wily ways, to stand strong in You and so deflect his attempts to trip me over.

Our **warrior's wardrobe**

**Ephesians
6:13–17**

'Therefore put on
the full armour of
God ...' (v.13)

The battle may be raging, but we've not been left without adequate protection. Obviously we can't dress ourselves in chain mail, but let's walk through our warrior's wardrobe and remember daily to put it on.

Nowadays, belts are more often accessories, but this one is essential to resist the tugging of enemy lies by securing our lives in truth. So, too, we protect our hearts by engaging with life 'in Christ'; for the breastplate of His righteousness guards us against a condemning urge to try and earn God's favour. We also need a firm foothold so as not to slip on life's ups and downs, and it takes the defence of the gospel message to maintain Christ's resilient peace – peace for our own hearts as well as for those with whom we share it.

If our shield is wearing thin it's our responsibility to build it up again, otherwise Satan's arrows might penetrate straight through! And don't forget it can be used in attack as well as in defence, for it's as we push against the enemy in faith that we make further progress. The head is still very vulnerable, however, requiring a helmet to encase our minds in Christ, protecting our thoughts before Satan takes them hostage. And finally, let's take up the invincible sword that is the Word of God. Wield it under the Spirit's command then watch the enemy fall!

Do remember to put it all on, for if you leave out truth or faith, for example, you'll offer Satan easy targets. But stand your ground, dressed in full armour, and he will surely flee. Admittedly he'll return with fresh waves of attack, but God will empower you to stand, and stand, and stand again against him.

**For prayer and
reflection**

**Take a few
minutes as part
of your waking
routine to
prayerfully put
on God's armour.
It may help to
write out
and place
this scripture
somewhere
obvious as a
reminder.**

Our **personal prayer Guide**

We've been reflecting on the infilling of the Spirit and His enabling and empowering in every area of our life, but a relationship with God would be no relationship at all unless it included prayer – the very means of our communication no matter what we're doing or who we might be with. God wants us to know Him as Father and friend, not just as servants (Eph. 1:17; John 15:15).

God is omnipresent, so He hears the prayers of the unsaved as they call upon His name, just as He hears the prayers of believers who simply pray with their minds. But if we want to pray with power then we need to pray in the Spirit. Being clever with words and confident in public may give an impressive appearance, but there's far greater power behind three whispered words inspired by the Spirit than a torrent of human thought and desire. Enabled by the Spirit we learn to intercede according to God's intentions (Rom. 8:26–27), protecting us from unwittingly praying contrary to God's will!

And let's not reserve this energised praying simply for special events, for Paul says to pray in the Spirit 'on all occasions'. Do you need a breakthrough at work, do you need help for your neighbour, do you long to know God more deeply, do you seek a physical healing, do you want to praise Him, are you struggling with your studies, do you often pray for your spouse, children, Sunday school, pastor, country and so on? Then ask the Spirit to guide you in prayer on all of these occasions. And how much more natural this will surely become by learning to live in the heavenly realms, armed for battle and empowered each day by lives that are filled with God's presence.

Ephesians 6:18–20

'And pray in the Spirit on all occasions …' (v.18)

For prayer and reflection

All-knowing, all-loving Creator God, teach me and empower me to pray.

251

Our picture **in perspective**

**Ephesians
5:18–20; 6:21–24**

'… be filled with
the Spirit.' (v.18)

D espite the cruel confines of prison, Paul sent a letter of encouragement to Ephesus. He was suffering physically in Roman chains, and yet he remained Christ's ambassador (3:13; 6:20). Here was a Spirit-filled man seeing the picture of his life from God's perspective – a life, therefore, that overflowed with praise and thankfulness.

Excesses of alcohol, food, exercise or shopping are some means that people use to escape difficult circumstances, overcome inhibitions or find pleasure when life seems dull. But Paul reminds the believers of a far greater power and pleasure that is found in being filled with God's Spirit. Life may well seem meaningless or harsh until we view it from God's perspective. He who conceived its unique design long before it came into being; He who dove-tailed our one special life with the lives of countless others – at a unique time, into unique circumstances, for His unique kingdom purpose. Only from such an eternal perspective can we genuinely give thanks in all circumstances. God never promised an easy ride or constant entertainment, but fulfilment is found as we walk hand-in-hand with His divine ways and purpose.

And so, as our painting nears completion, we can see all its colours blending beautifully as one – surrounded by, headed up and filled to the measure with God. Raucous songs are frequently heard on the binge-drinking streets of Britain, but how much more the expressions of praise when believers meet together. Believers, that is, who are filled to overflowing and united as one with the riches and blessings of Christ.

I too, therefore, pray for peace, love and grace '… to all who love our Lord Jesus Christ with an undying love' (6:24).

For prayer and reflection

**'… [glory] to him who is able to do immeasurably more than all we ask or imagine, according to his power that is at work within us … Amen'
(Eph. 3:20–21).**

Pioneering

Marion Stroud

Marion Stroud has published 26 books and writes and speaks regularly on writing and other topics. She is a European trustee of Media Associates, and works with this charity to train Christian writers in Eastern Europe and the developing world. One of her particular concerns is the needs of those who come to faith or regain their faith after marriage leaves them as lone worshippers in their families. She has written and spoken widely on this topic both in the UK and overseas. She is married to Gordon, a retired dentist, and has five adult children and 16 grandchildren, ranging in age from 4–21. Her most recent titles are two books of prayers for women *Dear God It's Me and It's Urgent* and *It's Just You and Me, Lord*. See more on her website www.marionstroud.com and read her blog *Living Life on Purpose* at marionstroud.blogspot.com

WEEKEND

Pioneering

For reflection: Jonah 1:1–10
'But Jonah ran …' (v.3)

A t nineteen, I wasn't entirely sure what I wanted to do or be, but of one thing I was certain. I didn't want to be a missionary. Living in the Far East as a child, I had met 'pioneer missionaries' for whom, to my young eyes, life seemed extremely tough. Back at an English boarding school, it was the 'Missionary Kids' who rarely saw their parents and always seemed to be short of cash. Fully intending to marry and have children I decided then that 'Marion' and 'missionary' didn't sit well together. And I stuck to my guns. When fellow students went to the Keswick Convention's Missionary meeting I scandalised them by staying defiantly in my tent. I wasn't going to give God a chance to tap me on the shoulder. No way! I wonder if He laughed?

These next few weeks we're looking at God's call to pioneer, going beyond our 'comfort zones' with Him. Does that send a shiver of anxiety or excitement down your spine?

If you're tempted to run like Jonah, remember that the 'belly of a big fish' is an uncomfortable destination too.

God so loved ... that He gave

Luke 23:26–46

'Jesus said, "Father, forgive them, for they do not know what they are doing."'
(v.34)

Last year, Armistice Day and Remembrance Sunday moved me in a way they had never done before. Watching elderly men proudly raising their standards as they blinked away tears, I had to swallow a lump in my throat, Was this because I now have adult sons whom I might have seen go off to war if I'd been a mother then? Was it the memory of a summer visit to a war cemetery where row after row of gleaming white headstones marked the final resting place of a generation of young men who gave their lives far away from home, so that I would not grow up under a totalitarian regime?

I don't know why, but I do know that I was overwhelmed by a sense of thankfulness and wished I could do more than buy a poppy to demonstrate how I felt.

Jesus was just a young man when He died. We're so familiar with the story that the full horror and wonder of it often escapes us. He didn't just go off to war when the call came, however heroic that may seem. He came to earth fully aware from the beginning that He was here to demonstrate God's love in action and then to die a horrendous death so that we could be part of God's forever family. I have known this since I was old enough to know anything.

Perhaps that is why the 'teenaged me' had come to accept it as part of the 'wallpaper' of my life and could see no particular need to share it with others. For it is only as we pause, not at a war memorial but at the cross, that the full pain and beauty of what happened there can begin to touch and move us.

For prayer and reflection

**Consider: 'The cross is the blazing fire at which the flame of our love is kindled ... but we need to get near enough to it for the sparks to fall on us.'
(John Stott)**

Love **so amazing**

Luke 7:36–50

'Therefore, I tell you, her many sins have been forgiven – for she loved much.' (v.47)

O ne of my favourite musicals is *Oliver Twist*. I especially like the song sung by Oliver to Nancy and Bet, where he offers to do anything to prove his thankfulness to them. They take it in turns to set him ever more difficult challenges, but his response is always the same: 'I'd do anything, anything for you.' An abandoned orphan had found somewhere to belong – even if it was among thieves – and he'd go to any lengths to demonstrate his gratitude.

The woman in today's story would have fitted in well with Oliver and Nancy. She was a woman with a reputation. So Simon must have been mortified when she gate-crashed his party. And she didn't just stand quietly at the door with many of the other townspeople, observing what was going on. That might have been just about allowable for a prostitute. But she got as close as she could to the man whom she seemed to know would love and accept her, rather than abuse and misuse her. The ointment was probably very valuable, but she poured it out, careless of the fortune she was lavishing on dirty feet. She wasn't bothered about who was watching and criticising. She did what she had to do with passion and abandon. Seeing Simon's disapproving scowl, Jesus asked him a question. Who would love most – the person who had been forgiven much or little? We know the answer.

What is your 'love level'? Have you lost sight of how much you've been forgiven, especially if, like me, you lack a 'gutter to glory' story? Remember, whether we've fallen short by a long way or a little, we're powerless to rescue ourselves. Simon needed Jesus every bit as much his uninvited guest.

For prayer and reflection

I don't want to be lukewarm, Lord. I owe You everything and without You I am nothing. Forgive my lack of love and set me on fire for You.

Do we have **a choice?**

'There are certain topics that we simply do not discuss when treating our patients.' Our lecturer fixed us with a stern glare to make sure we were all listening. 'Things like sex, politics, religion ... and, er, life-threatening diseases, especially cancer.'

In the years since I was a physiotherapy student, politics and religion – as opposed to a living faith – have definitely lost their place as top conversational taboos, while sex is probably discussed as freely in our hospitals as it is on TV chat shows. Even cancer gets mentioned from time to time. But the life-threatening disease of sin and what happens to us after this life is over – now that's a different matter entirely. Our leaders are so busy trying to be politically correct that councils ban Christmas lights in an effort to avoid upsetting people of other faiths and Easter is rapidly becoming the 'Spring Festival'. Why is it that any topic goes except for the good news that we know can change people's lives?

When I studied for an adult education certificate we had to prepare a topic and give a lecture to our fellow students as part of our course. The talk that got top marks was about feng shui – the Chinese art of arranging your home in a certain way so that life flows harmoniously. John didn't worry about appearing ridiculous, or offending those of other beliefs. He reckoned that he could change our lives with his ideas and he was passionate about it. The rest of the group loved it and hung on his every word.

Paul's passion was Jesus. He knew that he owed everything to the One whom he had once despised, and he was ready to risk life itself in order to pass on the news.

---

2 Corinthians 5:11–21

'... Christ's love compels us ... those who live should no longer live for themselves ...' (vv.14–15)

For prayer and reflection

Father, forgive me for fearing ridicule from others more than I fear You, and remaining silent while people are dying without ever hearing about You. Please give me boldness today.

But **what can I do?**

Judges 6:11–32

'… "how can I save Israel? My clan is the weakest … and I am the least in my family."' (v.15)

How did you see yourself when you looked in the mirror today? Did your eyes go straight to the part of your anatomy that you like least, and did you silently criticise your clothes or lament that you're having a 'bad hair day'? Do you often come into God's presence with a bowed head and heavy heart, because you're so aware of your shortcomings; and do you look at your Christian friends convinced that they are more spiritual, have more gifts or more value to God than you do? If so, then you will have a sneaking sympathy for Gideon.

He had what you might call a siege mentality. Instead of farming in peace he was part of a nation reduced to hiding in caves and mountain strongholds. The crops that the Israelites were able to plant were destroyed by marauding Midianites before they could be harvested. In addition to that his family belonged to an insignificant part of his tribe – no notable warriors there. He was confused about his theology, and certain about his own unimportance or ability to change anything. In fact he just wasn't impressed with himself at all.

But that didn't alter the plans that God had for him. You see God didn't see him as he was, but as he could be, and called him a mighty warrior.

Can you see any similarities with Christians today and the Israelites in the time of the judges? We often feel beleaguered and outnumbered and Satan seems to snatch away the people who make tentative steps towards faith before they have chance to grow. But let's remember God's word to Gideon if we feel that we have little to offer. Being insignificant in our own eyes doesn't disqualify us.

For prayer and reflection

Consider: Pioneer missionary Hudson Taylor said, 'When God wants to do His great works He trains somebody to be quiet enough and little enough and then He uses that person.'

Night **faith**

ideon might have heard audible words of encouragement from God but he still wasn't confident. But then would you have been if you'd been asked to do the equivalent of killing your father's bull, tearing down the family altar and then sacrificing it in full view of the town? I think I would have agreed with him that such a thing was best done under the cover of darkness! After all, there is radical and then there is RADICAL! Amazingly it all turned out OK.

Emboldened by this result, Gideon began to believe that God could use him to do the greater task of saving Israel. Then he had another faith wobble and asked God to confirm His guidance again. Our loving Father doesn't seem to have been angered by Gideon's cautious obedience or need for reassurance, and Gideon's fleece has become a byword for seeking for a sign from God.

Years ago God added two small children to our existing family of three – initially for three months and then indefinitely. That, for us, was a 'save Israel'-sized challenge, affecting everything we did, but especially how I allocated my time. Before this happened I had with great excitement signed contracts to write two books. But where would I find the time now? Despairingly I spread out my fleece. 'Father,' I prayed, 'if You want me to write, please give me a sign that is so extraordinary I can't possibly doubt it or argue it away.' Within weeks, a complete stranger offered me, a hopeless typist, enough money to buy 12 months' worth of secretarial help. I invested the lump sum and like the widow's cruse of oil, it lasted for nearly ten years, and ten books. Then, as the cash ran out, someone invented personal computers!

Judges 6:25–32

'But because he was afraid of his family and the men of the town, he did it at night ...' (v.27)

For prayer and reflection

Remember: God doesn't condemn our fears or questions. He just asks us to take the first step in the strength that we have, promising to meet each need as it arises.

WEEKEND

A vision and a vow

For reflection: Isaiah 6:1–8
'Whom shall I send? And who will go for us?' (v.8)

We call them 'mountain-top experiences', although of course they can take place anywhere. We've been at a conference or special service where inspiring preaching and wonderful music have made our spirits soar in wonder, love and praise. We feel as if we really have seen a glimpse of God's glory. Then we go home. And it can seem like being at a wedding breakfast after the bride and groom have left. Empty glasses, deflated balloons, dirty plates, musicians silent. A beautiful and meaningful occasion has become an empty shell.

Do you feel as if you're sitting amidst the 'ruins of the feast' today? Isaiah's 'mountain-top experience' didn't end when the glory faded, because he had had dealings with God that changed him forever. Humbled and forgiven, he put himself at God's disposal so that others could hear His word.

If the 'glory' has faded for you, why not spend a few moments this weekend thinking back to a time when God impacted your life.

In the light of that healing experience, will you say 'Here am I. Send me'?

Pioneering **with God**

t had all begun to go horribly wrong. Adam had decided to go his own way and within a few generations the earth was corrupt and full of violence. Sound familiar? Then onto the world stage steps the first biblical pioneer. Noah stands out among his generation for two reasons. He was righteous and he walked with God. And because of that God could use him.

Genesis 6:9–22

'Noah did everything just as God commanded him.' (v.22)

I wonder how Noah felt about it? There he was, quietly getting on with life, perhaps disturbed by the wickedness he saw around him yet feeling powerless to do anything about it. Then out of the blue God spoke to him. First came the bad news. God was going to destroy the world and everything in it. Then he heard the better news. Noah and his family would escape the Flood but first he had to build a boat. We're not told whether Noah was a carpenter. We don't even know if he knew much about animals. Domesticated farm animals perhaps, but lions? Neither of those things seems to have come into the equation. God saw the problem and he had the solution. What Noah had to do was obey.

It took Noah 120 years to build the ark and you can imagine some of the remarks he had to put up with from neighbours and friends. I suspect he gained the reputation for being very eccentric. Were his wife and sons embarrassed and dismissive of what they saw as wild tales? After all, up to this time it had never rained. Noah lived miles from the coast and he probably wondered how on earth he would collect, feed and house innumerable animals – without them killing one another! I think I would have asked myself whether I'd heard God correctly, wouldn't you?

For prayer and reflection

Question: Have you ever been faced with an ark-sized challenge? Did you say 'I'll pray about it', hoping that it would go away? Or did you say 'Yes, Lord', and just do it?

'But **I'm not qualified**'

**Genesis
11:31–32; 12:1–9**

'… they set out
from Ur … to go
to Canaan. But
when they came to
Haran, they settled
there.' (11:31)

**For prayer and
reflection**

**Are you in Ur,
Haran or moving
towards the
promised land in
your journey with
God? If you feel
stuck, what do you
need to
do in order to
move forward?**

What makes people spiritual 'pioneers'? Do they have to be charismatic, young and energetic, with the right family background? Must they have a clear vision of the work to which God is calling them right from the beginning?

Abraham is one of the pioneering giants of the Bible, but he didn't have any of those credentials. It seems that he and his father Terah had lived in a land where moon worship was the norm, and when they set out from Ur they did so without knowing exactly where they were going. What is more, they got halfway and then settled down in Haran rather than pressing on to Canaan.

It isn't clear whether Terah had died before Abraham was called to uproot his family again, but what is certain is that Abraham had accumulated wealth and possessions and he had to leave behind for the second time much that was comfortable and familiar. He could have tried to excuse himself on the grounds that he was from the wrong background, couldn't be expected to uproot his relations when they were happily settled and prosperous or that he had a dodgy religious pedigree. But he didn't allow his past to limit his future, or let his track record thus far disqualify him from further adventures with God.

Jackie Pullinger longed to share God's love overseas but none of the traditional missionary societies would have her. She was too young and she didn't have the right qualifications. As a musician she just didn't fit the mould. Worse still, she didn't know where God wanted her to go. Having tried every obvious avenue, she bought a ticket on the cheapest ship with the longest route, passing through the most countries and asked God to tell her where to get off.

But **I'm a failure!**

A t the beginning, Moses would seem to be perfectly qualified. First there was his miraculous escape from Pharaoh's murder squad, and his unlikely homecoming to spend his impressionable early years with godly parents. Then he moved on to the finest possible education and leadership training in Pharaoh's palace. He must have felt pretty confident that God's hand was on his life. Whether that confidence bred arrogance we don't know, but in trying to defend a fellow Israelite he killed an Egyptian and guilt and fear drove him far away from home.

Perhaps he thought that he had put himself beyond forgiveness after such a dramatic failure. But God never gives up on us. He knew that Moses needed to be equipped for his future mission, and desert survival skills would be a key part of that. Moses probably imagined that his years as prince of Egypt had been a waste of time, and that he was stuck in this rut for the rest of his days. However, Moses the shepherd was a character under construction, emerging from the wilderness as a man whom God could use. At exactly the right moment the bush burst into flame and Moses discovered that God still had a plan for his life.

Guilt is a crippling emotion and as women we seem to have a gift for blaming ourselves for everything, whether or not it is our fault. If we have things in our past that would seem to disqualify us from serving God we must refuse to listen to Satan's accusations or allow him to make us ineffective and afraid. The Bible tells us that if we confess our sins God will forgive us, wipe out the past and equip us for the future, just as He did with Moses.

Exodus 3:1–12

'Who am I, that I should go to Pharaoh …?' (v.11)

For prayer and reflection

'Search me, O God, and know my heart … and … my anxious thoughts. See if there is any offensive way in me, and lead me in the way everlasting.' (Psa. 139:23–24)

But **I'm the wrong age**

Joshua 14:6–15

'… my brothers … made the hearts of the people sink. I … followed the LORD … wholeheartedly.' (v.8)

Caleb was a pioneer to the core. As one of the ten men who had been sent to spy out Canaan, he was both an enthusiast and a man of faith. So he had brought back a glowing report. 'It's a great place', he said, 'and we should go ahead and take possession of what God has for us. He is on our side and He will deliver it to us, no matter how difficult it seems at face value. Never mind the giants and the fortified cities. The place is ours and we can certainly do it.'

Unfortunately, he was in the minority. The majority of the people not only dismissed his report but talked themselves into a state of abject terror. Going back to slavery in Egypt seemed preferable to going forward. And so the whole nation spent 40 years wandering in the desert, until the entire generation who had refused to trust God had died – except for Joshua and Caleb.

By the time they were in the land, Caleb was 85 years old, but he was still up for the tough option. The hill country had been promised to him and he had absolutely no doubt that he could conquer it. Why? Caleb took God at His word and said, in effect, 'God has said it, I've believed it; that settles it'.

How do you feel when you meet someone like Caleb? Do you shy away from his or her enthusiasm, quick to make comments like 'that didn't work last time' or 'we don't do that kind of thing here'? Do you inwardly disqualify yourself thinking, 'I'm too old, too busy or just not the type'?

Caleb did two things. He trusted God and followed Him wholeheartedly. Do you?

For prayer and reflection

Question: Although we may try not to think about it we have a stark choice. A wholehearted walk or wilderness wanderings. We can't do both. Which will you choose?

But **where is my mission field?**

Noah, Abraham, Moses and Caleb were men whose obedience to God involved them in dangerous and dramatic situations. But we don't need to travel long distances or face great physical danger in order to pioneer for God. Paul described his 'pioneering' work very simply. His aim was to go where people did not know about Jesus and no one else was telling them.

Perhaps you feel that this disqualifies you, since you live in a 'Christian' country. But a simple check amongst your neighbours or work colleagues would show you how deeply ignorant about faith issues the vast majority are. They might say that they believe in God, but the god to whom they refer is often created in their own image and bears little resemblance to the God of the Bible. And although they appear to be content with their lack of spiritual understanding, there is a barely recognised hunger eating away inside.

Claire and I often sat together to watch our small daughters dance. I knew little about her family except that her older daughters went to a school where my friend taught. 'A wild lot!' she said when I mentioned meeting Claire. 'Hosting parties where anything goes. Not the sort of friend I'd want for my daughter.' I'd asked Claire to bring Sally to play a couple of times, but on hearing this I was discouraged and didn't repeat the invitation. The girls moved on to other hobbies and we lost touch.

Several years later, I met Claire when she was offering Jehovah's Witness leaflets in the town square. I asked her how she'd become involved. She smiled. 'I'd wanted to find out about faith for years,' she said. 'Then the Witnesses came to my door and told me.'

Mark 5:1–20

'Go home to your family and tell them how much the Lord has done for you …' (v.19)

For prayer and reflection

Ask Jesus to show you those with prepared hearts and open ears among your friends and family, however improbable it may seem that they are seeking Him.

WEEKEND

Teamwork

For reflection: Mark 2:1–12
'Since they could not get him to Jesus because of the crowd,
they made an opening in the roof ...' (v.4)

Do you dream? We're told that everybody does, but few of us remember our dreams in detail. And what about daydreams and visions from God? My husband insists that God never speaks to him in this way, whilst I seem to have more dreams than I can possibly act upon. Or perhaps it's just that I often don't have the courage to step out alone.

Have you ever felt the Lord urging you to do something but have held back because of fear? Fear of being wrong? Fear of not having all the skills that would be needed?

Could it be done – with others? Why not revisit the dream this weekend and then ask God to show you who could help you bring it to fruition. The paralysed man undoubtedly wanted to get to Jesus. Without his friends he didn't have a hope. With them a miracle took place.

'All men dream but not equally ... the dreamers of the day are dangerous men for they may act their dreams with open eyes to make them possible.'

T.E. Lawrence

Press through – **family mockery**

1 Samuel
17:20–40

'You are not able
to go out against
this Philistine and
fight him; you
are only a boy …'
(v.33)

F amilies may be God's building blocks for society, but our nearest and dearest can be positively obstructive at times. If you've ever tried to lose weight you'll know what I mean. Your mother cooks your favourite food when you go for Sunday lunch and is then mortally offended when you refuse second helpings. Your aunt tells you that you're beginning to look haggard and your husband buys the jumbo-sized popcorn for your special evening in with a DVD.

David didn't get much encouragement from his family either. He'd been anointed by Samuel as God's chosen one to succeed the disgraced King Saul. But far from being treated with respect, he was still expected to look after the family flocks and carry food and messages between his father in Bethlehem and his soldier brothers in the Valley of Elah. What is more, when he rose to the challenge of fighting Goliath, his brother Eliab was furious rather than encouraging. His motives were criticised and his proposed methods made him a laughing stock.

David, however, wasn't discouraged. He took confidence in three things. He remembered the successes that God had given to him in the past. He trusted the skills and the tools that he had used many times. And above all he relied on God to deliver him when His honour was at stake.

When we hear the call of God to do something that takes us into uncharted territory it would be nice to have the encouragement of our family. But if we don't, should that stop us? What did Jesus do when He was criticised by His mother and brothers for taking things to extremes? He listened politely but refused to be deflected. In the end it is God to whom we are answerable.

For prayer and reflection

Father, I would love my family to support me. Please help them. But whatever happens help me to keep my eyes on You and my ears open to Your voice.

Press through – **impossibilities**

Joshua 6:1–20

'… do not say a word until the day I tell you to shout. Then shout!' (v.10)

The whole situation looked hopeless. Jericho was in lock down. No one could go in or out. And then God gave Joshua what must have seemed like very odd instructions. 'March right around the city in silence once a day for six days. On the seventh day march round seven times without a word. Then shout!'

I wonder how the soldiers received those instructions? They were used to plunging into battle and getting on with the job. Marching round the city and then going back to camp while the enemy laughed and jeered, must have seemed humiliating, and repeating the process for six days without any apparent result, an exercise in futility. Did the word go round that Joshua was losing his grip? Did they scare each other witless when they looked at this particular battle plan in the light of what had worked in the past? To do as God said might have seemed to be an act of folly. But, when they obeyed, the walls didn't just crack, they disintegrated.

Jericho walls come in all shapes and sizes but we'll all have to face them eventually. We too may feel that the way we're being led just doesn't make sense, and it's OK to express that puzzlement to God. He is always ready to listen to us when we come to Him in honest confusion. But by complaining to others, we simply spread discouragement and do Satan's work for him. Those Second World War posters that said 'Careless words cost lives', are as relevant today as they were 60 years ago.

So, in those circumstances, let's become 'faith whisperers', reminding ourselves and others what God has done in the past, or what He has said to us as we set out on this particular journey.

For prayer and reflection

A challenge: We sometimes fast from food but have you ever thought of fasting from criticism, negativity and despair, and feasting on praise, faith and confidence – not in ourselves, but in God?

Press through … **your prejudices**

How do your prejudices make themselves felt? You may reply indignantly that you're entirely open-minded and nothing is off limits to you. But think about the time you went to a church of another denomination. Did you inwardly criticise the loudness of the music and the length of the sermon, or feel uncomfortable when strangers shook you by the hand if you're not used to exchanging 'the peace'? And what about the last time you went abroad? Did you miss your daily newspaper or find the local habit of eating dinner very late in the evening or the shops shutting at noon, annoying and inconvenient? We all have our comfort zones and for some of us they're narrower than for others.

When I was young there were lots of unwritten rules about things that 'good' Christians shouldn't do, and people with whom they mustn't associate. The 'banned list' varied from the length of your hair and your hemline to the places you went to meet your friends. Coffee bars were in; pubs were definitely out! Today we may follow fashion or go to the pub without a qualm but view people involved in the club scene and chat rooms on the Internet with grave suspicion. We're concerned about immigrants and the homeless – as long as they stay in their own part of town. We say we're ready to be used by God – with the inward proviso that it is on our terms and within our own culture.

For Peter, eating non-kosher food or associating with the uncircumcised wasn't an option until God turned his thinking on its head. God's priority is that everyone should have a chance to hear about His Son, and He challenged Peter to do the unthinkable in order to touch the unreachable.

Acts 10:9–29

"'Surely not, Lord!" Peter replied. "I have never eaten anything impure or unclean."' (v.14)

For prayer and reflection

Father, please free me from my prejudices and fear of what others might say, and give me the courage to act in faith and obedience, whatever that means practically.

Press through … **Satan's ploys**

Esther 4:1–17

'… who knows but that you have come to royal position for such a time as this?' (v.14)

I f you see words like the 'Final Solution', 'Kosovo', 'Rwanda' and 'Darfur', what do you associate them with? Genocide!

This deliberate attempt to exterminate an entire people group has happened repeatedly throughout history and the book of Esther tells the story of one such attempt. This time it is a plot to exterminate the Jews captured by Nebuchadnezzar and now settled in Susa.

In summary it goes like this. Queen Vashti is deposed and in a nationwide search for beautiful virgins, the orphaned Esther is 'discovered'. It's a bit like the story of Cinderella without the glass slipper. But what the talent scouts don't know is that her ancestors were Jews. Keeping this a secret Esther wins the king's heart and becomes queen. The scene is set for a happy ending until her uncle Mordecai offends the king's favourite, Haman, and a retributive purge of all the Jews in the kingdom is sanctioned.

What would you have done in Esther's place? Risked your own life in an attempt to save many others, with no guarantees of success? Or kept quiet and hoped that the crisis would blow over? When I read of people like Corrie Ten Boom who hid Jews during the Second World War, and went to a concentration camp as a result, I wonder, 'Would I be brave enough to put my life on the line for others?'

For prayer and reflection

Think: If not me … who? If not here … where? If not now … when?

Some of us may be faced with such a challenge one day. But God's call to pioneer for Him isn't always dramatic or life-threatening in the physical sense. Each of us has been born at a certain time and brought into our particular 'kingdom' with a unique job to do.

The question is, will we prepare humbly and then step forward boldly when challenged to face the enemy?

Press through ... **to the end**

he Reubenites and the Gadites felt that they had journeyed far enough. The land around them was well suited to their flocks and herds and they just wanted to settle down. Going into the promised land would mean risking their families and their belongings and they wanted none of it. But Moses realised that if they settled down short of their goal, this would discourage the others and God's purposes would not be fulfilled.

The attitude of going 'so far and no further' is one to which many of us are susceptible. We see it in our churches, our Christian organisations and ourselves. We step out in faith and excitement, feeling that we're responding to God's call and fulfilling His purpose. We're passionate about the vision and make great initial strides. And then as things get hard, or don't turn out as we'd hoped, discouragement and weariness set in. It may come from the sheer enormity of the task, unsympathetic relations, fellow workers who fail us or even direct spiritual attack.

Pioneering requires persistence as well as passion. I'm not into long distance running; 5k is the most I've achieved so far. But friends who have taken part in the London Marathon report that the infamous 'wall' which runners are said to hit when they reach approximately the 20 miles marker is very real. Suddenly the whole thing seems impossible. The only solution is to hang on until the next flow of energy kicks in.

The writer to the Hebrews gives the spiritual solution. 'Let us fix our eyes on Jesus', he writes. 'Consider him who endured such opposition from sinful men, so that you will not grow weary and lose heart' (vv.2–3).

Numbers 32:1–15

'Why do you discourage the Israelites from going over into the land the LORD has given them?' (v.7)

For prayer and reflection

Father, when I'm weary and tempted to give up, help me to just love You more dearly, follow You more nearly and see You more clearly, day by day.

WEEKEND

Light up the fire

For reflection: 2 Timothy 1:3–12
*'... I remind you to fan into flame the gift of God,
which is in you ...' (v.6)*

When the days shorten we need new sources of light. In Britain we celebrate the downfall of Guy Fawkes with bonfires and fireworks, and the scent of burning leaves is one that many of us associate with autumn. But a good fire takes time and skill to create.

My father had the knack of getting any kindling to burn, whether it was damp or dry, in the garden or in the grate. With infinite patience he would add one little piece of wood after another, blowing gently into the embers until the flames sprang up.

Paul points out that the gifts God gives us can be damped down in our lives if they're not fed and fanned. If you are lighting a bonfire this weekend or using candles to brighten a dinner table, ask yourself, 'Do I need to ask the Holy Spirit to rekindle His gift in me? Is there rubbish in my life that needs to be taken out and burned?'

Whether we have become weary and allowed the pressures of life to dampen our fire, or just need more spiritual fuel to feed the flames, He is always ready and willing to set us ablaze again.

Pressures **and priorities**

I've always had a sneaking sympathy for Martha – which probably says something about me! Mary always gets the positive press, but supposing Martha felt trapped in her role as older sister? Maybe she had a reputation for being the 'hostess with the mostest' and felt compelled to come up with a marvellous meal because that was what people expected of her. Or maybe no one else would want to feed at least 13 hungry men. Could she have been longing to put down her responsibilities and listen as Mary did, but felt that she was on the treadmill of coping from which she just couldn't escape?

Today, when multi-tasking seems to be the norm, and where everything seems to be going faster and faster, many of us find it hard to distinguish the urgent from the important. So although we want to be totally available to God we just don't know how to recognise that 'one thing' for which we, like Esther, have 'come to the kingdom'. And so we continue to juggle umpteen tasks with an ever-increasing sense of panic or frustration. We mutter to each other about the need for 'heavenly emails' and wonder how we can discover that sense of serenity and purpose that Jesus seemed to have. He knew exactly where He was going and never appeared to be in a hurry, but at the end of His life He could say, 'I have finished the work that You gave me to do.'

Why not take these three questions to Jesus and keep pondering them until you get a sense of His answer:

- What is required of me that nobody but I can do?
- What brings the greatest return on time invested?
- What have You equipped me for that gives me the most joy?

Luke 10:38–41

"'Martha, Martha," the Lord answered, "you are worried and upset about many things …'" (v.41)

For prayer and reflection

Remember: We can accomplish in our lifetime only a fraction of God's work; but when we follow His leading, it enables us to do something, and do it very well!

Wherever **is this leading?**

John 2:1–11

'Do whatever he tells you.' (v.5)

nitially, it seemed an excellent idea. 'Let's invite our neighbours to coffee,' suggested my friend Ethel, 'and get someone to talk about something of general interest from a Christian viewpoint. I'm sure that they'd come, just to get out of the house.' 'Sounds great,' I responded absently, watching my toddler wobble towards the road. 'Where would you hold it?' She looked surprised. 'At your house of course! You've got a large sitting room and a room we could use for a crèche.'

That was a different matter entirely. We both had three children under five. I never seemed to get through my 'to do' list as it was and the thought of running something so identifiably Christian, as opposed to being active in church was not what I had in mind. I wrestled with God throughout the summer but eventually gave in and we ran that fortnightly coffee morning until the children reached school age and most of our neighbours returned to work.

We hoped that non-believers would become Christians but I don't know of any who did. However, several uncertain Christians grew in their faith and started serving Him in ways that they would never have contemplated before. And for Ethel and I it was the first step in God's plan for us. God has used Ethel's gift of personal evangelism worldwide and I became aware of the needs of women who are 'lone worshippers' in their families. This has resulted in books and articles for those who often seemed to be ignored in our couple-oriented churches.

It may seem odd to us that Jesus' first miracle appeared to have no spiritual edge. Helping with the catering – what's the point? But His glory was revealed and His disciples believed. Good enough?

For prayer and reflection

If the first step of obedience you're asked to take seems strange, remember that it is only a first step. Infinite possibilities lie ahead. So do whatever He tells you.

First things first

After a professional life governed by his appointment book, my husband still works best from a daily 'to do' list, tackling one thing at a time. My natural approach is very different. Being something of a perfectionist, I may start clearing away the breakfast things and quickly become distracted by all the other jobs that I can see need my attention in the kitchen. Before I know it, a five-minute job has taken me half an hour. We all have our own style and there are times when my form of multi-tasking can be very efficient. But if we are going to carve out time to follow God's leading in an already full life, there are times when we may have to practise 'planned neglect'.

When Jesus sent out His 12 disciples to preach and heal, He gave them very specific instructions. They were to go to a particular group of people, meaning that on this occasion others would be left out. They were to proclaim a specific message. Theological debate could take place another time. Healing was to be a major focus and in order to move fast they must travel light and live simply. And if some people refused to listen they were not to spend time agonising or persuading, but move on to those who would.

How are you with priorities? I believe that God has called me to write, but often struggle to find the time when other things seem more urgent. My days flow best when I copy the concert pianist who said, 'I play well only when my daily practice comes first. Until that is completed I deliberately neglect everything else.'

Remember that it matters what you put first, because by saying 'yes' to this commitment, you're saying 'no' to another one.

Matthew 10:1–15

'These twelve Jesus sent out with the following instructions: "Do not … Go rather … As you go …"'
(vv.5–7)

For prayer and reflection

Father, teach me what it means practically to put Your kingdom commission first, knowing that You will help me put all the necessary 'other things' in place too.

People pleasing

Mark 1:29–38

'Simon and his companions … exclaimed: "Everyone is looking for you!"' (vv.36–37)

D o you spend a lot of time keeping people happy? Women seem to have a natural desire to oil the wheels of relationships and in doing so we often find it difficult to say no. How often have you agreed to a request only to be furious with yourself moments later because you know that now something that you know you should be doing will be left undone?

Having a clear focus is important. First of all it simplifies your decision-making. When a friend of mine is on a diet, she refuses off-limit food by saying, 'No thank you. Biscuits aren't part of my eating plan at the moment!' I think she's brave but it works for her.

A clear focus also concentrates your efforts. Being busy with many things doesn't necessarily mean that you're more effective. The sun warms a room by shining through the window. But if you focus its rays through a magnifying glass you can light a fire that will burn the house down.

Jesus is the perfect example of a focused life. Stories of His healing miracles and His authority over evil spirits were spreading like wildfire. Everyone wanted to see Him, and the disciples were eager that He should be available. After all, they reasoned, popular support was necessary if the Messiah were to make an impact. It wasn't a good idea to disappoint the punters.

But Jesus had other ideas. He knew that His time on earth was limited and that He must reach as many people as possible with the good news of God's love and forgiveness. So He refused to court popularity with the few and miss being a blessing to the many.

For prayer and reflection

Reflection: Jesus got up early and prayed. Then He could answer the disciples with composure because He had received His direction for the day.

No **well-worn paths**

The way in which God fits us into His plan can seem quite confusing at times. Paul was Jewish to the core, and scholarly with it. You would have thought that he was the ideal candidate to reach other well-taught Jews. But God knew that he would do a great job with those 'beyond the pale' Gentiles – people who were despised, shunned and restricted to a certain part of the Temple. There were plenty of disciples witnessing to the Jews. And Paul doesn't appear to have argued or had doubts. He responded eagerly to God's call even though it led him through terrible suffering.

When our older daughter left university, she joined an organisation that recruited young people to work for a year alongside local churches in Malawi, Jamaica and Haiti. At first I prayed fervently that she wouldn't be sent to Haiti. Dangerous physically, with a witch doctor around every corner it was a spiritual minefield. What could she contribute in such a place? Guess where she went? And I came to realise what a privilege it was for her to briefly 'stand in the gap' (Ezek. 22:30) supporting her brothers and sisters in the poorest nation in the Western world.

It isn't always necessary to go across the world in order to go where others have not been. An Indian fisherman who had been a fervent Communist came to faith. He was a simple man who had never travelled far from home, and the area in which he lived was considered very dangerous for Christians from other places to visit. But he was there by right, and as he has talked to his friends and family about this Jesus whom he had come to know, over the last three years 150 people have come to faith.

Romans 15:17–22

'I have trailblazed ... the Message of Jesus ... This has all been pioneer work.'
(*The Message*)

For prayer and reflection

Father, I'm willing to stand in the gap. I trust You to equip me, show me where it is and how I can pioneer in that place for You.

WEEKEND

It's worth it

For reflection: 2 Corinthians 4:5–12; Hebrews 12:1–3
'Let us fix our eyes on Jesus ... who for the joy set before him endured ...' (Heb. 12:2)

I can't do it!' Robert threw his pencil down in despair. 'It's just too hard.' Reading, writing and spelling seemed impossible to our dyslexic nine-year-old. At last, a solution was being offered. But it was tough. He had to practise reading and spelling for 20 minutes every evening except at Christmas and on his birthday. And of course we had to be committed, too. It was hard for us all and at times we despaired. The goal that motivated us was to get Robert's reading age and his chronological age the same. When we succeeded, after two and half years of unremitting work, all the tears and struggles seemed infinitely worthwhile. Not only had Robert learned to read and spell, but we'd learned the lessons of patience, stickability and much more. We celebrated with gusto!

Paul suffered all sorts of hardships as he pursued his goal of evangelising the Gentiles. But the joy of seeing them respond made it all worthwhile.

If you're feeling 'weary in well doing' this weekend, take another look at your goal. And write down what you're gaining from the journey. The treasure that is wrapped up in the experience may be hidden, but it is certainly there.

Praying for the promises

Y ou have to hand it to Abraham. He was immoveable. If God had said that he would have a son then he believed it – however much the odds were stacked against it humanly speaking. He reminds me of that bumper sticker which says, 'Impossibilities we do at once. Miracles take a little longer', or the Queen in *Alice in Wonderland* who believed 'six impossible things before breakfast'. And, as we know, after years of waiting, and mistaken attempts to help things along, Isaac was born.

How do you cope when God seems to keep you waiting for His promises to be fulfilled? Do you get depressed and give up, concluding that you can't have heard from Him correctly in the first place? Or do you try to hurry things along like Abraham did? My friend Pat has an interesting approach. She says that some issues need to be put into an imaginary basket and left in God's care, like the infant Moses in the bullrushes. Her role then is to prayerfully watch to see what God is going to do and whether He wants to involve her. And others need to be put into an imaginary basket of a gas-filled balloon. When you release those, you just have to trust that the wind of God's Spirit will take them exactly where they need to go.

An essential part of adventuring with God is believing in His power to bring His promises into being, and that answers delayed aren't answers denied. I find this reminder to TRUST helpful.

Tell God what your problem is.
Remember that He cares and that He can
Unlock the situation.
Submit the outcome to Him and
Thank Him for His answer.

Romans 4:18–22

'… he did not waver … being fully persuaded that God had power to do what he had promised.' (vv.20–21)

For prayer and reflection

Father God, please give me Abraham's dogged faith, believing heart and determination to be Your instrument, wherever that takes me and whatever it costs.

'Feel the fear **and do it anyway**'

**Matthew
14:22–32**

'Take courage! It is
I. Don't be afraid.'
(v.27)

On my study wall I have a cartoon that makes me grin every time I look at it. Peter is walking on the water, but in this instance all the disciples are sheep. As Peter forges ahead on his hind legs, another of his woolly companions is balanced on the gunwhale, snorkel in place, saying, 'Right behind you mate.'

The rest are huddled together, bleating encouragingly but keeping as far out of harm's way as they can get. When this story is preached on, the emphasis always seems to be on Peter's failure. I don't think I've ever heard the rest of the disciples discussed at all. In my book, Peter is a success because he got out of the boat. He felt the fear and did it anyway. It was those who never tried at all who failed.

As you've considered God's call to pioneer this month, what has been your overall reaction? A dismissive shrug – this sort of thing is not for ordinary Christians? A feeling that going out on a limb is not what you signed up for because you've misinterpreted Jesus' promise of 'abundant life' to mean no problems? Or excitement tinged with uncertainty as to how taking a risk for God might impact your life? After all, we reason, taking a risk might make us look foolish. And that is something that we avoid like the plague. But if we allow that to bind us we end up afraid to be anything.

Helen Keller said, 'Security is mostly a superstition. It does not exist in nature, nor do the children of men as a whole experience it. Avoiding danger is no safer in the long run than outright exposure. Life is either a daring adventure or nothing.'

For prayer and reflection

Father, thank You for stretching out Your hand and saying, 'Come'. Help me to get out of the boat, knowing that it is totally safe to walk on water with You.

The power of praise

Helena Wilkinson

Helena Wilkinson trained in counselling at Waverley Abbey College and has subsequently taught there as a tutor. She is the author of nine books including the bestseller *Puppet on a String*, her personal account of overcoming anorexia, written when she was a teenager.
In 1994, she founded Kainos Trust, a charity for eating disorder sufferers, of which she was Director. In January 2004 the charity merged with Swansea City Mission. Helena is now based at the mission's retreat centre, Nicholaston House, on the Gower Peninsula where she runs courses.
She is a freelance writer and international speaker. For further information visit her website: www.helenawilkinson.co.uk

Joy of surrender

John 15

'Greater love has no-one than this, that he lay down his life for his friends.' (v.13)

When I was praying about what to cover in this month's notes I knew that I should write on surrender. Initially I entitled the notes '*The challenge of surrender*', for surrender is, without doubt, a challenge! But the word 'challenge' didn't sit well and, instead, I found myself drawn to the word 'joy'. I wonder if you would associate joy with surrender? If only we can get past the effort and pain of surrender, then I believe we can encounter the deepest joy.

We sing: 'I surrender all, all to thee, my blessed Saviour, I surrender all' ('I Surrender All' by J.W. Van Deventer). But the question is, do we really surrender all, or are we even prepared to?

Of late, I have been greatly challenged by the words of both J.W. Van Deventer's chorus and also those of Frances Ridley Havergal's hymn, 'Take My Life'. Both songs speak of giving more of ourselves to Jesus; of not giving Him just our lives, but submitting our very selves: our moments, our days, our hands, our feet, our voice, our lips, our worldly pleasures, our silver and gold, our intellect, our will, our heart, our love, our all!

The dictionary definition of surrender is to 'relinquish possession or control': to surrender to God means that we become fully His and not our own.

What aspects of your life do you feel are yet to be surrendered? Can you begin the process of relinquishing control? Jesus laid down His life for us. What does it mean that we too lay down our lives for Him? As we lay down our lives He becomes fully ours and we know the joy of full salvation, are filled with love and power and are truly blessed.

For prayer and reflection

Lord Jesus, You laid down Your life for me and I don't ever want to take it for granted. Help me to surrender more of my life to You. Amen.

Kept for **the Master's use**

One day I was talking with a friend about how certain things hadn't worked out in my life. I'd always held a picture in my mind of how my life would be as I got older, and things were not coming into line! For example, I would be happily married with children; instead I am single! One phrase stuck in my mind as my friend prayerfully brought her reply: 'kept for the Master's use'. She wasn't saying I wouldn't marry, but that I had been set aside for God's service. The question was, did I hold in my mind God's agenda for my life, or mine? What about you?

In *The Word for Today* (UCB notes 10 Jan 2006), the author writes, 'Do not ask God to bless your plans, ask Him to show you His; they are already blessed. When the time is right the plan will be clear, the people in place and the resources available.' There is a distinct difference in how things work out when we are flowing with God's plans rather than endeavouring to swim against the tide in an effort to maintain our own!

When I think of a surrendered life one particular person comes to mind, the hymn writer Frances Ridley Havergal. She had a deep walk with the Lord, radiated the love of her Saviour and had an attractive personality. In her short life she received a number of proposals of marriage – all of which she declined! Biographer T.H. Darlow says, 'in the best sense of a phrase which she would *never* have presumed to employ, she was a bride of Christ'. She had learnt the joy of consecrating not only her life, but each aspect of it.

A consecrated life is one 'set apart as sacred; dedicated to some service or good'.

Psalm 32

'I will instruct you and teach you in the way you should go …' (v.8)

For prayer and reflection

Lord, help me to lay down my own agenda, plans and ideas and to seek Your will for my life. Amen.

Our lives **for Jesus**

Philippians 2:1–18

'… for it is God who works in you to will and to act according to his good purpose.' (v.13)

We saw yesterday, and it is affirmed in today's reading, that what counts in life is that we follow God's instruction and His will for our lives; and that surrender is about bringing our desires in line with His. Many times in my life I have been given the verse 'Delight yourself in the LORD and he will give you the desires of your heart' (Psa. 37:4).

To my shame, on several occasions I have found myself saying to God, 'You still haven't given me the desires of my heart.' I had taken delight in the Lord and yet what I longed for still evaded me. Do you ever feel like that? I came to realise that I would only see the fulfilment of my heart's desires when they matched God's desires. Plus, I had failed to put into operation the verse which follows: 'Commit your way to the LORD; trust in him and he will do this' (v.5). Without my way surrendered, how could my desires be the same as His?

The title of today is 'Our lives for Jesus' and this means not just surrendering our desires, but giving Him all of ourselves. Like me, do you tend to give some bits and hold others back? Surrender requires us no longer to compartmentalise our lives: following God's way in one area of our lives and our own way in another!

Can you spend a few moments thinking about whether you have compartmentalised your life and said to God: 'In this part of my life I'll follow You, but in *this* part of my life I'm doing things my way.'

One thing is certain, Jesus will take the life that is offered to Him and He will keep that which is entrusted to Him. But can we appreciate Him keeping our lives if we don't fully comprehend the importance of surrendering them?

For prayer and reflection

Thank You that there is no safer place than my life in Your hands, Lord. Amen.

WEEKEND

Christ for us!

For reflection: 1 John 4:10
'This is love: not that we loved God, but that he loved us and sent his son as an atoning sacrifice for our sins.'

When the concept of surrender seems to be hard work, it's good to remind ourselves that the foundation for us sacrificing our lives is that Christ first sacrificed His life for us. It is not that we have loved Him but that He has loved us. Rather than condemning ourselves for not loving Him enough, do we not need to understand more deeply His love for us, out of which our love for Him will overflow?

God's love for us, despite our sin, is awesome. Hosea chapter 3 speaks of the woman beloved and yet adulterous. Are we too not like that at times – overwhelmingly loved by God despite our unfaithfulness? His love still flows out to us in abundance even though, at times, we look away from Him with eyes that wander towards the world, seek earthly pleasure and self-gratification, put our trust in people above Him and indulge in false comfort and hope.

Can you spare a little time this weekend to consider the ways in which this applies to you?

Moments **to remember**

Ecclesiastes 3:1–8

'There is a time for everything …' (v.1)

I recently had to make a rather embarrassing phone call. I couldn't access my internet banking because there was some information I had forgotten. 'What is it that you can't remember?' the lady asked as I called the bank for help. 'My memorable data!' I chuckled! It couldn't really have been that memorable if I'd forgotten it only two months after setting up the account! But to me it was just another bit of data in my already overloaded brain which was bursting at the seams with passwords and pin numbers!

Yet, is it not the case that some data sticks clearly in our minds? Could this be data which relates to a significant event rather than a scrambled attempt at creating something 'memorable'? I recall clearly the day I was saved over 20 years ago: the people, the sequence of events, my emotional and physical reactions and my immediate actions. Why? Because it changed me forever – it was truly memorable! By no coincidence, the day before I was saved I'd had a revelation that I had miserably failed in my attempts to make my own life work, and I had begun to let go of control and to surrender my moments to the Lord.

Ecclesiastes 3 reminds us that indeed our times are not our own: that there is a time for everything. Soon after I became a Christian and read Ecclesiastes, I questioned if there was any point in surrendering my moments if God had it all worked out anyway! But now I tend to look at it differently – God has a plan for my life but my holding on to my moments adds unnecessary complexities. It reminds me of the Israelites taking 40 years to enter the promised land, when in fact it was only 'a stone's throw away'.

For prayer and reflection

Lord, I want my memorable moments to be those that You have touched, not those that I have endeavoured to fill with my own agenda. Amen.

Moments **to surrender**

I wonder how different our days would be if our moments really were kept for Jesus! Psalm 118 reminds us that today (and every day) is the day that God has made; let us rejoice and be glad in it.

Psalm 118:1–24

'This is the day the LORD has made …' (v.24)

How much do you plan your days and your moments, and how much do you leave your day open to God's leading? And are you happy to see your plans change? I work a lot to deadlines and a fairly high degree of structure is necessary. But I used to plan my time to the minute and become quite stressed if anything unplanned got into my 'work slot'. I might change what I was doing but inside I could hear myself calculating how many hours I'd have to add on to the day to make up for 'wasted time'.

Recently God has been bringing about a significant change: as I commit my moments to Him I find that my work is taking less time and if other things, led by Him, do come along and take the 'designated work slot' then amazingly the inspiration needed for my work flows at twice the pace! He is in the process of teaching me that if I can trust Him with my moments then He will give back to me more than I have given.

When we consider how so much of our life is directed by our own sense of being driven, it's good to remind ourselves of how Jesus operated completely out of God's leading. In response to being 'picked up' on working on the Sabbath, Jesus gave them this answer: 'I tell you the truth, the Son can do nothing by himself; he can do only what he sees his Father doing, because whatever the Father does the Son also does' (John 5:19).

For prayer and reflection

Lord, I give You my days, I give You my hours, I give You my moments, and I wait with excitement to experience each moment filled by You! Amen.

Unclasped hands

Exodus 30:22–33

'… and consecrate them so that they may serve me as priests.' (v.30)

With what do your hands tend to be filled – work, baggage, burdens, 'must dos'? In Exodus 29 and 30 we read of the consecration and anointing of priests. '… In this way you shall ordain Aaron and his sons' (29:9). The Hebrew word for 'ordain' has a connection with hands. There appear to be many different usages of '*yâd*' including 'uplifted hand' describing prayer towards the sanctuary (Psa. 28:2); a public blessing (Lev. 9:22); and 'fill the hands', which refers to consecration (Exod. 29:9–35; 16:29).

The Hebrew word for 'consecrate' is '*qâdâsh*'. It means to make clean, to dedicate, sanctify, purify, to be selected, be pure, be holy, be devoted. A derived meaning is 'being separated', signifying 'an act or a state in which people or things are set aside for use in the worship of God … withheld from ordinary (secular) use and treated with special care as something which belongs to God.'[1]

Looking briefly at this consecration process we see that the priests were washed (signifying that they must be clean who bear the vessels of the Lord), and clothed with holy garments (signifying that not only must they put away the pollution of sin, but put on the graces of the Spirit). The high priest was anointed with oil (as a token of the pouring out of the Spirit upon him, to qualify him for his work). In addition, sacrifices were made for the covenant of priesthood: a sin offering (as atonement); a burnt offering (as dedication of themselves wholly to God, as living sacrifices); a peace offering (joyful communion with God).[2]

Is there anything you feel you want to bring before God in order that you can come with clean hands, empty and ready to be filled?

For prayer and reflection

Lord, I lay before You all that my hands have been holding on to. Amen.

1. NASB Lexical Aids to the Old Testament.
2. Matthew Henry's Commentary.

Led by the Lord

How powerful our hands would be if they were surrendered to God at all times! Each moment of the day we are being led to use our hands by God, but do we realise it? We may be led to write a letter, make a phone call, reach out with compassion, help lift another's burdens, turn the pages of God's Word.

Exodus 33:12–23

'My Presence will go with you, and I will give you rest.' (v.14)

As a Christian writer, I pray about what I write and, at times, I have been led powerfully by God, but recently I was listening to a talk on the life of Frances Ridley Havergal and I was struck by her admission that she didn't write a single word until the Lord directed her!

In the same way, a minister friend of mine in South Africa once shared with me how God had directed him to change the way he evangelised. He regularly carried out door-to-door evangelism, but God told him to go only to the households that He led him to. The result was that when he did this the people in the household were ready to receive the gospel and respond.

The first part of Psalm 37:7 reminds us, 'Surrender yourself to the LORD and wait patiently for him' (God's Word Translation). Are you able to do as the psalm suggests – surrender and wait patiently? In his book *The Purpose-Driven Life*, Rick Warren points out that 'there are three barriers that block our total surrender to God: fear, pride and confusion.' Which of these speaks most to you – fear, pride or confusion?

A.W. Tozer said, 'The reason why many are still troubled, still seeking, still making little forward progress is because they haven't yet come to the end of themselves. We're still trying to give orders and interfering with God's work within us.'

For prayer and reflection

Lord, teach me to wait patiently for You and not endeavour to take control. Deal with my fear, pride and confusion. Amen.

Fearless feet

'How beautiful on the mountains are the feet of those who bring good news …' (v.7)

H ave you ever found yourself walking or travelling somewhere and your feet are just taking you? I recall a wet, blustery day about 13 years ago when my feet took me out of work, onto a train and into a church in a town I'd never been to before! The first person I met at the door has prayed for me every day since!

On another occasion, at the age of 22, God led me to step into new territory when He called me to leave southern England suburbia to work amongst the rural Zulu people in Southern Africa. The political climate was such that everybody bar one person advised me not to go, but I knew God was leading and I went. It changed my life!

If our feet are to move for God, our gaze must be always upon Him and our ears open to hear Him. When I went to the Zulu township I was a relatively new Christian and working my way round the Word of God. Without having previously read it, I was given by God Psalm 91 – a promise of protection. I faced many a danger but His Word was true – no harm befell me.

Proverbs 3 reminds us to keep God's commands if we do not want our feet to stumble: 'My son, do not forget my teaching, but keep my commands in your heart … Then you will go on your way in safety, and your foot will not stumble …' (vv.1,23).

Ephesians 6 speaks of 'feet fitted with the readiness that comes from the gospel of peace' (v.15). The message of salvation is called the 'gospel of peace'. We are to take the gospel of peace wherever we tread, not just in word but in action. The New Testament Greek word for peace, '*eirēnē*', shows that the absence of strife is brought about by God's mercy granting freedom from the distresses that are brought about as a result of sin.

For prayer and reflection

Lord! I give you my feet! Show me where you want them to tread and help me to step out in Your name, bringing Your love and truth to others. Amen.

WEEKEND

His broken body

For reflection: Isaiah 53:5

'But he was pierced for our transgressions, he was crushed for our iniquities; the punishment that brought us peace was upon him, and by his wounds we are healed.'

It may seem a strange time of year to be thinking of Jesus' body broken for us but we cannot separate His birth and His death. Jesus surrendered His whole self, body, soul and spirit, in death, that we might live!

As we spend time over the next few weeks thinking of surrendering different aspects of our lives, how about looking at the different aspects of Jesus' life that He surrendered for you?

His hands were pierced 'when the whole weight of His quivering frame hung from their torn muscles and bared nerves; literally uplifted in parting blessing' (Frances Ridley Havergal). His hands were tender, healing, faithful hands, pierced that our hands might be as His to those we meet.

What about the rest of His body? His feet, His voice, His lips? Can you meditate on how each of these were operational in His life?

What aspect of these challenges you at this moment in your life?

Sacred songs

Exodus 15:1–18

'… I will sing to the LORD, for he is highly exalted …' (v.1)

How often do you stop and think about the words you sing in church? Have you ever found yourself singing a hymn that you have sung for years and suddenly, in the middle of singing it, you are impacted by how meaningful the words are? As you sing, your spirit engages with the biblical truths in the lyrics. In contrast, have there also been times when, to your shame, it dawns on you that rather than being lost in worshipping God, you are listening to the sound of your own voice or concentrating on other people's voices. Can you hit that note? Can others hear you? Maybe you sing the words but your mind drifts off to think of other things?

Do you ever stop to think of the type of song you are singing? There are different types of songs recorded in the Old Testament: a joyous song (Gen. 31:27); a triumphant song (Judg. 5:12); a purification song (Neh. 12:46); a love song (Song of Solomon).

The song in our passage today, 'The song of Moses and Israel', appears to me to be a triumphant song. The Israelites are declaring the might and power of God ('The LORD is a warrior; the LORD is his name', v.3); who He is to them ('The LORD is my strength and my song; he has become my salvation', v.2); and what He has done for them ('Your right hand, O LORD, shattered the enemy', v.6). What about the lyrics of the songs that we sing? Are they declaring the power, might and majesty of God or are they making us 'feel nice'?

If you could sing your own song to the Lord today, what would you like to say?

For prayer and reflection

Lord! I give You my voice! May it proclaim Your might, Your majesty, Your power. And may it honour You. Amen.

Heart **of worship**

ooking at 2 Samuel 22 and 23, we read David's song of praise and his last song. David was a man who knew what it was to worship God. He wasn't singing songs that other people had written but instead he says, 'The Spirit of the LORD spoke through me; his word was on my tongue' (2 Sam 23:2). He worshipped God from the depths of his being and as he did, he was taken to the deep places with God.

Yesterday we looked at the words we sing and the giving of our voices to the Lord. When we sing, we worship, but worship is far more than just singing. Rick Warren points out, 'The heart of worship is surrender'. John 4:24 declares, 'God is spirit, and his worshippers must worship in spirit and in truth.' It's interesting that in Romans Paul spends 11 chapters speaking of God's grace and mercy, and our life in Christ, and then in chapter 12 challenges us to surrender ourselves fully and to offer our bodies as living sacrifices, which is our spiritual act of worship (Rom. 12:1).

Worship is not so much what we *do*, but what we *are*. We are not called to *do* worship, but to *be* worshippers. To worship God is to be preoccupied by Him and become more like Him – 2 Corinthians 3:18 points out, 'And we, who with unveiled faces all reflect the Lord's glory, are being transformed into his likeness with ever-increasing glory, which comes from the Lord, who is the Spirit'.

Are God's characteristics being imprinted on us as we worship Him? As Joe King, worship leader and songwriter, points out, 'Unless worship changes us, it's not worship – it's just songs ... God wants our worship to be living and our living to be worship.'

2 Samuel 22:26–51

'Therefore I will praise you, O LORD, among the nations ...' (v.50)

For prayer and reflection

Help me to worship You in spirit and truth, Lord, I pray. Amen.

Guarded lips

Philippians 4:1–9

'... put it into practice. And the God of peace will be with you.' (v.9)

Proverbs 18:21 reminds us that 'the tongue has the power of life and death'; what we say and how we use our lips is very powerful. Proverbs speaks of life and death. Life signifies living purposefully, whereas death signifies destruction. The root word referred to in the Old Testament for 'lips' includes speech, language, thoughts and motivation. Our passage for today exhorts us to think on those things that are right and pure – not only must we *think* on that which is admirable and lovely, but we must *speak* it too!

Thinking good thoughts may not sound too difficult, but if we are at all honest, to always think good thoughts is quite a challenge! Do we affirm, speak with love and retain righteous thoughts about others? Sadly, women are known for gossip, but Scripture encourages us to guard our lips. Proverbs 18 is very direct in what it has to say about mouths and lips! 'A fool's lips bring him strife ...' (v.6). 'A fool's mouth is his undoing, and his lips are a snare to his soul' (v.7). Proverbs also tells us of the futility of lips that do not speak that which is true and noble. 'Truthful lips endure for ever, but a lying tongue lasts only a moment' (12:19). That which our lips utter, our lives must reflect and not contradict God's ways.

Matthew 12:34 reminds us that 'out of the overflow of the heart the mouth speaks'. We need to surrender our lips to the Lord, but even more must we surrender what we hold in our hearts. 'Search me, O God, and know my heart; test me and know my anxious thoughts. See if there is any offensive way in me, and lead me in the way everlasting' (Psa. 139:23–24).

For prayer and reflection

'May the words of my mouth and the meditation of my heart be pleasing in your sight, O LORD, my Rock and my Redeemer' (Psa. 19:14).

Chosen words

Today we continue with the importance of guarding our words. The NASB translation of 2 Timothy 2:16 exhorts us to 'avoid worldly and empty chatter for it will lead to further ungodliness'. 'Worldly' refers to that which lacks relationships of affinity to God; 'empty chatter' refers to chatter that is devoid of spiritual character, and fruitless in terms of moulding the Christian life. I wonder how much of our talk fits these descriptions or has the tendency to come precariously close! The consequence of 'empty chatter' is that we will be led into ungodliness. The New Testament Greek for such ungodliness, '*asebela*', speaks of a lack of reverence and a neglect of duty towards God, our neighbour and ourselves. Perhaps most of us would rightly declare that our talk is not lacking in reverence; but does it include neglect of duty towards God, our neighbour or ourselves?

Proverbs 12:18 reminds us again of the choice we have in how we use our words, and the consequence of our decisions – 'Reckless words pierce like a sword, but the tongue of the wise brings healing.' Oh that our words would bring healing to others and to ourselves at *all* times. James 3 and 4 have much to teach us on chosen words and conduct. James 3 speaks of the taming of the tongue, and the fact that the tongue has the tendency to be restless and full of poison! It goes on to teach us about two kinds of wisdom – worldly and godly. '… wisdom that comes from heaven is first of all pure; then peace-loving, considerate, submissive, full of mercy and good fruit, impartial and sincere' (3:17). The answer as to how we attain such wisdom appears in James 4: 'Submit yourselves, then, to God …' (v.7).

2 Timothy 2:14–26

'Avoid godless chatter, because those who indulge in it will become more and more ungodly.' (v.16)

For prayer and reflection

Thank You, Lord, that if I come near to You, You will come near to me and You will purify my heart. Amen (James 4:8).

Priceless pennies

1 Timothy
6:10–20

'… nor to put
their hope in
wealth, which is so
uncertain, but to
put their hope in
God …' (v.17)

The concept of surrendering our finances is something with which many people struggle. Various passages in the Bible, our reading today included, indicate that it's not wealth per se that poses a problem, but our love of money and the temptation to put our hope in wealth rather than in God. In our minds, money and possessions bring with them a certain level of security, but is this true security? Paul, writing to Timothy, speaks of hope in wealth as uncertain and yet society teaches us the opposite.

Ecclesiastes 5:10 tells us, 'Whoever loves money never has money enough; whoever loves wealth is never satisfied with his income. This too is meaningless.' It's no doubt true that money has attached to it a certain insatiable hunger. Paul exhorts Timothy to teach others not to seek richness in lasting things but in good deeds, generosity and willingness to share (1 Tim. 6:7–18).

Proverbs 11:28 emphasises that it is where our trust is placed that is so vital, 'Whoever trusts in his riches will fall, but the righteous will thrive like a green leaf.' 'The word expresses the sense of wellbeing which results from knowing that the "rug won't be pulled out from under you" … The folly of depending on any other type of security is strongly contrasted with depending upon God alone.' (NASB, Lexical Aid to the Old Testament)

If your finances were truly surrendered to God would it change how you spend your money? If you have not fully surrendered this area, do you know what holds you back? Could it be fear of not having sufficient? Fear of loss of control? Fear that the 'nice' things won't be allowed? Fear of the future and not making adequate provision for it?

For prayer and reflection

Lord! You say that I cannot serve two masters. Show me in what way I need to change in attitude and practicality in the area of finance. Amen.

WEEKEND

Characterised by quality

For reflection: Matthew 6:33
*'But seek first his kingdom and his righteousness,
and all these things will be given to you as well.'*

Scripture emphasises that we are to seek first
God's kingdom and His righteousness
(Matt. 6:33); if we do this, then we will lack no
good thing (Psa. 34:10). We are blessed if we both keep God's
statutes and seek Him with all our heart (Psa. 119:2).
The word 'blessed' is used in both the New and Old
Testaments and in New Testament Greek the word is
makarioi, which means to be characterised by the quality of
God. It indicates being indwelt by God, and refers to God's
nature and kingdom being in us.

In this context it also means to be fully satisfied.
Satisfaction is not the same as happiness: what is being
brought to light is a deep satisfaction that is a result of
Christ's indwelling.

What brings you satisfaction at the moment? Is it a
satisfaction irrespective of circumstance, and does it result
in continuing growth in maturity and Christlikeness? The
satisfaction we need is that which comes through submitting
our *hurts* to the Lord, drawing close to Him because 'the
closer we get to God the more like Him we will become'
(David Roper).

Committed minds

'… but be transformed by the renewing of your mind.' (v.2)

Recently my year-old computer stopped working! I knew it wasn't dead because it was 'whirring', but the screen was blank. It turned out that I needed a completely new processor, without which I was powerless to do anything constructive! It's similar with our minds: if our minds are not surrendered that can affect the rest of our being!

The mind also seems to be one area that Satan loves to attack. In 2 Corinthians 10:4–5 Paul exhorts us to take captive every thought and make it obedient to Christ. He understands fully the effect of a mind that is not captive to Christ. Have you ever consciously surrendered to God your mind – your thought-life, emotions and intellect?

The Lord makes the most of what is unreservedly surrendered to Him. Whatever we give Him He will use. Not only will *He* use our surrendered minds to His glory but *we* are to use that which we have surrendered to honour Him and bless others. As I write this I am reminded of the account in Acts 3:6 where Peter heals the crippled beggar. 'Then Peter said, "Silver or gold I do not have, but what I have I give you. In the name of Jesus Christ of Nazareth, walk."' He used that which He had been given and didn't worry about that which he didn't have! So often we spend vast amounts of energy concentrating on that which we don't have and fail to see that which we do!

For prayer and reflection

Lord, thank You that You can change me! Renew my mind, I pray. Amen.

If you can, spend time today focusing on the cross and allowing God to renew your mind and revive in you the abilities He has given you. I would urge you to lay down wrong beliefs about yourself, others and God, and 'Discover for yourself that the Christ of the Cross can change you' (Vernon Grounds).

My will **or His?**

As well as a battle taking place in our minds, another area where battles frequently take place is in our wills! Rick Warren warns, 'the greatest hindrance in your life is not others, it is yourself – our self will, stubborn pride, and personal ambition. You cannot fulfil God's purposes for your life while focusing on your own plans.' Just when we have dealt with self and are enjoying our newfound journey with Jesus, our will rears its ugly head again!

Do we pray 'my will be done' or 'Thy will be done'? We must lay down our will for, 'Prayer does not consist in battering the walls of heaven for personal benefit or the success of our plans. Rather, it is the committing of ourselves to carrying out God's purposes' (G. Ashton Oldham).

True surrender of the will is, without a doubt, based on complete confidence in the One to whom it is surrendered, and yielding ourselves to the One in whom we have put our trust. 'Then this will of God which has seemed in old far-off days a stern and fateful power, is seen to be only love energised ... So, as the fancied sternness of God's will is lost in His love, the stubbornness of our will becomes melted in that love, and lost in our acceptance of it' (Frances Ridley Havergal).

Isaiah 55 has many a time challenged me, with gentleness and love, concerning my ways, to surrender my will. I can see God smiling at me as I do things my way, saying, 'Come to Me, My path is much more rewarding.' The reward? As Isaiah says, '... you will go out in joy and be led forth in peace' (v.12).

Isaiah 55

'"For my thoughts are not your thoughts, neither are your ways my ways," declares the LORD.' (v.8)

For prayer and reflection

Lord, I give You my regrets, my problems, my past, my future, my ambitions, my dreams, my weaknesses, my habits, my hurts, my will. Amen.

Confidence in Him

'In God, whose word I praise, in God I trust; I will not be afraid.' (v.4)

C.S. Lewis once said, 'The more we let God take us over, the more truly ourselves we become – because He made us.' Yesterday we touched on the concept of surrender only being possible if we have confidence and trust in the One to whom we surrender. Is there anything holding you back from fully trusting God? Trust means a firm belief in the reliability, truth or strength etc of a person and requires a confident expectation. It involves a firm reliance on the integrity, ability or character of that person. Do you see God as fulfilling these? I do! And more!

We can have trust in the everlasting strength of God – '... the LORD, is the Rock eternal' (Isa. 26:4). We can have trust in the goodness of God – 'The LORD is good, a refuge in times of trouble' (Nah. 1:7). We can have trust in the lovingkindness of God – 'How priceless is your unfailing love!' (Psa. 36:7). We can have trust in the bounty of God – '... God, who richly provides us with everything for our enjoyment' (1 Tim. 6:17). We can have trust in God's care for us – 'Cast all your anxiety on him because he cares for you' (1 Pet. 5:7). We can have trust in the fact He won't forsake us – '... for you, LORD, have never forsaken those who seek you (Psa. 9:10). The list could go on!

Our trust in God leads to enjoyment of perfect peace (Isa. 26:3). Our trust in God leads to prospering and being blessed (Prov. 16:20). Our trust in God leads to rejoicing in Him (Psa. 5:11; 33:21). Our trust in God leads to the fulfilment of the desires of our hearts (Psa. 37:3–5). Our trust in God leads to deliverance from enemies (Psa. 37:40). Our trust in God leads to safety in times of danger (Prov. 29:25). Our trust in God leads to stability and security (Psa. 125:1).

For prayer and reflection

Thank You, Lord, that You are trustworthy at all times. Amen.

Heart **of stone**

' f you don't surrender to Christ, you surrender to chaos.'[1] There's no doubt that an un-surrendered heart can lead to internal and external chaos! Is this also so in a life given to Jesus but with a heart that has not fully been given over to Him? Our hearts are naturally: sinful (Heb. 3:12); deceitful (Jer. 17:9); weak-willed (Ezek. 16:30); full of flattery and falsehood (Psa. 12:2); rebellious (Jer. 5:23); hard and obstinate (Ezek. 3:7); stony (Ezek. 11:19); proud (Prov. 21:4); perverse (Prov. 17:20); foolish (Rom. 1:21); corrupt (Psa. 14:1).

In Psalm 51 David recognises the results of his deceitful heart and cries out to God to change it. This is one of the most powerful passages in the Bible concerning conversion and forgiveness. It was written after David had committed adultery with Bathsheba and subsequently had her husband, Uriah, killed in battle (2 Sam. 11:2–17). David's repentance involved: godly sorrow, verbal confession, turning from sin, forgiveness, restoration to God's favour, rejoicing in salvation and the desire to testify to others about God's grace.

David asks of God, 'Create in me a pure heart'. The Hebrew word used for 'create' indicates an activity that can only be performed by God. It means to make, produce, engrave and carve. That which is purified (cleaned) has had all dirt removed. In the Old Testament, the word used for heart is commonly interpreted as man's inner or immaterial nature. In the Bible the whole spectrum of human emotions is attributed to the heart; wisdom and understanding reside in the heart.[2]

Can you spend time talking with God about the state of your own heart?

1. E. Stanley Jones. 2. NASB Lexical Aids to the Old Testament.

Psalm 51

'Create in me a pure heart, O God …' (v.10)

For prayer and reflection

O Lord, You know my imperfections. I give my heart to You and ask You to begin a cleansing process in me. Amen.

Heart **of flesh**

1 Kings 8:54–61

'But your hearts must be fully committed to the LORD our God …' (v.61)

We saw yesterday that only God can change our hearts – the creating of a new heart is an activity performed by Him.

God can make our hearts: clean (pure) (Psa. 51:10; Matt 5:8); good and noble (Luke 8:15); faithful (Neh. 9:8); discerning (1 Kings 3:9); contrite (Psa. 51:17); sincere (Heb. 10:22); glad (Psa. 16:9); wise (Prov. 2:6); cheerful (Prov. 17:22); steadfast and trusting (Psa. 112:7). And more!

In our passage today we see a picture of returning from sustained prayer, giving praise to God and affirmation of His might, majesty and faithfulness, amongst other things, and giving exhortation to the people of Israel to ensure their hearts are fully committed to the Lord and that they live by His decrees and obey His commands. However, we also see a difference between Solomon and his father, David. King Solomon's rule began with wealth, glory and power, but it ended in disgrace. He lacked the spiritual toughness of David and he compromised on some spiritual principles to achieve his goals.

I see a humbling and softening of David's heart following the recognition of his wrongdoing and his deep, deep repentance. It just goes to show that the hard times in our lives can bring us to a place where we are open for God to do major work on us. But we still have a choice over whether we let Him. In Psalm 119 the psalmist calls upon God with earnest cries for a heart of flesh, 'Keep me from deceitful ways; be gracious to me through your law. I have chosen the way of truth; I have set my heart on your laws … I run in the path of your commands, for you have set my heart free' (vv.29–30,32).

For prayer and reflection

Thank You, Lord, that You have made a way for my heart to be free by my choosing the way of truth. Amen.

WEEKEND

His heart for you

For reflection: Isaiah 40:11
*'He tends his flock like a shepherd: He gathers the lambs
in his arms and carries them close to his heart;
he gently leads those that have young.'*

How do you see God's heart for you? Is it based on the adult role models you had as a child? So often we project onto God our own experiences of those 'in charge' and, sadly, the role models aren't always positive.

Personally I love the image of God as a shepherd. I see gentleness in God's heart as He holds us as vulnerable lambs close to His chest. His heart rhythmically beats with life, and radiates warmth and protection. His love is strong, bright, fruitful, energising and all-embracing.

His heart for you and me is anything other than passive. With each beat resounds His very nature and character declaring that He is Master, Saviour, Friend and King.

Jesus said, 'I am the good shepherd. The good shepherd lays down his life for the sheep' (John 10:11). All His Godhead and all His manhood concentrated in His ceaseless love for you and me!

Can you spend time this weekend receiving God's heart for you?

Created **to love**

**Philippians
1:1–11**

'And this is my prayer: that your love may abound more and more …'
(v.9)

God has created us to love. 'We have a sealed treasure of love, which either remains sealed, and then gradually dries up and wastes away, or is unsealed and poured out, and yet is the fuller and not the emptier for the outpouring' (Frances Ridley Havergal).

The key to fruitful love is the source of love. If we draw upon that which is of our own making there is effort and a limited supply. But if we draw upon that which God gives us, the more we give the more we have! However much love we do or do not have naturally (and for some the heat from life's hardships has all but dried up their pools of love), there is a well of love of which there is an endless supply – God who is love. The nature of that love is different too! God's love is not an absorbing, but a radiating love, unlike our own love that often consumes.

2 Corinthians 5:14 tells us that 'Christ's love compels us'. Something that compels is rousing, strong, brings about interest, conviction, attention and admiration.

For prayer and reflection

I give You my capacity to love, Lord. Thank You that You have created me to love, but help me to draw on Your resources and not simply my own. Amen.

There is nothing weak or ineffective about the love of Christ. In the same way, our receiving His love to pass on is not without positive consequence. As we love others with the love which Jesus has given us, we draw them closer to His love. We do not love that they may love us, but that they may love Him. The evidence that the love we pour out is from Jesus and not of our own making is that it doesn't occur in isolation. Love is, after all, just one part of the fruit of the Spirit, 'But the fruit of the Spirit is love, joy, peace, patience, kindness, goodness, faithfulness, gentleness and self-control' (Gal. 5:22).

Love **knows no limits**

O ver the past few days we have held in our mind's eye the image of God as a shepherd and have, I hope, become increasingly aware of His great love for us through His Son Jesus, which in turn compels us to love others.

In today's reading we have an equally powerful image of God's tender, life-giving love in the Song of Moses. The theme of the song is the name of the Lord, His loving care of His people, His righteousness and His mercy; which are contrasted with the unfaithfulness of Israel.

In verse 10 the passage speaks of God's love for Israel as the 'apple of his eye', which some versions translate as the 'pupil of his eye'. The pupil is the part of the eye upon which sight so greatly depends. In verse 11, reference is made to the eagle. The eagle recognises when her young are ready and kicks them out of the nest. But she flies close by, ready to swoop under those that do not fly but fall, and carefully catches them in her vast expanse of wing. The mother eagle has huge regard for her young and in teaching them to fly she protects and encourages them to imitate her own movements. In the same way God is incredibly diligent of us, His children, and He too longs that we would imitate Him. God's love for us encourages growth and is protective at the same time.

In what new way can you take on the manner of His love?

Dennis Fisher once said, 'Our greatest liberty lies in serving the One who created and redeemed us.' I'd like to add, not only serving Him, but imitating Him and sharing His very nature with others through our transformed lives.

Deuteronomy 32:1–14

'He shielded him … he guarded him as the apple of his eye ...' (v.10)

For prayer and reflection

Lord, Your love sets me free! Let me never become complacent of that and let me share more of You with those around me. Amen.

A **special people**

'In him we were also chosen …' (v.11)

'Love so amazing, so divine, demands my soul, my life, my all!' (Isaac Watts). We say to God, 'Take my love and use it for your purpose' and are instantly reminded that because of God's love for us, which is so amazing, so divine, He deserves more than simply our love. Can we give Him our soul, our life, our all?

Thinking in terms of our inheritance as believers, I find it helpful to look back at God's relationship with Israel. In Deuteronomy we read, 'For you are a people holy to the LORD your God. The LORD your God has chosen you out of all the peoples on the face of the earth to be his people, his treasured possession' (Deut. 7:6). Chosen because God wanted them to be chosen, not because He was obliged to choose them!

Can you put that in a personal context for a minute? What does it mean to you to be chosen, to be holy, to be God's treasured possession? Does receiving this afresh stir in your spirit the desire to give more of yourself to Him?

The word used for 'holy' here is '*qâdôsh*'. This is an important Hebrew word meaning selected, pure, holy and consecrated. Israel was holy, a nation which was separated for God's service. If you have put your faith in Jesus you too are set apart, and through your inheritance in Christ are holy (if not yet in terms of your practice, then certainly in terms of your position!).

For prayer and reflection

Help me, Lord, to give You more of myself. Amen.

The root of the word 'chosen' involves a careful, well-thought-out choice. Have you ever considered that you are a careful, well-thought-out choice of God's? Does that cause you to want to change your actions at all?

Crown **of consecration**

W e saw yesterday that we who are in Christ are a chosen people – people who are set apart. Jesus reminds His disciples 'As it is, you do not belong to the world, but I have chosen you out of the world ...' (John 15:19).

Frances Ridley Havergal wrote, 'There is no consecration without separation.' In Hebrew the word 'separation' stems from a word meaning 'consecration'. '... the symbol of his separation to God is on his head' (Num. 6:7). Separation in this context refers to the priest, who was separated from anything secular and wore an engraved plate over his forehead declaring that he was a consecrated person. But the word 'separation' is also used in the context of a royal crown or diadem which was a token that someone was separated from the people at large and indicated royalty (NASB Lexical Aids to the Old Testament).

In 1 Peter we are reminded that we are a chosen people, a royal priesthood, and in Romans Paul reminds us of the part that we have to play within the honour of being chosen: 'Give yourself to God ... Surrender your whole being to him to be used for righteous purposes' (Rom. 6:13, TEV). And William Booth (founder of the Salvation Army) challenges us with the fact that 'The greatness of a man's power is in the measure of his surrender.'

As we draw our reflections on surrender to an end, spend a little while with the Lord considering the aspects of yourself which still require surrender, and pray either 'change my', 'take my' or 'use my' life, moments, days, hands, feet, voice, lips, silver, gold, intellect, will, heart, love, and self.

'Victory comes through surrender. Surrender doesn't weaken you; it strengthens you' (Rick Warren, *The Purpose-Driven Life*). It brings great joy!

1 Peter 1:13–2:12

'But you are a chosen people, a royal priesthood, a holy nation, a people belonging to God ...' (2:9)

For prayer and reflection

Thank You for the joy of surrender, Lord. Amen.

Titus — a call to
radical discipleship

Heather Coupland

Heather loves working alongside her husband Simon, who
is a vicar in Surrey. She has recently been diagnosed with
Fibromyalgia and is learning how to pace herself, which is a
constant challenge for someone who loves to be busy! She
thrives on being part of the local church community and really
enjoys connecting with mums and their pre-school children,
mainly so she can have as many cuddles with their little ones as
possible! She loves writing Bible reading notes and hopes one
day to write a book. She also likes reading, going to the theatre,
going out for coffee and shopping with her daughter Pippa.

Titus – radical discipleship

Titus 1:1–4

'To Titus, my true
son in our common
faith …' (v.4)

I wonder if you like short stories or prefer epic novels which span generations and are too heavy to read in bed! I confess that I love novels I can escape into, rather than a short story which seems to be over before I've decided whether I like the main character or not. I therefore approached the book of Titus with a slightly negative bias. How much good teaching, relevant to my life, could come out of its paltry 46 verses? How misguided I was. Even though this is one of the shortest books in the whole Bible, its teaching has incredible relevance for us today.

Titus, like 1 and 2 Timothy, is primarily concerned with pastoral care in the new churches that Paul has planted. Titus has been travelling with Paul and has now been left in Crete by himself to get on with the work that had been started there. He was a Greek convert and a trusted companion and fellow missionary of Paul (2 Cor. 8:23). He was obviously a capable leader and co-worker who had already sorted out trouble in Corinth. He had also accompanied Paul on a strategic trip to Jerusalem to investigate the position of non-Jewish converts in the church there (Gal. 2:1–3).

So what does the letter Paul wrote to Titus on an island in the Mediterranean have to say to us today? Plenty! This book is a call to radical Christian discipleship. It is about living out the Christian life so that our lives are transformed, leading others to be attracted to the gospel and to experience this transformation for themselves.

The book of Titus is not always comfortable reading, but as we open our hearts to its message let's be committed to obeying the commands we find there and to experiencing the fruit of that obedience in our own lives.

For prayer and reflection

Lord, as I open my heart to Your Word, give me a real excitement at all You want to say to me through it. Amen.

WEEKEND

Prepare the way!

For reflection: Mark 1:1–8; Isaiah 40:3–5

One of the busiest months of the year inevitably is December, and yet it's the month when I always long for more time to prepare my heart properly for all that lies ahead.

A few years ago I became frustrated that December came and went without my having any real sense of the spiritual build-up to Jesus' birth. Last year, therefore, I was determined to let God prepare my heart *amidst* the busyness rather than longing for the busyness to stop. I was intentional about bringing my anxieties to God in the middle of what was going on.

I wanted to meet with Him as I wrapped the presents and did the shopping, truly letting Him be Emmanuel, God with us – God with *me*. I realised that if we wait for the perfect time to prepare our hearts it will never happen, so let's meet Him where we are and rejoice that He wants to speak to us, whatever we are doing.

Who are you?

Titus 1:1–4

'Paul, a servant
of God and an
apostle of Jesus
Christ ...' (v.1)

The first verses of Titus are packed with theology: Paul preaches a mini-sermon before even saying hello! His introduction to this letter is one of the longest in the New Testament, but you won't find any waffle or wasted words here. What I love is the confidence with which Paul introduces himself. I'm impressed with the way he asserts that he is, first and foremost, 'a servant of God'.

Today's society often defines people by what they do rather than simply by who they are. I don't have a full-time job, but do lots of voluntary work in my church. My days are full and varied with all kinds of interesting activities, and yet at social functions, when people ask me what I do, I get completely tongue-tied and my mind goes blank. As a full-time vicar's wife, I have no official job title that explains what my function is, and so I find myself desperately trying to justify the fact that I don't actually have a 'proper job'. Paul wouldn't have had this kind of problem. He was utterly confident and comfortable in his calling and his role. We do find out that part of his job as a servant of God was to preach (v.3), but that's not the most important part of the package. Paul's preaching comes out of the fact that he is a servant, and not the other way round. Jesus also exhibits servanthood, telling His disciples that '... the Son of Man did not come to be served, but to serve ...' (Matt. 20:28) and washing their feet (John 13).

Are we confident in our calling to be servants of God? Does what we do flow out of the security of knowing who we are, or do we join in with society and desperately try to define ourselves by what we do?

For prayer and reflection

Lord, thank You that You have called me to be Your servant before anything that I do. Help me to rest in the security of that precious calling on my life. Amen.

What does your **faith rest on?**

I know that there have been many times in my Christian life when I have relied too much on my feelings and have desired experiences of God, rather than trusting in the truth He has given me in His Word.

In the opening verses of Titus, Paul seems to want to remind his readers of why he is serving God. He's not doing it because it makes him feel good, but because of things like faith (v.1), truth (v.1) and hope (v.2). He wants Titus to remember that he is serving 'God's elect' (v.1). This isn't just any group of people, but people chosen by God to live as a community, blessed with His grace and obedient to Him. Their lives are to be examples to the people around them, showing God's nature in the way they live. These new Christians in Crete live among godless and wicked people who want to deceive them at every opportunity. They can't afford to let their faith rest on their feelings or they will soon give up.

I wonder how swayed you are by your feelings? My husband and I have helped to lead many Alpha courses. Nearly every time there are several people waiting for the ultimate experience of God which will make believing easy and their relationship with God unshakeable. Paul tells Titus that our faith rests on a firmer foundation than our experiences; the certain hope of eternal life. If our spiritual lives are governed by our feelings, then we won't send out a very consistent message to the people among whom we live. We need to learn deep in our hearts that our faith rests on the promises of a God who 'does not lie' (v.2), and Who can be trusted completely.

Titus 1:2

'... a faith and knowledge resting on the hope of eternal life ...' (v.2)

For prayer and reflection

Please help me, Lord, to rely on the promises in Your Word and not on my emotions. Thank You that You are the same yesterday, today and forever. Amen (Heb. 13: 8).

Getting on with **the day job**

Titus 1:5

'... straighten out what was left unfinished and appoint elders in every town ...' (v.5)

Having laid the spiritual foundation for this letter, Paul now moves on to what he wants Titus to do practically – and it's not going to be easy. Titus is to travel from town to town developing the leadership structure of each church and completing what Paul had started. What a daunting prospect! Titus is like a management consultant drawing out leadership potential in each place and encouraging the newly-appointed elders to fulfil their roles.

In many ways Titus's job is very straightforward. He has Paul's instructions to follow and a task to accomplish – end of story. Or is it? As we read this letter, we see what massive spiritual implications Titus's role has for the churches and also for the communities around them. If Titus picks lousy leaders who go their own way and take no notice of the advice they have been given, then the new church will become a laughing stock and the opponents of the gospel will have won a victory.

I wonder how you view the practical tasks you do each day, the people you mix with and the relationships you form. Are these things just a part of your job or do they have more significance than that? They do to God! Many people put little value on what they do if there is nothing obviously 'spiritual' about it. We need to recognise that Jesus is Lord of our whole lives, wanting to be a part of everything we do. Paul made this point when writing to the Colossians: 'And whatever you do, whether in word or deed, do it all in the name of the Lord Jesus, giving thanks to God the Father through him' (Col. 3:17).

It's good to remember that in God's eyes there is no divide between the spiritual and practical areas of our lives.

For prayer and reflection

Lord, thank You that You want to be involved in every part of my life. Help me not to exclude You from anything I do. Amen.

High standards for all!

M y husband is a vicar, so reading about the necessary characteristics of an elder (and his family) makes me understandably rather nervous!

'… he must be hospitable, one who loves what is good, who is self-controlled, upright, holy and disciplined.' (v.8)

It's important to note that Paul is writing to a very young church. In his first letter to Timothy (1 Tim. 3:6), where he is writing to a more established church, Paul stipulates that a leader *must not* be a recent convert. Here in Crete, however, no such advice is given as the whole church is made up of new believers. In this situation we might feel that anyone who has an ounce of leadership potential ought to be immediately appointed as an elder. But no, Paul is adamant that the elder's character and lifestyle must match the message that he is preaching. He must be someone who can face any situation with God-given wisdom and self-control, showing himself to be someone who is serious about following Jesus' teaching. The word 'blameless' here frightened me a little, so I was relieved to read in a commentary that it doesn't mean perfect, but rather refers to a person whose life is characterised by moral integrity. Then I read on about family life and the behaviour of children and felt challenged again, because Paul really does set very high standards for those involved in leadership. And that's when I was struck by a radical thought: aren't these qualities that should be reasonably expected of *any* follower of Jesus Christ? Shouldn't we all be hospitable (Rom. 12:13) and self-controlled (Gal. 5:22), loving what is good (Phil. 4:8), and living lives that attract people to the gospel?

If the Church is to be a witnessing community showing non-believers how to 'live the life', shouldn't these verses apply to all of us?

For prayer and reflection

Read these verses again, applying them to your own life. Pray for your church leaders, too, that they will be able to live what they preach.

Hold on

'… hold firmly to the trustworthy message as it has been taught …' (v.9)

P aul is emphasising here that the elders must hang on to the truth with which they have been entrusted. It is vitally important that they teach people the Word of God in order to prevent the new converts from being tempted to follow one of the many false teachers who have appeared on the scene.

We might think that hanging on to sound doctrine was only of importance where churches were being planted and Christians were real pioneers, but it is still something that we need to do today. These new believers were discovering how to follow Jesus' teaching amidst much spiritual and doctrinal confusion, and many new believers today find themselves in a similar situation.

Over my years as a Christian, there have been many different fads and trends in the churches I have attended and in the books I have read. At some meetings I went to as a teenager, you were thought of as a second-class Christian unless you spoke in tongues. Later on it became a mark of God's anointing if you shook or laughed. I'm not saying that any of these things are intrinsically wrong. The danger comes when these things become our whole focus, and the Word of God, the 'trustworthy message', is relegated to second place.

The Bible is the benchmark by which we must test everything and on which our lives are to be built (2 Tim. 3:16). Jesus Himself teaches that obedience to His words should be the foundation on which our lives are built (Matt. 7:24–27). If God chooses to bless us with laughter or tears as we worship, let's thank Him, and be even more determined to get to know Him and His Word better in gratitude for what He has done.

For prayer and reflection

'I have hidden your word in my heart that I might not sin against you' (Psa. 119:11). Give me a hunger for Your Word, Lord and speak to my heart as I read it. Amen.

WEEKEND

People with a message

For reflection: Malachi 3:1–4

The Bible is full of people with a message to deliver. In the Old Testament we think of Moses and the prophets who spoke out the words God gave them. In the New Testament, and particularly at Advent, we think of John the Baptist (Matt. 3), preparing the way with his message of repentance. Then, at Christmas, we think of the angels bringing the good news of Jesus' birth (Luke 2:8–20).

Further on, we see Paul as a passionate messenger for the gospel as he travels and plants churches. Do you live your life as someone with an important message to deliver? Do you make the most of every opportunity to communicate the good news of Jesus to those around you?

Let's remember not to get too cosy when we prepare for our individual Christmases and we celebrate all that the message of the angels means to us. And let's also remember: the message that came two thousand years ago still needs delivering today.

Don't be **deceived**

Titus 1:10–16

'For there are many rebellious people, mere talkers and deceivers …' (v.10)

For prayer and reflection

Pray for your church leaders to teach the truth and live lives that point to God. Let's also pray for discernment for ourselves – that we will hold fast to God's Word and not be led astray by teaching that does not come from Him but from man.

Paul wants to warn Titus about the type of people among whom he is working. Cretans had a reputation for being lazy and untruthful, and now into this unstable society come false teachers whose aim is to confuse the new converts with their clever arguments. Titus must protect his new converts and be on the lookout for these rebels. This is why his elders must be above reproach and be able to teach truth and refute error. Paul emphasises the importance of sound doctrine in verse 9 because he knows how much spurious and unhelpful teaching is available to those who will listen. Titus and the elders he appoints must know how to spot false teaching and how to deal with the teachers.

The elders' impeccable character is emphasised so that they can show up the errors of the false teachers by their conduct, and not just by their teaching. Paul says that false teachers are 'mere talkers', who try to deceive with words, but whose lives don't match up to what they say.

Titus must also ensure that the Jewish converts do not take back on board Jewish customs in order to be part of some special super-spiritual group. Wandering teachers often offered new rituals or doctrine, claiming that these would bring people closer to God. They then demanded money for divulging these secrets, proving how corrupt their hearts were. They weren't motivated by wanting to bring about unity in the newly formed churches nor were they interested in teaching the truth and training people in godliness. Motivated only by selfish gain, they were to be avoided at all costs.

Where does **purity** come from?

Titus 1:15

'To the pure, all things are pure ...'
(v.15)

My husband receives a Christian book catalogue which has several pages of Christian diet books. Some of these books have very sound nutritional advice, which is great. Some publications, however, come close to inferring that if we follow strict dietary guidelines, we can have greater intimacy with God. This is exactly what some of the false teachers wanted people on Crete to believe over 2,000 years ago! The false teachers said that in order to really know the true God, you had to abstain from certain foods because they were impure. Paul wants Titus to tell people to reject these ideas completely because they go against everything he is trying to teach them about the grace of God, which is a gift and cannot be earned by correct behaviour and eating the right things.

Jesus Himself gave clear teaching on this whole issue in Mark 7, telling the crowd that nothing a person eats of drinks can affect their purity (v.15). Paul wants to stress that our purity as believers does not come from following certain rules about diet or taking part in rituals. We have a purity that comes from having been made clean on the inside through faith in Christ. It's all about what *He* has done and not about what *we* have done. What a relief!

These false teachings come from people who have fundamentally misunderstood Christ's message of grace and faith. Paul even goes so far as to say that because they need regulations to achieve their own purity this demonstrates that they are themselves corrupted. They aren't teaching people to trust in Christ and live in freedom, but are weighing them down with legalism which brings condemnation rather than liberation.

For prayer and reflection

Lord Jesus, thank You that You have made me right with God through Your death on the cross and that it's nothing to do with what I've done. Amen.

Actions versus words

Titus 1:16

'They claim to know God, but by their actions they deny him.'

As we move further into this letter it is noticeable that the same themes crop up repeatedly. Paul was desperate for these church communities to understand the gospel and he longed for them to influence the non-believers around them by being examples in what they said and did. To this end he was determined to get his point across in as many different ways as possible. He uses passionate language here to emphasise the futility of the false teachings that are being presented. Verse 16 reminds us of 2 Timothy 3:5, where Paul talks of some people in Ephesus having 'a form of godliness but denying its power'.

I am deeply challenged by these verses. Do my actions on Monday morning contradict what I have said and prayed on Sunday? Do I profess to trust God and then waste time worrying about my children, job, health, finances etc? I was greatly impressed by the faith of a gentleman from our church who came forward for prayer recently. He had been ill and wanted us to pray for healing. As well as asking for healing, we also prayed that he would know God's peace. As we prayed, the gentleman interrupted us, saying that he didn't need prayers for peace because he trusted in God!

For prayer and reflection

Let's use this time to confess where we haven't always acted in a way that matches what we say we believe.

Do I really 'walk the talk'? I don't know about you, but I long for my relationship with Jesus to permeate every single part of my life. I hope that this verse could be rewritten about my life saying, 'Heather claims to know God, and the truth of that can clearly be seen in all she does.' Wouldn't that be a great epitaph? It would be better still if that's what people say about you and me while we are still around!

Are we **teachable?**

I wonder if you are the sort of person who reads the instruction manual before you try out a new appliance, or do you think you'll be able to figure out how it works by playing with it? My husband often reminds me that I very nearly broke the food processor we were given as a wedding present because I was in such a hurry to try it out. I didn't want to 'waste' time reading the instruction booklet.

In the Christian life we have to learn that the formation of our character into the Christlikeness that God desires takes time. We don't become Christlike overnight or by sleeping with the Bible under our pillows! We need teaching and training and lots of patience with ourselves (and with each other), as we learn and change. We need to read God's Word and let its truth challenge and change the way we live our lives. We need to follow the Maker's handbook!

How willing are we to be taught? Are we prepared to take time to learn things properly, or do we get discouraged that our lives aren't being transformed quickly enough? Paul knew that if Titus trained the people well, they would be able to pass his teaching on to others and become trainers themselves.

We must also take the responsibility for passing on the lessons God has taught us. However ill-equipped we feel as teachers, we all have people around us over whom we have some sort of influence. There will always be ways in which we can pass on what we have learnt to our friends so that we can encourage and therefore also teach them. So let's look out for opportunities to learn new things from God, and also grasp the opportunities we have to pass on to others what we have already learnt.

Titus 2:1–5

'Teach the older men … teach the older women … Then they can train the younger women …' (vv.2–4)

For prayer and reflection

Give me a teachable spirit, Lord, and help me to play my part in passing on Your truth to others. Amen.

Be an **example**

Titus 2:1–8

'In everything set them an example by doing what is good.' (v.7)

O n Friday we were thinking about how good it is to pass on to those around us what God has been teaching us in our own lives. Paul now says to Titus that as well as teaching people how to live by the words he speaks, he must also set the new Christians an example by the way he lives his life among them. He must be a role model by living out the truth of all that he is teaching. Surely we are called to do the same. What a scary thought!

In fact the whole book of Titus is about new Christians learning to be role models to the non-believers around them. These new converts are embarking on a radically different way of life from the people among whom they live. They will be watched closely to see whether they fall at the first hurdle or whether they stick at it. We've already considered this month whether our actions live up to our words, but this verse really challenged me in relation to my preparations for Christmas. Will I be setting an example as to how the real meaning of Christmas should be celebrated? If I'm married, will I be showing love, respect and kindness to my husband and children (vv.4–5)? If I'm single, will I be self-controlled at the Christmas party while watching my friends overindulge? Will I be just as irritable as everyone else amidst the stress, greed and overindulgence?

Paul knew how vital it was for non-believers to see Christians living out their faith, swimming against the tide and making others curious about the gospel. As we celebrate Christmas, perhaps by inviting people into our homes or to our carol services, or perhaps by gathering together with family and friends, let's endeavour to show people what Christmas really means to us.

For prayer and reflection

Lord, I pray that people will be able to see how much You mean to me as I prepare for Your birth. Amen.

WEEKEND

Onwards and upwards

For reflection: Psalm 16

Advent is a good time for some serious heart-searching about our relationship with God as we look back over the past year. Confession is obviously an important part of that, and one we shouldn't neglect, but so is thanksgiving. It's great to take some time to think of all that God has done for us and all that He has meant to us as we've travelled through the year. Even if there have been hard times, we can acknowledge that He was with us through it all. Thanksgiving can encourage our faith as we recognise God's love, care and intervention in our lives.

In the year ahead, let's cultivate an attitude of thankfulness to God for all He has done in us and for us, and let's lift our hearts in praise as we realise how much He means to us.

Read through the psalm and join with David as his heart overflows with praise and thanks to God.

Attractive teaching

Titus 2:9–10

'… so that in every way they will make the teaching about God our Saviour attractive.' (v.10)

Paul has been aiming his teaching at each specific group within the household, and now it's the turn of the slaves. In 21st-century life we can relate to teaching for men and women within the family, but slavery is something a little further from our experience. Perhaps we think that Paul should have demanded the abolition of slavery in places where the gospel had been accepted, but that wasn't on his immediate agenda.

We must read these verses in the light of first-century life. Part and parcel of society, slavery wasn't going to disappear overnight. The important thing was that newly converted slaves should not now despise their non-Christian masters, thinking themselves superior to them. If these slaves felt that they had a right to be equal with their masters and treated them now with contempt because, as Christians, they were serving a different kind of Master, how would that have looked to the people of Crete? It would have made the enthusiastic teaching of Paul and Titus very unattractive and unpopular to non-Christians – and also have nullified everything else they were working so hard to do. In these verses, Paul emphasises that Christian slaves, just like Christians in any walk of life, must be good ambassadors for the 'sound doctrine' they have been expounding. So what does this teaching, aimed at slaves, have to say to us today? Do we ever look down on people who have yet to discover faith in Christ? Are we sometimes more polite to people in church than to work colleagues or family members who aren't Christians? If we want the teaching we live by to be attractive to those around us, then we have to adhere to its principles wherever we are and whoever we are with.

For prayer and reflection

Lord, please help me to live a life that makes Your gospel attractive to those around me. Amen.

The gospel **in a nutshell**

I have really enjoyed and been challenged by preparing these notes on Titus. It has been a great opportunity to study this book in more depth than usual. When we read very quickly, as I often do, we can miss nuances or small words that, although seemingly insignificant, are there to make an important point in the text.

I found it fascinating, for example, that after a passage teaching on the qualities that should be shown in the characters of believers, Paul launches into this wonderful verse that sums up the gospel. In the NIV translation, verse 11 begins with the word 'for': not a very eye-catching word, nor one that has us reaching for our dictionaries, but an important word here, nevertheless. With this word Paul is showing Titus exactly why he has exhorted the Cretans to live in such a way as described in Titus 2:2–10. They should follow these instructions for living *because* 'the grace of God that brings salvation has appeared to all men'. He doesn't want them following rules just for the sake of it, but because God has done something amazing for all people and he wants them to respond with joy and gratitude. This joy and gratitude will then lead to behaviour which will make their message attractive (v.10) and will stop the Word of God from being maligned (v.5).

Having just split the teaching up for various groups within the community, Paul now wants to emphasise that this grace is for everyone. It's for young and old, slave and free, believer and non-believer. This grace appeared in the birth of Jesus, and it's what we are preparing to celebrate.

Titus 2:11–14

'For the grace of God that brings salvation has appeared to all men.' (v.11)

For prayer and reflection

Take a few moments to sit before God, perhaps with your hands open in your lap. Let God fill you with an assurance of His love for you and thank Him for his 'indescribable gift' (2 Cor. 9:15).

The power **to say no**

Titus 2:12

'For the grace of God (v.11) … teaches us to say "No" to ungodliness and worldly passions …' (v.12)

This verse is such good news. It's almost too good to be true! Can the grace of God in my life really teach me to renounce all those ungodly and unhelpful thoughts, attitudes and patterns of behaviour that I hate so much? The great news is *YES*, it can. The more I understand God's amazing grace, the more I will be motivated to say no to the things that hold me back from being the woman He wants me to be and living the life that He wants me to live. I'm getting quite excited as I write this! If I grasp afresh what Jesus had to go through because of my sin and rebellion, and if I begin to understand that He chose to do it because of His love for me, then surely my desire will be to say no to anything that opposes His ongoing work in my life.

Do you wish it was easier to say no to greed, jealousy, pride, gossip, hating yourself …? Take a look at Jesus. Soak in His love for you and meditate on the fact that you are now a forgiven and precious child of God. Do you still want to consciously choose to turn away from Him? Do you want to tell Him by the way you live your life that it was all a waste of time, and that you'd rather wallow in your sins?

I'm not saying that it's simple to turn away from everything ungodly in our lives, but I do believe that learning to say no is part of the process of sanctification that God starts when we choose to follow Him. Paul wants to encourage the new Christians in Crete. He wants them to know that, through the amazing grace of God, they now have the resources to say *NO* to the way they behaved before they believed in Jesus.

For prayer and reflection

Why don't you take a few minutes today soaking in Jesus' love for you and thanking Him that He has given you everything you need for life and godliness (2 Pet. 1:3).

Eager **to say yes**

Yesterday we talked about how we've been given the resources to say no to the things that would turn us away from God. Sometimes non-believers think that the whole Christian life is about saying no and that a Christian's favourite word is 'don't'. It is our responsibility to show people that we don't say no to things just for the sake of it. We say no to some things so that we can say yes to others. We say no to ungodliness so that we can live 'self-controlled, upright and godly lives' (2:12). Paul wants the recipients of this letter to be intentional in their desire to be 'energetic in goodness' (2:14, *The Message*). He wants them to say no to the lifestyle they pursued before they believed, so that they can spread the good news of the gospel to those around them.

I must admit that I'm not always eager and determined to do what is good. I'm often lazy and self-centred and need God's help to do the right thing. The good news is that God has given us not only the power to say no, but also, by His Holy Spirit, the resources to say yes. When we're feeling weak and saying yes to God seems difficult, we need to remember that '... God did not give us a spirit of timidity, but a spirit of power, of love and of self-discipline' (2 Tim. 1:7). If Jesus is Lord of my life, it is now possible to lead a life that is genuinely 'energetic in goodness'.

Often when I take bread and wine at communion, I imagine Jesus giving me whatever I need at that moment. It might be peace about a situation or courage to do the right thing. I might need a dose of joy or be desperate for guidance. I'm encouraged by the book of Titus that God really wants to enable me to live the self-disciplined, godly life I long for.

Titus 2:14

'... a people that are ... eager to do what is good.' (v.14)

For prayer and reflection

Please help me, Lord, to be a person who is eager to do what is good. Amen.

Jesus – kindness and love

Titus 3:1–8

'But when the kindness and love of God our Saviour appeared, he saved us …' (v.4)

I f you are reading these notes in the run up to Christmas, you may wonder how I am going to include the subject of Jesus' birth. I thought we would probably have to set Titus aside for a couple of days while we took time to think about Christmas. I was quite wrong, however, because we reach the climax of this letter, and of this Advent season, at exactly the right time. The Revised Common Lectionary (the set readings) for the Church on Christmas Day actually includes this passage from Titus, because it is so relevant as we look at Jesus' coming and all that it means for us.

Paul is encouraging Titus to remind the Christians in Crete of the contrast between the lives they lived before they believed in Jesus ('At one time we too were …' v.3) and their lives now ('But when …' v.4). Life was empty and chaotic for them, and many lives were being destroyed by greed and hatred. Paul longs for them to understand that they have been saved from the consequences of their old lives because of God's 'kindness and love'; not because they earned or deserved it, but just as a gift.

Whether we had a dramatic conversion experience or whether our understanding of the gospel was more gradual, we can still look back and see how God has changed us. He's washed away our past and given us His Spirit, and now He calls us to come to Him to receive all that we need to become more like Him.

Let's express our gratitude to Jesus today for all that He has done for us.

For prayer and reflection

Thank You, Lord, for the difference that knowing You makes to my life. Thank You that Your love and kindness towards me never run out. Amen.

WEEKEND

'Cast all your anxiety on him'

For reflection: 1 Peter 5:7
'Cast all your anxiety on him because he cares for you.'

I must admit that even though I've been a Christian for over twenty years and am now involved in the running of my local church, Christmas can sometimes come and go without my taking in its real meaning very much. I fall into the trap of being preoccupied with the next event, meal, visitor, church service etc. I can worry too much and pray too little and then wonder what went wrong.

Christmas can be a difficult time for many people, Christians and non-Christians alike. It is a time when issues of loneliness, bereavement or rifts in the family come to the fore and we can find ourselves feeling full of anxiety rather than full of faith.

The great thing is that Jesus knows life isn't always easy (John 16:33), and He longs for us to come to Him with our anxieties and to exchange those anxieties for the peace we need. Why don't you do that now?

Jesus Christ **our Saviour**

Titus 3:6–7

'... so that ... we might become heirs having the hope of eternal life.' (v.7)

The six-year-old daughter of a friend of mine caused rather a stir in her school when she announced to her friends that Santa Claus was dead! Her family have never subscribed to the story of Father Christmas, so Harriet had been told that the whole thing was based on the story of St Nicholas who lived a long, long time ago. The logical conclusion to her therefore was that Father Christmas had also died.

Life and death, and time and eternity are very different in the spiritual realm. Here we are today celebrating the birth of a baby who was born over 2,000 years ago and who died a horrendous death some 30 years later. He then came back to life and is with us by His Spirit today. No wonder some people think it's unbelievable! We can know His presence and experience His guidance and help in our lives, and all this 2,000 years after He was born. Amazing! Even more amazing are the consequences that His life, death and resurrection have for us who believe in Him today. We are going to live forever with Him.

When we became God's children we also became heirs with Jesus; our inheritance is the gift of eternal life given to us by the baby in the manger all those years ago. What's more, we don't have to wait until we die for this gift, because we have begun living this supernatural life already. What a gift to receive again on Christmas Day! It's not the sort of present that can be wrapped up and put under the tree because it's a gift that can't be seen. It's the gift of a Saviour, to free us from our sins; the gift of Immanuel, God with us (Matt. 1:21–23). Let's thank God with our whole hearts today for His goodness to us, as we celebrate this most precious gift of all – the gift of His Son Jesus.

For prayer and reflection

O come let us adore Him, Christ the Lord.

An **excellent** and profitable life

'These things are excellent and profitable for everyone.' (v.8)

As I've studied the book of Titus I have enjoyed observing Paul's passion for the people to whom he is writing. It must have been hard being so far away and having so little communication with people he loved so much. I'm sure that if the Internet had been invented he would have been emailing Titus with new instructions every five minutes!

In much of Paul's writing we can see that he is a very passionate person, longing for people to grasp the truth of the gospel and to pass it on to others. What he says can be complicated and sometimes controversial, but I do appreciate the balance here in his letter to Titus between grace and behaviour. Paul knows that people can try to follow all the rules for right living, but that the lives of those same people can be dry and joyless. He has experienced at first hand what understanding God's love and grace means. He has been able to sing hymns of praise while chained up in a prison cell! Paul wants Titus to both model this balance between freedom and right living and to teach it. Above all, he wants him to stress God's mercy and generosity so that people will follow the teaching about relationships, church leadership and other important matters out of overflowing hearts and not with burdens of duty on their backs.

Paul knows that understanding the gospel and living godly lives motivated by all that God has done will lead to a community that is a blessing to those both inside and outside its borders, believers and non-believers alike.

This teaching from Paul is 'excellent and profitable for everyone': it blesses those who follow it and it blesses those who watch them. I long to live an excellent and profitable life. Do you?

Help me to follow You, Lord, not with gritted teeth but with a joy-filled heart. Amen.

Differences and **divisions**

Titus 3:9–11

'But avoid …
arguments and
quarrels about the
law, because these
are unprofitable
and useless.' (v.9)

Yesterday we heard about what is 'excellent and profitable'; now Paul warns Titus of what is 'unprofitable and useless', and to give him instructions about how to handle divisive people.

Paul is tackling a problem which sadly still exists. Within our churches there will be different personality types, different levels of Bible knowledge, different spiritual experiences and different social backgrounds. Even so, these don't have to cause divisions. We mustn't be frightened of our differences, because diversity can be a positive thing and need not create disunity. When church leaders try to stamp out the differences in their congregations, they are on their way to forming a cult rather than building a church.

We must, however, be careful that our differences don't lead to divisions within the Body of Christ. Any group of people within a church who concentrate on their differences can create a split, which can lead to much hurt and confusion. In Corinth (1 Cor. 1:10–13), factions grew up around powerful personalities and the people became divided. Paul had strong words about how to treat people who caused division. Although it's uncomfortable, we need to recognise how much damage disunity can do, and take appropriate action. Jesus highlights the importance of confronting all kinds of sin within the Church in Matthew 18.

For prayer and reflection

Help me to be a peacemaker, Lord, and to appreciate the diversity there is within Your family. Amen.

In Ephesians 4:3 Paul says that we should, 'Make every effort to keep the unity of the Spirit through the bond of peace', and that's what we each have a responsibility to do. Are we sometimes caught up with emphasising our differences, or do we work for unity and long to bring glory to God through the united witness of our church?

What's so amazing about grace?

Titus 3:12–15

'Grace be with you all.' (v.15)

'May the grace of our Lord Jesus Christ, the love of God, and the fellowship of the Holy Spirit be with us all evermore, Amen.' We may be familiar with this prayer, known as 'the Grace', which is sometimes said at the end of church services or prayer meetings. It is based on 2 Corinthians 13:14 and is Paul's farewell to the Christians in Corinth. Paul loves to end his letters with a reminder of the unfathomable grace of God, and his letter to Titus is no exception. I confess that I must have said 'the Grace' many times without really focusing on what I was saying. It can so easily become the way we end a meeting, rather like the way 'Amen' has become a signal that our prayer is over.

Paul wasn't just using these words as the ending to his letter; he was summing up the essence of what he had been writing about. If the new believers in Crete didn't take on board anything else that he had said, then at least let them remember that it's all about God's grace. I love Philip Yancey's imagery when he says that the word 'grace' '... contains the essence of the gospel as a drop of water can contain the image of the sun'.[1]

The world can compete with the Church in many areas of doing good. It can set up charities and help the poor and abused in our society, but it cannot offer grace to the people it helps, only the Church can do that. The dictionary defines grace as 'the undeserved mercy of God', and understanding this word can have a dramatic effect on our lives. When I really grasp what grace means, I can walk out from living under condemnation; I can stand tall as the person God created me to be. I can stop striving in my own strength and let God empower me with His Holy Spirit.

1. Philip Yancy, *What's So Amazing About Grace?* (Zondervan, 1997).

For prayer and reflection

Lord, I pray that You would open my eyes to understand Your amazing grace. Amen.

What are you **passionate about?**

**1 Corinthians
15:1–11**

'For what I
received I passed
on to you as of first
importance …'
(v.3)

In magazines I've read interviews with celebrities who have been asked which historical figure they would like to have a meal with. I think it would be exciting to have supper with the apostle Paul. I might be too nervous to eat anything, but it would be pretty amazing! I would want to ask so many questions about his life, his conversion and what made him tick. Most of all I would want some of his passion to rub off on me, because to me that is one of his most desirable characteristics.

As I've read Paul's letter to Titus, what has come across to me again and again is the depth and strength of feeling Paul has for both his subject and the people to whom he is writing. As a Jew he had a good grounding in Scripture, but what drove him on more than any amount of knowledge was a passion to share what God had done in his life.

What are you passionate about? Is it to see God do new things in your life? Is it to share your testimony with others? I don't just mean a testimony about your conversion. Paul had an amazing conversion but didn't actually write about it that often. I mean a testimony from last month, last week or even yesterday. Are you letting God challenge, change, bless and heal you as you walk with Him in your everyday life, so that you always have something to share of what God is doing in and for you?

Let's resolve to be women who are passionate for God. That doesn't mean that we have to travel to far-flung places like Paul did. It simply means letting God work in our hearts so that we can't help telling other people about Him.

**For prayer and
reflection**

**Lord, I pray that
You would give me
a passion for Your
name in the year
ahead. Amen.**

You ain't seen nothing yet!

For reflection: Jeremiah 29:10–14

'"For I know the plans I have for you," declares the LORD, "plans to prosper you and not to harm you, plans to give you hope and a future."' (v.11)

I wonder what sort of year you have had. Maybe it has been a peaceful one where nothing unpredictable has happened, or maybe it's been a year of turmoil to which you will gladly say goodbye. Whatever it has been like, God goes before us into the next year and will be with us every step of the way.

Even if we've had a great year, with a real sense of God moving in our lives, He still has more for us. Sometimes at New Year we can get stuck looking back to all that has been. It's good to take time to do that, but it is also good to look forward to all that will be and to realise how much more of Himself God wants to give us.

Let's echo Dag Hammarskjöld's prayer when he says, 'For all that has been, Thanks; For all that will be, Yes!'

WAVERLEY ABBEY TRUST

We are a charity serving Christians around the world with practical resources and teaching. We support you to grow in your Christian faith, understand the times in which we live, and serve God in every sphere of life.

waverleyabbeycollege.ac.uk

waverleyabbeyresources.org

waverleyabbeyhouse.org